LIBERALISM AND SOCIAL JUSTICE

Liberalism and Social Justice

International perspectives

Edited by

GIDEON CALDER
Cardiff University

EDWARD GARRETT
Middlesex University

JESS SHANNON

Routledge
Taylor & Francis Group
LONDON AND NEW YORK

First published 2000 by Ashgate Publishing

Reissued 2018 by Routledge
2 Park Square, Milton Park, Abingdon, Oxon OX14 4RN
711 Third Avenue, New York, NY 10017, USA

Routledge is an imprint of the Taylor & Francis Group, an informa business

A Library of Congress record exists under LC control number: 00132803

ISBN 13: 978-1-138-72793-9 (hbk)
ISBN 13: 978-1-138-72790-8 (pbk)
ISBN 13: 978-1-315-19069-3 (ebk)

Contents

Foreword

Doc. PhDr. VLASTIMIL FIALA, CSc
Head of the Department of Politics and European Studies,
Palacky University, Olomouc

Versions of the papers which comprise this book were originally presented at the conference 'The Liberal Order; the Future for Social Justice?', held at Palacky University, Olomouc, in July 1999. The conference was the fourth in a series of collaborations between the University of Brighton and universities in the Czech Republic on the broad themes of liberal politics in post-1989 Europe. Palacky University, founded in 1573 in the ancient metropolis of the Hana region, welcomed over eighty leading academics and professionals, coming from the United States and Australia and from across Europe – as well as students and lecturers from Olomouc itself. It was with special gratitude to the financial and organisational support of the Open Society Fund that we were able to play host to delegates from all over eastern Europe and the former Soviet Union.

The conference took the form of several streams comprising papers of kindred themes, devoted to different aspects of liberalism: political, economic, philosophical, cultural, legal and historical, culminating in a panel discussion of recent events surrounding the Nato bombing of the former Yugoslavia. A representative sample of papers is collected here. The selection process has not been at all easy, but we believe that what follows conveys the variety and diversity of opinions expressed at the conference, as well as the constructive, open-minded spirit in which it was conducted.

It was an honour for our Department to host this conference and our thanks must go to Bob Brecher, and to the organisational team – Henry Miller, Jess Shannon, Gideon Calder, and Edward Garrett. This conference would not have been possible without the help and support of the students of the Department of Politics and European Studies.

Translated by Jan Němeček.

Acknowledgements

The editors would like to thank the University of Brighton and Palacky University, Olomouc for their support of the conference from which this book derives. Other, special thanks are due to Henry Miller and Jan Němeček as conference co-organizers; to Richard Bridgens and Jack Spink for their financial assistance; to the Open Society Fund for so generously funding many of those who attended from eastern Europe, and to Vlastimil Fiala for his extraordinary tolerance as a host. Claudia van Draker was an inspiration throughout. Most of all, we'd like to thank all of those participants (featured in this volume or not) whose contributions to the conference helped make it a success.

Introduction

GIDEON CALDER, EDWARD GARRETT AND JESS SHANNON

At the beginning of the third millennium the liberal appropriation of the political space appears increasingly complete. Yet it is not without its critics, and in particular it is the capacity of liberalism to provide for social justice which is coming under question.

The problems themselves in this regard are not hard to find. For example there are the facts of global poverty and inequality, and the role the ever expanding market plays in their production. Welfare systems are being rethought and dismantled in the face of a dwindling commitment of citizens to extensive welfare provision. Challenges are brought to liberalism's claims to structure genuinely inclusive societies – human rights for example, it is argued, forming a particularly liberal discourse.

Within the academy these issues have been addressed more or less explicitly. Firstly, there is the status of liberal theory itself. Under attack from various quarters liberals have tended to retreat from universalism to a more 'localised' liberalism. On what grounds is this liberalism to be supported? Does it lean over into an impossible relativism? What ethical or epistemological scope is there for claims which go beyond the liberal acceptance of pluralism? Secondly, there are the responses to changing political, economic and social structures. Most important here perhaps is the process of globalisation. Not only do these changes jeopardise social justice; they also change the way in which it might be brought about. Thus the focus moves beyond individuals, the normal agents of change of liberal theory, to 'community', and to the 'new social movements'. Equally, there is a growing acknowledgement of the internationalisation of social justice. Thirdly, there are the specific explorations of specific issues.

This collection of papers gives some indication of this work. It is a collection perhaps distinguished by its breadth – of academic and national backgrounds, and by the different perspectives on liberalism arising from this. The wider societal influence of academic debates should by no means be presumed. However, it would seem fair to say that an understanding of how best to provide for social justice needs at least some such dialogue between these different backgrounds. It is as a small contribution to this process that this book should be seen.

That said, a certain wariness of liberalism (shared by at least one editor of this volume) is often found, for various reasons, in western European humanities and social science departments. With this in mind, we felt it important to begin this book with a paper which responds to a more historically ruptured recent past. In the opening paper here Gulia Taghiyeva explores the precarious nature of liberalism and democracy in Azerbaijan following the dissolution of the Soviet Union. She draws particular attention to the difficulties of creating a liberal political culture in a country with different political and cultural traditions, but emphasises the dangers of 'western' political societies not underpinning this process.

Liberalism, of course, is no neat package either in theory or practice. While for some, its methodological individualism links it inextricably to the logic of free market capitalism, for others, more left-leaning, its egalitarianism is key. A version of this tension – between welfarist left-liberals and neo-classical liberal economists – emerges in Doris Schroeder's discussion of the assumptions behind the arguments of recent Western European proponents of cuts in state benefits provision. Schroeder argues that the 'lazy-scrounger' argument on benefit provision, familiar enough in recent political rhetoric in Germany and the UK, arises from ideological expediency rather than from substantiated factual or psychological evidence. Next, in a wide-ranging cultural survey, Ian Duncanson points to tensions between liberal values and those forces of economic and cultural conservatism with which they can be said to form the Western 'liberal democratic' establishment. Looking mostly at the mass media and universities in Australia, he argues that these have acted precisely against the fostering of genuine debate. Such debate, he argues, is a crucial aspect of any putative overlap between liberalism and social justice.

However 'liberalism' is defined, some form of pluralism is surely a constitutive principle; the appreciable diversity of lifestyles, values, priorities and beliefs is often taken in itself as necessitating liberal politics. Chapters four and five deal with the nature and scope of pluralism as an ideal. Separating out different senses of the term, and using a combination of philosophical and more personal examples, Alison Assiter shows some of the pitfalls and aporias involved either in assuming a plurality of identities, or in assuming any common (universally human) denominator beneath the surface appearance of difference. She argues that whatever the importance of pluralist values, sensitivity to difference should not imply a relinquishing of the very idea that there might be a true set of 'emancipatory values' to which, in case of conflict, we might refer. Stephen de Wijze's paper takes a contrasting angle on pluralism. He explores how the notion of the 'reasonable' is used by liberals as a way of founding the most inclusive conception of justice possible in pluralistic societies. He develops and defends the importance of the reasonable whilst stressing that it has its basis in a pre-existing commitment to the democratic ideal and thus does not have a universal, ahistorical appeal.

Chapters six to eight each focus on a particular theorist in relation to liberalism. A founding text of modern liberalism is of course J.S. Mill's *On Liberty*. It is here perhaps more clearly than any other text that we see emphasised the importance of the individual living out their own life plan. Judith Grbich's paper takes issue with such a reading of this classic text. She emphasises how the 'freeman' has his 'doubles', that a liberal politics is dependent on others paying for it; in particular Grbich's paper explores the part Mill's text played in the construction of this process. Kalle Pihlainen's paper looks at the relationship between liberalism and social justice through Sartre's philosophy, and in particular its emphasis on the situatedness of the human subject. Sartre objects to the generalizations which liberal theory employs in discussion of 'the individual', as if this figure can be abstracted from the specific circumstances which *make* us individual. This is the 'esprit analytique' of Pihlainen's title. His conclusion is that, read the right way, Sartre's thinking points in the direction of a more satisfactory account of the relation between the chosen and unchosen aspects of our situation than the analytic spirit is able to provide, and thus to a more concrete respect for individuality. Meanwhile discussing Richard Rorty's work (with that of Rawls, amongst the most cited of Anglophone contributions to current liberal thinking) Justin Cruickshank suggests that Rorty fails to find a non-metaphysical basis for liberal beliefs which appeals instead to the historically contingent practices of Western democracies. As Cruickshank sees it, a main shortcoming of the 'ethnocentric', pragmatist version of liberalism Rorty espouses is that adequate consideration of social justice *requires* precisely the sort of thinking which Rorty would reject as metaphysical speculation.

Chapters nine and ten consider the often opposed concepts of the community and the individual. The liberal emphasis on the individual and its ignoring of the importance of community threaten, some argue, the very possibility of the liberal polity sustaining itself. Drawing extensively on writings from the post-socialist countries, as well as from Hegel and Foucault, Lubica Učník's paper attempts to unravel the meaning of the contested concept of the individual. Importantly, and relevantly, this unravelling takes place in the post-socialist context of the individual's supposed rescue from the 'rubble of collectivism'. A particularly interesting feature of the challenge to liberalism that the emphasis on community has brought has been the dialogue that has developed between the academy and the politicians. Petri Koikkalainen's paper explores this dialogue in the arena in which it has been most apparent, that of America. In particular he explores how 'community' is used in political rhetoric in ways that suggest a paradigm shift away from a liberal consensus.

Shifting focus to more global concerns, the final four chapters make fresh and important contributions to discussion of problems arising from liberalism's application as an organising principle of *international* social justice. Immigration issues provide an appropriate starting point. Traditionally both universalistic and individualistic in its methodology, liberalism has had an ambiguous relationship with the institution of the nation-state, entailing as it does that some are treated as insiders, and others outsiders. Phillip Cole, in his paper, explores Michael Walzer's communitarian attempt to provide criteria for community membership. It is an approach, says Cole, beset by problems and lacunae which point beyond its own internal coherence to more general questions facing any political philosophy which has at its core a commitment to the moral equality of humanity. With this commitment in place, any immigration policy runs the risk of inconsistency, or of sheer arbitrariness – risks which Walzer's work fails, ultimately, to avoid.

Despite its ambiguous relationship with nationality, liberalism has traditionally seen the nation-state as the forum for political action, and – most importantly here – as the space within which social justice is to be provided. Majid Yar's paper explores how globalisation threatens the nation-state as a signifcant level of political organisation. However, he suggests, the response to this threat does not lie (solely) in the development of global institutions of political power, but also in the growth of localised political organisation that we see today. It is unsurprising by extension that in this changing context of political organisation the imminent demise of the modern territorial state has been both declared and celebrated. In his paper Daniel Kofman warns against such premature proclamations, taking issue particularly with the arguments of Onora O'Neill and Thomas Pogge. As Kofman notes, the question of why sovereign power should be organised territorially has been in large part ignored by liberal thinkers; his paper both explores this question and suggests why it is a vital one for liberals to engage with.

Given these pressing issues of global change liberalism's theoretical capacity to provide for international social justice is of vital import. In his paper Byron Kaldis identifies liberalism's disassociation from ethical questions and its prioritising of the political as the central problem in its attempts to provide for social justice. Drawing on Rousseau particularly he suggests that only a significantly expanded, and therefore altered, liberalism can make convincing claim to be the future for international social justice.

Our scope in this collection ranges, then, from ideological conflict within newly liberalising states to liberalism's relationship to global capitalism; from the assertion of individual and group identities to that of territorial rights; from the nature of difference and equality to the theoretical tools and assumptions required for that nature adequately to be addressed. We hope that this dialogue, as with the conference from which these papers are sourced, might have value as much for the rare internationality and scope of the perspectives represented as for the matters they individually raise. Our positing of the liberal order as a given and of social justice as a goal may be less than hotly controversial. But neither should the commitment of the contributors here to the spirit of the latter (regardless of their orientation to the first) be up for serious doubt.

1 Liberal Democracy in Transitional Azerbaijan: Challenges and Prospects

GULIA TAGHIYEVA

Introduction

Liberalism was developed as a philosophical theory with the aim of defending the individual in the face of growing power of the state in the sixteenth and seventeenth centuries. Within liberalism, social justice is mainly understood in terms of individual rights, freedoms and choices. In a conflict between interests of an individual and those of the community or the society in which the individual exists, liberals have traditionally tended to protect the former against the latter. Hence liberalism is inevitably antagonistic towards a non-liberal society such as a traditional Islamic community where majority interests are seen as superior to those of an individual, or an authoritarian type of the state regime where the individual's will is subordinate to that of the ruling elites.[1]

The liberal-democratic type of the state where both strong liberal traditions and culture are developed is widely believed to provide the best conditions for the protection of human rights. Indeed, as theoretical discourse and empirical evidence have shown, democratic states seldom fight wars, at least against each other (Huntingdon, 1991); state violence is less likely to occur in democratic states (Gurr, 1986) and they are based on free and peaceful competition for power (Linz, 1992). Furthermore, democratization in Western countries took centuries; it was an extended process often involving coercion and violence and passed through bloody revolutions and numerous civil wars. Nevertheless the longevity and gradual character of this process ensured the profound character of democratic culture and the enhancement of liberal traditions, which are now deeply embedded in the state system and institutions and in the minds of private citizens.

This paper focuses on transitional Azerbaijan, which presents an example of a society where neither cultural traditions nor the type of the political regime inherited by the country is favourable for promotion of human rights.

The country has yet to accomplish the processes of political liberalization which is defined

> in terms of protecting and promoting civil rights such as freedom from torture and degrading punishment, arbitrary arrest, and imprisonment; freedom of speech, faith, opinion, and assembly; and also the right to life, security and the ownership of property. A broader definition of political liberalization includes the right to seek or nominate for public office and the right to form and join political parties through an orderly electoral process. Thus conceived, political liberalization means democratization (Monshipouri, 1995, p. 12).

There are many factors conditioning the tumultuous and peculiar character of Azerbaijan's and other Newly Independent States' (NIS)[2] transition to democracy.[3] The necessity of simultaneously carrying out democratic and economic reforms appeared to be a formidable task for the former Soviet republics, for their communist legacy provided neither conditions for a market economy, nor respect for democratic principles and individual rights. The third issue which made transition in the NIS a unique and complicated process was that of territory and state-building, issues not faced by most other countries undergoing democratization.

The three issues (i.e. the territorial issue, including state-building, the issue of democratization and that of transition to a market economy) composing the well known phenomenon of the 'triple transition' (Offe, 1996b) challenged virtually all of the NIS and generated common problems for the newly democratizing states. Nonetheless, in spite of the common legacy and the common challenges, these countries differ radically from each other in terms of the speed and character of their transformation, for 'all of them have their own specific problems, stemming from historic or religious traditions, their demographic situation, the gravity of inter-ethnic tensions, etc' (Müllerson, 1995, p. 61).

The peculiar character of democratization in Azerbaijan has been determined by a cluster of pre-transitional and transitional factors. These include the task of building a strong and stable state, the division among its elites, the country's cultural and ethnic diversity and its involvement in the armed conflict caused by the secessionist movement of ethnic Armenians in Nagorno Karabakh that threatens its independence, statehood and territorial integrity. Among other factors historical experience, cultural traditions and religion play crucial roles for they appear to be the very foundation upon which the whole structure of new democracy is being built and upon which its durability will depend in many respects.

As I suggest in this paper, the issue of state-building (which in transitional Azerbaijan is inseparable from, and indispensable to, national issues and democratization) is a formidable task for the country's current and future elites. In this regard, the elites' attitudes to the tasks which are to be accomplished in the course of transition play a crucial role; for elites are a determining factor in the transformation of the regime, influencing democratization significantly. I will also suggest that there are cultural peculiarities that conditioned lack of popular support and a lack of commitment by the elites to the goals of democratization in Azerbaijan. Finally I will argue that a gradual progress in their promotion may bring about better results and that some changes in the Western approach towards transitional Azerbaijan are needed to facilitate this process.

Given the environment within which democratization in Azerbaijan is occurring, it is still not clear what type of society is emerging in the course of transition. However, I will attempt to draw some tentative conclusions about perspectives on liberalism, democracy and human rights in Azerbaijan.

Democratization and problems of 'stateness'

Virtually all scholars who address the conflicting logic between 'stateness' and democratization, point out the dependency of the latter on the former, holding that the existence of an independent state is a pre-requisite to democracy (Huntington, 1991; Linz and Stepan, 1996; Offe, 1996a.). In the case of Azerbaijan, the very existence of a modern state with its institutions and procedures, and the legitimate authority over its territory is open to question. Although Azerbaijan is recognized by the UN and the international community as a sovereign state with the borders and territory the republic had before the collapse of the USSR, the tasks of creating a state and (concomitant with it) the formation of the nation which have yet to be accomplished.

Having no experience in state-building, let alone nation-state-building,[4] Azerbaijan was forced to begin its existence as an independent state in 1991 in a situation where part of its population (ethnic Armenians living in Nagorno-Karabakh) refused to acknowledge the state's authority over the territory they occupied. By 1993, 20 per cent of the republic – including not only Nagorno Karabakh but also a few neighboring districts – were beyond the control of the Azerbaijani state. Separatist movements took shape in 1993-1994 in the north and the south of the country, occupied by Lezgis and Talishs respectively, indicating that not all ethnic groups in Azerbaijan were willing to accept citizenship of the new state. Thus territorial and national issues were added to the state project and reform agenda, putting into question the legitimacy of the state's authority over its territory and undermining the opportunity to carry out democratic reforms. It is considered that 'if there is no significant irredenta outside the state's boundaries, if there is only one nation existing ... in the state, and if there is low cultural diversity within the state ... [only then] can leaders of the government simultaneously pursue democratization policies and nation-state policies' (Linz and Stepan, 1996, p. 25).

As historical experience shows,[5] a liberal democratic state with its institutions and procedures protecting both individual and minority rights contributes to political stability and allows for peaceful resolution of political, social and ethnic conflicts in society. Introducing democratic measures, such as enforcing individual rights and granting equal citizenship, presumably produces a similar effect in a democratizing multicultural society too (Linz and Stepan, 1996, p. 33). If so this would allow for a gradual accomplishment of the tasks of the state's project and require from the elites a balanced and cautious policy approach. Yet, the elites in Azerbaijan have often had to act under emergency circumstances making decisions influenced not as much by the interests of the democratizing state as by the demands of 'stateness'[6] and by their own struggle for power. Moreover, this has created more favourable conditions for those rulers following authoritarian trends in their governance to gain support of a public longing for 'strong power'.

Under these circumstances, creating a strong, 'Weberian' type of the state inevitably became a primary task for the Azerbaijani elites. It became less important whether assertion of the state's authority was ensured through repression, violation of human rights, coercion and forcible subjugation of different political community groups (ethnic minorities, political parties, or contending elites) or through voluntary cooperation and overall consensus, so long as this could guarantee political stability and guard against potential challenges.

Elites in transition

The exclusive role of the elites in the newly democratizing states stem from the fact that public control of the government and public participation in governance have yet to be established through developing civil and political society, democratic institutions and procedures and 'constitutional checks and balances and the free marketplace of ideas' (Mansfield and

Snyder, 1998, p. 317). Given that transition in these countries was evidently controlled by elites from the very beginning, elites became either a driving force of, or an impediment to, the regimes' transfomation. In terms of the prospects of democratization, elites[7] in the transitional states probably play the most crucial role compared to other determinants of the process for all newly democratizing states. This is irrespective of whether the transition was initiated by the elites or imposed on the country in question. The former Soviet Union is an example of both cases, where republican elites had to follow reforms initiated by the elites at the 'centre'. In other cases, 'serving as primary agents of change at the time of transition, Eastern European elites enjoyed an unprecedented autonomy' (Wasilewski, 1998, p. 163). In other countries, Azerbaijan included, elites had the role of reformers thrust upon them from Moscow and they eagerly accepted it in the face of emerging political forces struggling for power.

In short, a theoretical model of the least turbulent democratic transition in terms of change among the elites, would involve appearance of new leaders in politics, the economy, the social sphere and imply the readiness of old elites to cooperate with them in order to accomplish transitional tasks. It should be noted that consensus among elites implies an agreement not only about the goals of democratization and ways of attaining them, but also about the fundamental rules of political competition. This implies that 'at the individual level ... [a]ll must adhere to democratic procedures and a priori accept the uncertain outcomes of competition. At the level of political organizations this consensus means that none of the major political parties challenges the system of government' (ibid., p. 171). Finally, as a result of discrete elite change, democratic forces would prevail in all the main positions in the government, the economy and the judiciary, which would contribute to the stability of the new regime and, facilitate the process of democratic and economic reforms.

As often happens, reality differs from this 'outline'. In Azerbaijan, as in some other former Soviet republics with relatively strong authoritarian traditions in politics,[8] the elites were less inclined to promote democratization. In addition, the formidable task of solving the Nagorno-Karabakh conflict affected the process of state building and made Azerbaijan communist elites look on the new opposition as an additional destructive and destabilizing factor. For the elites it was a choice between compromise with new political forces and repression against them.

The choice of either democratic or non-democratic methods of state-building became one of the key issues in the dispute between the contending elites, notably between the communists and democrats. While in power, the communist elites and the democrats demonstrated different approaches to the democratization project and sought their own ways of legitimizing their authority and strengthening power with fluctuating success. Faced with the dilemma posed by the need to pursue the goals of democratization and state- building simultaneously, they either intended to promote democracy and were not able to, or they gave priority to strengthening the state's power and left democratization goals behind. However, the struggle for power and absence of consensus regarding power sharing among the old and the new elites delayed both the creation of modern state and democratization of Azerbaijan.

Thus, it is not surprising that the course of democratization in Azerbaijan since 1988 has been a continuous struggle between old party elites and new ones, where temporary victory of one side or another was often predetermined by the escalation of the Nagorno-Karabakh conflict and social turmoil concomitant with it. This struggle finally resulted in the return of Aliyev, the former communist leader of Azerbaijan, to power in 1993.[9] Despite the negative attitude of the internal opposition and foreign states to this return, Aliyev's 'triumph was welcomed by the general public ...' (Zinin and Maleshenko, 1994, p. 114). This phenomenon can be partly explained by the fact that the Azerbaijani people were exhausted by losses in war, economic hardships and political turmoil, and received Aliyev as a saviour who brought about long-awaited civil peace and political stability. Within six years of Aliyev's presidency, the republic had been through a series of events vital to both its political and economic development. The latest ceasefire agreement, which came into force in May 1994, is mainly observed, although no tangible success in the talks over Nagorno Karabakh's status and the return home of Azerbaijani refugees has been achieved.[10]

The strengthening of state authority during the six years of Aliyev's presidency presents a sharp contrast with the situation between 1988 and 1993, when the country experienced three enforced changes of its leaders, one civilian and two military coups, social and ethnic turmoil, continuous defeats in the war over Nagorno-Karabakh and a worsening economic situation. According to official statements, the country has been successfully moving towards creating a stable democracy, a market economy and a secular state governed by law. However, attainments in the sphere of state-building and economic reforms have evidently been achieved by 'sacrificing' the goals of democracy to political stability and safety of the ruling elites.[11]

In spite of a series of concessions made by the government under pressure from the opposition as well as from the international arena to democratize the state, the years from 1993-1999 have been characterized on the one hand by a further concentration of power in the hands of Aliyev and his supporters and on the other, by intensifying the persecution of those who either opposed the regime or were considered the enemies of the President.

The continuation of this policy and violation of civil and political rights raises serious doubts as to the truly democratic character of the presidential election campaign in October 1998. Aliyev's re-election asserted (despite the radical opposition's efforts) the legitimacy of power which he lacked in 1993, and enhanced the authoritarian tendencies of his rule. The country now seems farther from attaining the goals of democratization (i.e. developing democratic institutions, strong civil society and a market economy) than it was five years ago.[12]

It is not surprising to find a lack of a commitment to democratization goals among those who were, like Aliyev, long in power in the old regime and who have usually become 'staunch standpatters of democratization' (Huntington, 1991, pp. 296-97). Although this factor is considered to be a serious impediment to democratization, it will not last long. In general, it is argued that old communist elites cannot become leaders of democratic reforms for many reasons. They are often hostile to the very idea of changing from 'the centralized elite hierarchy of communist rule to an array of differentiated political, economic, military, state-administrative' elites including 'the media and other elites that are distinct and powerful competing groups' (Higley, Pakulski, and Wesolowki, 1998). The more diverse character of elites implies that non-ruling elites have access to decision-making processes. Moreover, new actors appearing on the political scene are often potential and real adversaries to the old elites, who oppose a radical regime transformation in order not to lose the privileges they had. Finally, given the public attitude to the communist legacy and its representatives, transition to democracy and the peaceful change of power makes their position insecure and threatens to exclude them from the power-seeking process.

Elite change is seen as a necessary condition for further promotion of democracy and market economy. The gradual replacement of former *nomenklatura* holding key positions in the administrative system is needed so that democratic forces prevail in all the main positions in the government facilitating the process of democratic and economic reforms.[13]

Historically, the communist era finished with the collapse of the USSR and, eventually, the old communist elites will leave the political scene in Azerbaijan, allowing for '[s]ome form of leadership change [which] has to precede movement towards democracy' (Huntingdon, 1991, p. 296). But such a change *per se* guarantees neither an ultimate victory of democratic forces, nor the success of democratization. It is necessary that the new elites, albeit a coalition government or a 'pure' democratic regime, have learnt lessons from the past in order to avoid the dangers faced by an Azerbaijan in transition. Those dangers include for example, the possibility of a weak and unstable democracy emerging, a failure to develop liberal and democratic traditions and to promote human rights. Other dangers include a revival of nationalism and neglect of ethnic minority groups' interests which in turn, may lead to inter-ethnic tension. The danger of losing a part of the state's territory and its sovereignty as a result of Azerbaijan's defeat in the struggle for its integrity cannot be excluded. Finally, the departure of so dominant a figure as the incumbent president, whose personality serves as a deterring factor to any potential contender, may create a dangerous vacuum of power. Given the weakness of democratic institutions allowing for the peaceful settlement of social and political disputes in society, it is plausible to suggest that the struggle for power after Aliyev may once more lead to 'unchecked and violent power struggles between elites, with the regime ... oscillating between democratic and authoritarian forms ...' (Higley et al. 1998, p. 1-2). This power struggle will not only make the outcomes of transition difficult to predict but will also continue to suspend transitional reforms.

Liberal values versus Azerbaijani traditions

Aliyev's political success and longevity as a political leader in post-Soviet Azerbaijan reflects a wider trend of erstwhile communist elites' reappearance in various parts of the old Soviet sphere. It indicates 'the resiliency of the strong authoritarian trend inherent in the traditional Muslim societies of the former USSR and its significant impact in shaping the socio-political dynamics of the new republics' (Zinin and Maleshenko, 1994, p. 114). Generally, the political, social and cultural context in which the process of democratization began in Azerbaijan presents a sharp contrast to a Western type of society with its respect for individual freedoms and values. Like the overwhelming majority of the former Soviet republics, Azerbaijan started its transition from a post-totalitarian, but still highly authoritarian regime, in the late 1980s. It became fully involved in this process as an independent state since 1991. The Azerbaijani inherited a country which was until recently was a part of the Soviet Union, where the very thought of individual liberties was considered hostile to communist ideology with its strictly hierarchical political structure and its favouring of the collective interests over those of the individual.

Even adoption of a new constitution,[14] which has been an important step in the democratization process,[15] has not guaranteed promotion of liberal democracy and protection of human rights. This is because they are neither endorsed by state policy nor have the leadership's willingness and capabilities to ensure their protection to create the conditions for their implementation. It is difficult to expect a democratic constitution to work effectively in a society with the legacy inherited by Azerbaijan. The country emerged as a fragment of the state of the USSR in which the independence of the three branches of power and the accountability of the ruling elite to the electorate were strictly limited, if not abolished, by the totalitarian character of the regime – a state in which the rule of law was replaced by the authorities' arbitrariness, in which the courts were corrupted, and the very notion of law and justice was consequently undermined in the eyes of the population.

The negative effect of the total neglect of civil and political rights on democratic development in Azerbaijan was enhanced by the communitarian character of the society with its subordination of personal liberties to traditional values. As devastating as the Soviet regime might have been for the traditional Azerbaijani society, it was not able to supplant the alternative system of rules, such as extended local, clan and kinship ties and to uproot close family and community ties that survived repression and remained virtually intact.[16]

In terms of rules and practices, traditional Azerbaijani society, particularly in rural areas, 'tended towards communitarian nationalism' (Maley, 1991, p. 187). It would be naïve to assume that a few years of independence could destroy traditional rules and practices; and the 'main values, mentality, modes of behaviour – what collectively could be called political culture – have remained practically intact [in Azerbaijan]' (Zinin and Maleshenko, 1994, p. 114). Conservation of many customs inherent to the traditional society has facilitated the process of revival of Muslim traditions. Moreover, the combination of preserved traditional values with revival of Islam has made the promotion of democracy in Azerbaijan especially difficult. As empirical evidence shows, 'In practice, with one exception [of Turkey], no Islamic country has sustained a fully democratic political system for any length of time' (Huntington, 1991, p. 307).[17]

Being by their nature antagonistic to liberal democracy, traditional Islamic values present a serious challenge to the democratization project in Azerbaijan. Their revival not only indicates a weakness of liberal traditions and a lack of public adherence to democratic goals, but it also explains the 'resistance', often covert, to the implementation of 'alien' democratic rules and laws, which comes from within society.[18] Although the Azerbaijan

Republic is declared to be a secular state and has joined a series of international covenants on human rights, Islamic customs and rules permeate virtually all spheres of ordinary people's life. These have been eagerly promoted as corresponding more to national mentality since the country gained state sovereignty.

Whilst not denying that the nascent democracy in Azerbaijan is seriously challenged by revival of Islam, seeing it exclusively as a menace to the future of Azerbaijani society would be to oversimplify the issue. There are at least two reasons why the re-emergence of national and religious values should be taken seriously. Firstly, this process can be seen as a natural process of Azerbaijani people rediscovering their own history, culture and language which were ignored and almost assimilated during the Soviet era.[19] Understood as such, this process entails the liberation of the Azerbaijani people from their totalitarian legacy and communist ideology and allows for flourishing and open exercise of religious and cultural traditions forbidden by the Soviet power. Secondly, return to traditional religious customs occurred as a result of free choice for the Azerbaijani people and, thus, should be accepted with due respect, while the democratization project was partially imposed on the society from outside and apparently has less popular support.[20]

This does not imply, however, a denouncement of the promotion of liberal democracy in Azerbaijan, but rather requires an understanding of its peculiarities in Azerbaijani society which differs so radically from European countries. It is also important that a priority in promotion and observation of individual rights and freedoms should be given to those (e.g. freedom of press and the right to fair trial) which serve as necessary prerequisites for the implementation of other liberal and democratic rights such as, for example, the right to peacefully change government.

Conclusion

Although the necessity to urge democratic reforms is constantly emphasized in foreign and domestic political leaders' daily rhetoric, both the general public and scholars are more skeptical about the pace and the outcomes of the process of democratization in post-Soviet Azerbaijan. Surprising as it may seem, scientific analysis of the conditions and challenges concomitant with democratization in the country lead to the conclusion that ordinary people draw on the basis of common sense and intuition: Azerbaijani society is not ready for the extensive and fast introduction of democratic reforms from outside. In particular, a too rapid democratization and liberalization in Azerbaijan in 1989-1993 resulted in mass impoverishment, the marginalization of vulnerable groups such as children, the elderly and disabled, in political instability, in violent armed conflict and on the whole in the unprecedented gross violation of human rights. This is a long-term project which includes the three most serious challenges transitional Azerbaijan faces. They involve building a strong and stable democratic state; achieving consensus among the most influential elites about power sharing, the decision-making process and the goals of the transition;[21] and progressive development of a liberal political culture in society, particularly among the younger generation. In so far as the appropriate culture has not yet developed, '[t]here is little that can immunize these new democracies [in the NIS] and market systems against the dangers of opportunism, defection, erosion, and opportunist subversion of the newly introduced rules' (Offe, 1997, p. 65).

The most urgent issues for Azerbaijan remain those of territory and state, i.e. state-building, and democratization. There are two major alternatives in terms of the state which have yet to emerge in the course of transition in Azerbaijan – authoritarianism and democracy, with variations on the type of regime within both. The issue of building liberal democracy in the country will remain precarious at least in the near future. Revival of a totalitarian regime is also implausible, given how far Azerbaijan has progressed from its post-totalitarian past. The possibility of a weak and unstable democracy is still open, as are the dangers of the emergence of authoritarian nationalism.

Indeed, nationalism remains a serious challenge to democracy. An authoritarian nationalist regime may emerge because the movement for independence in Azerbaijan was 'more [of an] anti-Soviet nationalist movement' than an 'anticommunist democratic' one (Huntington, 1991, pp. 293-94). A nationalist approach still dominates the ideology of the majority of political forces in Azerbaijan. Given that the national issue has not been 'tested' in Azerbaijan yet, it may arise as a backlash against the movement from the 'iron' arm of authoritarian power, as seen previously in the former USSR. Authoritarian nationalism might be chosen as the means of solving delicate issues of citizenship in multi-ethnic Azerbaijan, resolving the relationship between (1)'titular' nationality and conserving minorities, and (2) the representative rights of the latter in the process of nation building. The fact that opportunities and protection depend on the connection with ruling elites leaves ethnic and cultural minorities groups insecure and lays the foundation for potential conflicts. In particular, it may leave the door open to national discord, for overall national consensus about the political order and the form of governance has yet to be achieved.[22]

The only positive alternative to the undesirable and dangerous tendencies in current processes would be to pursue simultaneously goals of stateness and democratization in order to create a democratic state. It is not an easy task for current and future elites, given that the country is now midway between an authoritarian regime and a democratic one. One must consider also the presence of other factors overtly unfavourable to democracy in Azerbaijan, such as the partial imposition of the 'transitional project' and the lack of public belief in democratic values.

In addition, the authoritarian tendencies undoubtedly restrict the speed of the transition in Azerbaijan and make its outcomes more uncertain. On the other hand, as theoretical premises suggest, and empirical evidence confirms, unchallenged rulers have less political motives to violate civil and political rights (Linz, 1992; Goodin, 1992). The experience in Azerbaijan has shown that since Aliyev strengthened and stabilized his authority, some steps towards democratization have been undertaken.

An assessment of Azerbaijan's progress towards democracy and state-building, its human rights record, the role of the elites in transition and the conditions in which the democratization began can lead to rather gloomy conclusions about prospects for democracy in the country. As the ten years of transition in Azerbaijan have shown, no tangible results have been achieved so far. The facts that immense international economic and political support, huge investments, humanitarian aid and other forms of assistance neither brought prosperity nor helped to produce a fully fledged democracy in Azerbaijan, leads to the assumption that in order to make international 'intervention' more effective, some changes to the Western approach to Azerbaijan are needed. This is because transitional Azerbaijan may not have enough capabilities to make the succeeding stages shorter and less arduous, if no significant support from outside is provided. Thus, Western support for fulfilling transitional tasks should be continued. At the same time a policy should be aimed at *prioritizing* the transitional tasks in the country. Their *gradual* accomplishment needs to be enhanced by influential external and internal supporters of democratization and among those in the West who can play a crucial role.

Azerbaijan's intention to strengthen cooperation with democratic states and inter-governmental international organizations along with its aspirations to join European institutions, provides the international community with good opportunities to produce a more positive impact on the transition in Azerbaijan. Moreover, foreign 'intervention' in Azerbaijan is not only desirable but almost required, given that the 'democratic project' has mainly been imposed on the country and remains to a certain extent 'alien' to it.

The policy of a gradual introduction of democratic reforms will bring a more realistic approach to the process and bring about better results in terms of democratization. As an indispensable part of the promotion of democracy, the close and scrupulous monitoring of civil and political rights by the West is vital, while the underlying historical, social, economic, cultural or religious factors should be taken into account (Müllerson, 1995, p. 81). This approach is necessary to avoid excessively rapid reforms, which may become counter-productive, and to ensure the constant progress of democratization.

It may take a long time before liberal democracy is built in Azerbaijan. Yet, the peculiarity of the transition and specific country conditions, may produce a pattern significantly different from the 'classical' Western model, even if Azerbaijan does become the first successfully liberalized and democratized Islamic country.

Notes

1 Dependence of the type of the political regime in a society on existing ethnic, cultural and religious traditions is illustrated by the fact that the overwhelming majority of Muslim countries in the world are highly authoritarian. This correlation will be observed with regard to Azerbaijan later in the paper.

2 NIS stands for the Newly Independent States which emerged after the collapse of the USSR.

3 The modern notion of a democratic state implies a liberal-democratic type of the regime, although initially liberalism and the doctrine of democracy were developed as different philosophical and political concepts. Strictly speaking, there can be a non-liberal democratic state, but in this paper the term 'democracy' will be used as interchangeable with the term 'liberal democracy'.

4 Azerbaijan's only experience of having a state in a modern sense was limited to the two years of the Azerbaijan Democratic Republic, born soon after the failure of the Bolsheviks to extend the October revolution to Baku in 1918, and defeated after the 'restoration' of Soviet power in the republic in 1920.

5 The most unfavourable conditions, i.e. ethnic diversity in the USA, the relative weakness of the state of Luxembourg and the legacy of the fascist regime in Germany, do not usually lead to political instability and gross violation of human rights in a democratic society. The situation in non-democratic states is the opposite: the state violates the rights of the subjects even when there are not challengers to the ruling elites nor conflict situations threatening them. This argument might be illustrated by the examples of some contemporary Islamic countries such as Iran and Saudi Arabia.

6 In general, 'stateness' implies existence of certain attributes to state such as defined territory, legitimacy of the government in the eyes of the population,

exercise of the state power over its subjects, international recognition of the state boundaries and other conditions necessary for a unit to be a state.

7 In this context, elites are defined as persons/groups of persons who occupy key positions in the state administrative system and in the structure of extra-state spheres, such as political opposition parties, civil associations, business corporations, military forces, religious organizations, trade unions and the media. The place of 'non-ruling' elites in society is determined by the fact that they exert substantial influence on the process of political decision-making in the country alongside those in power (Higley, Pakulski, and Wesolowki, 1998).

8 These traditions were inherited from the strict hierarchical administrative system of governance in the former Soviet Union and strengthened by the communitarian type of society. On the whole, the undemocratic character of the regime excluded public participation in the political decision-making process.

9 Although a detailed analysis of the history of post-Soviet Azerbaijanis is far beyond the scope of this paper, a few comments on the political background to Azerbaijan are needed. In September 1991, Ayaz Mutalibov, the former party leader, was elected as the first President of Azerbaijan, but the growing strength of the opposition and its driving force, the Azerbaijani Popular Front (APF), on the wave of new defeats in the armed conflict over Nagorno Karabakh, led to his fall in May 1992. On June 7th 1992, the APF leader Abulfaz Elchibey won the presidential election, in which five candidates were on the ballot. The new Azerbaijan's leadership was determined to adopt new democratic institutions instead of old communist structures. During the year of the APF government, the parliament adopted laws regulating the activities of political parties, public associations and the mass media. About 30 political parties, more than 200 public organizations and about 500 newspapers were registered and began functioning. However, the development of events in 1992-3 showed that democratic forces that were inexperienced in politics were unable to deal with the challenges of state-building. All of the efforts of Elchibey's government to pursue simultaneously the goals of the 'triple' transition appeared to be futile: it failed not only in overcoming the country's problems of statehood, but also in introducing 'any reliable preconditions for a democratic regime' (Zinin and Maleshenko, 1994, p. 114). Threatened by a coup d'etat in June 1993, Elchibey endorsed Aliyev's election as chairman of the Parliament and fled Baku in mid-June. In October 1993, Heydar Aliyev easily won the presidential election.

10 Nonetheless, cessation of hostility allowed Aliyev to concentrate more efforts on the problems of stateness and economic reforms, and also contributed to his image as an initiator of peace talks over the conflict in the eyes of the international community.

11 An experienced and astute politician, Aliyev constructed his power in transitional Azerbaijan by adapting his political agenda to circumstances, while securing his and his elites' position via the methods of compromise and repression. There are only a few forces remaining in overt opposition to the current ruling elites: several political parties created long ago, a few unregistered human rights groups and civil associations and the opposition and

independent media. However, all of these are excluded from political decision-making – the opportunity for power-sharing was deliberately eroded and the ruling elites now comprise a dominant elite of a patrimonial type. The New Azerbaijan Party created by Aliyev became a ruling party resembling in its structure and hierarchy the former Communist Party: all key positions in the government, the military and judiciary are occupied by the members of the 'President's' party. Under Aliyev's power, the state project has become more 'personalistic', i.e. aimed more at strengthening his own legitimacy and authority, although some democratic procedures and attributes have been incorporated into the state's activity.

12 Some positive changes achieved in the country's movement towards democracy since 1991 should not be disregarded. There are about 40 political parties functioning in the republic, at least 10 of which are considered the opposition. In addition, a number of new professional associations and non-governmental organizations (including human rights and women's groups) have appeared; opposition and independent media exist alongside the official media; and the country has gone through several multi-party and multi-candidate presidential and parliamentary elections. However, government policy towards the opposition political parties, the incipient democratic press, human rights groups and civil associations follows one common pattern: the government tolerates their existence, but does not hesitate to use repressive measures against them to protect its interests.

13 For more detailed discussion on this issue see Higley, Pakulski, and Wesolowki, (1998).

14 The new Constitution ratified in November 1995 provides for a wide range of civil and political rights. It entitles every citizen, irrespective of race, nationality, religion, sex, origin, and political party and social unity affiliation and public associations to inviolable, undeniable and inalienable rights and freedoms. They include, inter alia, the rights to life and property, the freedom of thought, speech, conscience and information, and the right to elect and to participate in the political life of the society and the state. Not all of the provisions of the constitution meet the requirements set out by the relevant international covenants on civil and political rights, but the major problem is its due observation in a society where the rule of law has yet to be established.

15 A democratic constitution is often cited as a foundation which 'the durability of the democratic institutions and procedures can be assumed to rest on ...' (Offe, 1996a, p.257).

16 This is particularly true for the rural areas of the country, while Baku, the capital, has been more influenced by the processes of 'Russification' and 'Westernization'.

17 However, recent events in Turkey, e.g., the official policy towards the Kurdish issue and covert pressure on the democratic press and opposition raise deep doubts as to whether democratic culture in the country is fully-fledged and developed.

18 Liberal democracy and the traditional Islamic society differ radically from each other in basic principles and attitudes towards individual rights and the good of the society. A liberal democratic state is ruled by civic law and is characterized by public participation in making decisions about vital issues regarding social and political life of the society. In contrast, it is religious rules and traditional customs that determine all spheres of the community life in an Islamic society, where the common good is seen as superior to individual interests and a narrow circle of ruling elites make decisions regarding the life of the community.

19 It should be noted that the Azerbaijani alphabet was changed three times during Soviet era and was finally replaced by Cyrillic. The communist leaders of the former USSR made all possible efforts to cut Azerbaijan's connection with other Muslim countries.

20 Liberal and democratic ideas were known in Azerbaijan, like anywhere else in the former Soviet Union, and there were a few dissidents in the republic in the 1970s and 1980s, but these ideas were not widely spread or supported by local traditions and political culture.

21 However, such a consensus may or may not lead to a more democratic alternative, for it does not necessary imply mass participation in these processes and may exclude some groups of the population from them, e.g. ethnic minorities. Thus, achieving consensus among elites is a necessary but not sufficient condition for successful democratization.

22 Aliyev's so far successful attempts to 'freeze' the national issues instead of addressing them may turn out to be a fatal problem for his successors.

References

An-Naim, A. (ed.) (1992), *Human rights in cross-cultural perspectives: a quest for consensus*, University of Pennsylvania Press, Philadelphia.

Donnelly, J. (1989), *Universal Human Rights in Theory and Practice*, Cornell University Press, Ithaca and London.

Dunleavy, P. and O'Leary, B. (1987) *Theories of State. The Politics of Liberal Democracy*, Macmillan, Houndmills.

Elster, J. (1993), 'The Necessity and Impossibility of Simultaneous Economic and Political Reform' in D.Greenberg et al., (eds), *Constitutionalism and Democracy: Transitions in the Contemporary World*, Oxford University Press, Oxford.

Frank, P. (1994), 'Problems of Democracy in Post-Soviet Russia' in I. Budge and D. McKay (eds) *Developing Democracy*, Sage Publications, London.

Gurr, T. (1986), 'The Political Origins of State Violence and Terror' in M. Stohl and G. A. Lopez (eds), *Government Violence and Repression. An Agenda for Research*, Greenwood Press.

Higley, J., Pakulski, J., and Wesolowski, W. (1998), 'Introduction: Elite Change and Democratic Regimes in Eastern Europe' in J. Higley, J. Pakulski and W. Wesolowski (eds), *Postcommunist Elites and Democracy in Eastern Europe*,

Macmillan, Basingstoke.

Hunter, S. (1997), 'Azerbaijan: Searching for New Neighbors' in I. Bremmer and R. Taras (eds), *New States, New Politics: Building the Post-Soviet Nations*, Cambridge University Press, Cambridge.

Huntington, S. (1968), *Political Order in Changing Societies*, Yale University Press, New York.

Huntington, S. (1991), *The Third Wave Democratization in the Late Twentieth Century*, University of Oklahoma Press, Norman and London.

Kukathas, C., Lovell D. W., and Maley W. (eds) (1991), *The Transition From Socialism: State and Civil Society in the USSR*, Longman, Cheshire, Melbourne.

Kymlicka, W. (1995), *Multicultural Citizenship: a Liberal Theory of Minority Rights*, Clarendon Press, Oxford.

Linz, J. (1992), 'Types of Political Regimes and Respect for Human Rights: Historical and Cross-national Perspectives' in A. Eide, and B. Hagtvet (eds), *Human Rights in Perspective. A Global Assessment*, Blackwell, Oxford.

Linz, J. and Stepan, A. (1996), *Problems of Democratic Transition and Consolidation: Southern Europe, South America, and Post-Communist Europe*, Johns Hopkins University Press, Baltimore.

Mansfield, E. and Snyder, J. (1998), 'Democratization and the Danger of War' in *International Security*, Vol.20, No.1, Summer 1998, pp. 302-334.

Monshipouri, M. (1995), *Democratization, Liberalization and Human Rights in the Third World*, Lynne Reinner, Boulder, CO.

Müllerson, R. (1995), 'Perspectives on Human Rights and Democracy the Former Soviet Republics' in I. Pogany (ed.), *Human Rights in Eastern Europe*, Edward Elgar, Cheltenham.

Offe, C. (1996a) *Modernity and the State: East, West*, Polity Press, Cambridge.

Offe, C. (1996b) *Varieties of Transition*, Polity Press, Cambridge.

Offe, C. (1997) 'Cultural Aspects of Consolidation: A Note on the Peculiarities of Postcommunist Transformations' in *East European Constitutional Review*, Vol.6, No.4, Fall 1997, pp. 64-68.

Poggi, G. (1978) *The Development of the Modern State: a Sociological Introduction*, Hutchinson, London.

Rubin, B. (1998), 'Conclusion: Managing Normal Instability' in B. Rubin, and J. Snyder (eds), *Post-Soviet Political Order: Conflict and State Building*, Routledge, London.

Swietochowski, T. (1995), *Russia and Azerbaijan: a Borderland in Transition*, Columbia University Press, New York.

Taghyieva G. (1998), *Transition to Democracy: Azerbaijani Pattern?* MA Dissertation, Essex University, UK.

Wasilewski, J. (1998) 'Elite Circulation and Consolidation of Democracy in Poland' in J. Higley et al. (1998).

Zinin, Y. and Maleshenko, A. (1994) 'Azerbaijan' in M. Mesbahi (ed.), *Central Asia and the Caucasus After the Soviet Union: Domestic and International Dynamics*, University Press of Florida, Gainesville.

2 Unemployment Benefits: Social Justice or 'Social Hammock'?

DORIS SCHROEDER

Over the past decade, the welfare state has come under sustained attack not only from quarters which never approved of its policies but also from social theorists who used to support it. One area of concern is the alleged impact of welfare provision on work incentives. As Patrick Minford (1992, p. 117) puts it: 'If you can have the good life anyway, why bother to work and strive?'. The 'work incentives' argument against the welfare state is based on assumptions about human nature and reflections on modern state systems. Human beings, it is maintained, are characterised by an in-born desire for repose and an aversion to work. This disposition has been suppressed during most of human history. Work has been accepted as an unpleasant but unavoidable evil; a necessity to ensure survival. The emergence of the welfare state, however, untangled the age-old relationship between work and subsistence. Hence, huge numbers of malingerers are nowadays attracted by the availability of income without effort, according to opponents of welfare provision.

Frank Field (1996, p. 16) believes that the current British welfare system destroys work incentives, honesty and effort whilst 'recruiting a nation of cheats and liars' (ibid., p. 11). To target this alleged problem, the government launched an anti-fraud Website in May 1999 (http://www.dss.gov.uk/hy/bfraud) with tips on how to report benefit cheats. In North America, Charles Murray (1996, p. 23) claims that welfare has created the so-called 'underclass'; a social group allegedly characterised by nonwork, alcohol abuse, delinquency and general fecklessness. Lawrence Mead (1986, pp. 22, 197f) argues that nonwork fostered by welfare provision causes serious behavioural problems such as crime, family breakdown and illegitimacy in an ever growing 'parasitic class'.

Western libertarians and conservatives gained unexpected support when state communism collapsed. 'We pretend to work and they pretend to pay us' (Fukuyama, 1992, p. 11) is how Soviet workers described their relationship with communist rulers; suggesting that neither did they earn much nor did they work hard. The work incentives argument is seen as pivotal to explanations about the breakdown of communism. Joseph Stiglitz (1994, p. 68) writes that the 'failure to provide incentives is generally viewed as a central reason for the failure of the Soviet System'. Harold Perkin (1996, p. 203) claims that Soviet workers put all their effort into 'malingering, absenteeism, alcoholism on the job, and avoiding work by whatever means they could'. According to him (ibid.), 'a system that pays people to cheat and shirk rather than work constructively ... is a formula for disaster'.

System collapse has already occurred in the East and now opponents of the welfare state predict a similar fate for the West. But are their fears justified? Is the welfare state at risk of being overwhelmed by a growing majority of wilful idlers? This article sets out to invalidate this claim on three counts. First, it will be shown that psychological research lists powerful and widespread non-pecuniary work incentives. Second, empirical evidence will be given which contradicts the assertion that benefit fraud is a frequently occurring problem. Third, an analysis of the 'lazy scrounger' debate in Germany will reveal inconsistencies and ideological elements in the positions adopted by opponents of the welfare state.

Work incentives – the 'narrow' and 'broad' views

There are three possible ways to trigger unwanted action: use threats, employ coercion or provide incentives. If you want to help a friend stop smoking, you could explain the likelihood of dying from lung cancer, throw all her cigarettes away or promise a trip to Greenland after three smoke-free months. In all cases, the action itself – giving up smoking – is unpopular but external pressures might help to bring it about. The concept of incentives as external stimuli for action implies that the required action contravenes natural motivations. Incentives can be seen as a bribe to achieve goals where natural inclinations are lacking. The mere addition of the word 'incentives' to an activity therefore indicates that the action is unpleasant and does not come naturally. Hence, 'work incentives' denotes that work is an activity without intrinsic value which requires external stimulants in order to be carried out. Two different views on the nature of work incentives will be presented: the 'narrow' view and the 'broad' view.

One basic principle has been implemented in welfare states throughout the West: 'nobody should get from welfare that which he or she could get from working' (Macarov, 1980, p. 38). This rule – which even has a name in German (*Lohnabstandsgebot*) – has been advocated both in Anglo-Saxon and West European countries (Macarov, 1970, p. 15; Kühl, 1996, p. 37). It is based on the belief that rational individuals cannot be expected to work unless their earnings exceed benefit levels (Dex, 1989, p. 15). According to this view, there is only one incentive which can tempt human beings from repose to work: money. This is why it is crucial to maintain a significant gap between income from work and income from social services. If the gap narrows, income available through the state would present too pleasant an alternative to work. Or in the jargon of welfare state critics: The state would provide a 'social hammock' for 'work shy individuals' and 'shirkers' (Muhr, 1994, p. 57). This position will be called the 'narrow' view on work incentives because it acknowledges only one incentive: money.

Research from the field of 'occupational psychology' and studies on unemployment show a different picture. Their findings on non-pecuniary work incentives can be condensed into the following table under three headings: 1) Extrinsic incentives to work; 2) Intrinsic incentives to work and 3) General characteristics of work. This division of incentives into three main groups has been made for ease of presentation but also because some incentives only apply to some jobs. Prestige, for example, an extrinsic incentive, is not normally associated with plumbing.

Table 1
Incentives to Work

Extrinsic incentives	**Intrinsic incentives**	**General characteristics of work**
Prestige, status	Pride of accomplishment	Time structure
Respect, acceptance	Happiness	Social contact
Power	Self-respect	Purpose
Income	Identity	

Extrinsic Incentives to Work

Extrinsic incentives to work will be understood as reasons for work based on positive external events or reactions. A money transfer from employer to employee at the end of the month is such an external, positive event for the employee. It is also the only work incentive accepted by the narrow view, thereby carrying heavy weight. However, there are other motivations for work than obtaining money, the most important extrinsic of which are: prestige (status), respect (acceptance) and power.

Prestige is singled out by John Kenneth Galbraith (1962, p. 274) as a highly motivating factor for work. He argues that one offends the advertising man, the business executive, the professor, the poet, the tycoon and the scientist by alleging that their prime motivation for work was pay. Although pay is 'not unimportant ... prestige – the respect, regard, and esteem of others – is ... one of the more important sources of satisfaction' (ibid.).

In a psychological study on the motivation to work, Lutz von Rosenstiel (1996, pp. 51f) finds three motives which can be categorised as extrinsic: money, prestige and enhanced attractiveness leading to better chances in the 'marriage market'. In *Incentives to Work*, David Macarov (1970, pp. 82f) identifies acceptance and recognition by fellow workers as well as the attainment of a sense of power, both of which can be called extrinsic. The field of occupational psychology, which mainly deals with work incentives, has established that status is a powerful force behind the decision to work (McLaughlin, Millar and Cooke, 1989, p. 122). Based on these three studies, prestige (status), respect (acceptance) and power are listed in the above table as non-pecuniary extrinsic incentives. The group is completed by adding income, which is recognised as a work incentive by both the narrow and the broad view.

Intrinsic Incentives to Work

Extrinsic incentives are characterised by the fact that they cannot be achieved in Robinson Crusoe situations. Lookers-on and team or opposition players are fundamental to the concepts of power, respect and prestige. In contrast, intrinsic incentives are independent of bystanders; they are felt from within rather than being acknowledged from outside. The most important intrinsic incentives are pride of accomplishment, happiness, self-respect, and identity.

Pride of accomplishment is named as a highly enduring work incentive by A.J. Speakman in *Work Study and Incentives* (1951, p. 12). He claims that every human being possesses instincts of craftsmanship and ambition which lead to initiative and enthusiasm for work and feelings of satisfaction and pride of accomplishment.

Sigmund Freud (1970, p. 89; Mazlish, 1975, p. 62) connects happiness with work; he even contends that 'work is indispensable for human happiness'. Half a century after Freud's death the American psychologist Mihaly Csikszentmihalyi (1996, p. 14) draws the same conclusion. He has been examining the requirements of happiness for over twenty years. In meticulous empirical research he has found that work contributes greatly to happiness; not monotonous labouring, but highly concentrated work which ends in what he calls 'flows', euphoric streams of creative activity. According to Csikszentmihalyi, 'flows' are experienced not only by obsessed scientists and heart surgeons but also by welders, farmers, joiners etc. The flow-like feeling of satisfaction depends on reaching the personal ability limit and not on the regard a job carries in a community. The important factor is to be neither over- nor under-challenged.

A third intrinsic incentive from the above list is self-respect, the meaning of which is frequently discussed in philosophical literature. John Rawls (1995, p. 125), for example, suggests that self-respect has two aspects. First, self-respecting people believe that their concept of the good and their plan of life is worth putting into practice. Second, they expect that it lies within their power to execute these plans. What is important in our discussion is the relationship between self-respect and independence. Elizabeth Telfer (1995, p. 111) claims that 'a man with self-respect... will have the quality of independence'. The second aspect of Rawls' definition also suggests that independence is an important prerequisite for self-respect. Being dependent often means being drawn into the life plans of others and having to fit into theirs rather than carrying out one's own. How do self-respect and independence come into the work incentives debate? According to research into unemployment carried out by Graeme Shankland (1980, p. 29), most able-bodied people without paid work want to have a job to improve or 'maintain their independence and self-respect'. Receiving unemployment benefits robs claimants of self-respect, dignity and confidence, according to Paddy Ashdown (1997, p. 16). A similar view is taken by McLaughlin, Millar and Cooke (1989, p. 122) whose study on benefit receipt showed that unemployment is not only tedious and boring but also highly stigmatised and hence inconducive to self-respect.

Identity, the last intrinsic work incentive from the above table, is characterised by the same feature as self-respect. It is usually taken for granted when present but its lack often follows from unemployment. In psychology, identity is understood as the establishment and maintenance of a balance between personal individuality and the entirety of role expectations in any given social setting (Kwiatkowski et al., 1985, p. 195). The supreme social expectation in the post-war West is to hold a job in order to provide for oneself (Lister, 1999, p. 234). This expectation explains why unemployment can interfere unfavourably with the sense of identity. Elizabeth Wilson (1977, p. 177) writes that the ability to provide for a family is seen as an essential part of manhood and thereby a proof of virility. Once a man loses his job he is often confronted with a feeling of lost identity both in his eyes and in the view of his wife. However, lack of identity in periods of non-employment is not an essentially male problem. Studies about women who care for young children or look after dependants show that staying exclusively at home is often associated with low morale and poor mental health (Pascall, 1986, p. 57). Gillian Pascall tries to explain this by suggesting that the wife / mother / carer identity on its own is not rewarding but often demoralising and stigmatised in our society. Women appreciate having an identity separate from the household and an identity derived from work gives them self-confidence, a feeling of being in touch with the world and a better relationship with their family, according to Sue Sharpe (1986, p. 57). Identity completes the group of intrinsic incentives which also comprises pride of accomplishment, happiness and self-respect.

General Characteristics of Work

One of the most influential studies of unemployment in the post war period was carried out by Maria Jahoda et al., who researched the impact of job losses on people's lives over a long period of time. The essence of their studies is conveyed by the following extract (Jahoda et al., 1975, p. 83 – my translation):

> Whoever observed the tenacity of the working classes to fight for more leisure ... could come to the conclusion that there is at least one gain in the misery of unemployment: unlimited free time. But a closer look shows that this free time is a tragic gift. Dissociated from their work and without contact with the outer world, workers have lost the material and moral possibilities to make use of their time. They, who do not have to hurry anymore, do not make any new beginnings and gradually decline from a regulated existence into unbounded emptiness. When they run back over a section of their free time, nothing comes into their mind which would warrant the effort to talk about it.

This excerpt from Jahoda's research confirms Paul Jackson's (1994, p. 115) claim that unemployment is an overwhelmingly negative experience for the majority of those concerned. According to William Robson (1977, p. 121), unemployment means misery and hardship for individuals and a waste of human resources for society. It even has medical implications. Studies showed a straightforward correlation between rising unemployment and higher levels of mental health problems such as depression and psychotic morbidity (Rifkin, 1995, p. 195). The majority of those concerned view unemployment as an act of violence, according to Oskar Negt (1995, p. 7). They feel that it is an attack on their physical and mental integrity; a robbery and expropriation of their abilities which are no longer in demand. These experiences can lead to severe personality disorders (ibid.). In the long term unemployed, doctors even observed symptoms similar to those of dying patients such as loss of vitality, resignation and general weariness (Rifkin, 1995, p. 195f). Even the short and medium term unemployed experience symptoms that are normally only correlated with the loss of a friend or a relative, namely ill health, chronic lethargy and feelings of despair (Grint, 1991, p. 41). A study in West-Yorkshire undertaken in 1983 also revealed a rise in male impotence amongst the unemployed (Franks, 1999, p. 139). In the words of Dennis J. Snower (1994, p. 41): 'For most people the state of unemployment is far from agreeable; it commonly brings with it illness, family problems, and loss of self-esteem'.

Why does unemployment cause such an amount of misery? Apart from the previously mentioned extrinsic and intrinsic benefits of employment, it is the more mundane general characteristics of work which are missed strongly by unemployed people from all strata of life, namely: time structure, social contact, and purpose.

What do the unemployed do when they are not looking for jobs? Research showed that men do not usually start to share domestic responsibilities with their partners, neither do they begin moonlighting or charitable work. One study showed that unemployed of both sexes spend much more time watching television and sleeping compared to previously (Warr, 1985, p. 165). In general, observations suggest that unemployment robs people of the will to begin any kind of constructive activity (Grint, 1991, p. 45). Instead, some try to keep up appearances by leaving the house during what they perceive as working hours. This indicates that they cling to outdated time structures instead of establishing new ones. Others lose all sense of time and despite abundant leisure are often persistently unpunctual for job interviews. The above findings show that structures taken for granted by those in work are destroyed through unemployment: 'structures of time, routine ... and social networks' (ibid.).

Another characteristic of work which might be lost during unemployment is social contact. Peter Warr (1985, p. 165) sees two reasons why interpersonal contacts are significantly reduced in periods of unemployment. First, if there is no work place to go to, there are no colleagues to meet during working hours. Second, unemployment often leads to lack of money and a need to reduce social events (pub, tennis, parties etc.) for financial reasons.

The third general characteristic of work is purpose. According to Charles Handy (1985, p. xii) the link between purpose and work is not embedded in human nature but stems from the fact that modern Western societies are employment societies, i.e. wealth is generated and distributed through jobs. He describes work in employment societies as the 'financial and the social lynchpin of most people's lives and ... the source of much of the meaning of their existence' (ibid.). If individuals are made redundant in this type of society their purpose of life is being called into question, according to Handy. A good source for studies on the link between work and life purpose are feminist publications. According to Daniel Rogers (1978, p. 209), the feminist movements of the 19th and 20th centuries equated idleness with constriction, work with purpose and paid work with freedom. They demanded engagement in work to escape suffocation, play a part in society and give purpose to life (ibid., p. 196). A feminist case study unfolded when East Germany was reunited with the Federal Republic in 1990. In 1989, 90 per cent of East German women were in paid work. Four years later, nearly a third had lost their jobs. With the imposition of the West German system, most mothers found it impossible to juggle careers and children. Part time work is not freely available, schools finish at one p.m. and most nurseries do not accept children under three. Although some mothers were pleased to stay at home, most 'were embittered by the loss of purpose and income' (Fisher, 1995, p. 160).

The above studies reveal numerous incentives to work other than income, but are they all relevant in the work incentives discussion? Extrinsic incentives only apply to the upper echelon of highly regarded jobs. Those who claim that welfare provision causes work disincentives, are not suggesting that barristers, scientists or surgeons will stop working when benefit levels reach parity with earnings. Not only do their jobs carry prestige, respect and power but they are also highly paid and income could never be satisfactorily substituted by benefits. This restriction must, however, not be made as strongly for intrinsic incentives. 'Flows' of happiness linked with work are experienced without reference to social regard. Similarly, loss or lack of identity and self-respect are related to the experience of unemployment in general, rather than not being, specifically, an architect or IT consultant. The only type of work which was excluded from the benefit of intrinsic incentives was monotonous labouring. Could it be that the work incentives argument applies to this type of job? Although it might be very hard to believe that mundane, boring or dirty jobs have any sort of attraction, research did show that they are often preferred to unemployment because they provide purpose, time structure and social contact. The majority of unemployed feel that stigma, purposelessness and boredom outweigh any gain in leisure, according to McLaughlin, Millar and Cooke (1989, p. 122). Fifty per cent of those questioned said they would even prefer employment if they could secure a higher income from social security (ibid.).

The general conclusion which can be drawn is that benefits do not compensate for everything which is missing from a life without employment. Accordingly, the assertion that work will be replaced by benefits at every opportunity must be considered doubtful. To further strengthen this claim, empirical evidence on benefit fraud will be presented.

Benefit fraud

The issue of benefit fraud and workshyness seems to reveal different positions held by libertarians / conservatives and liberals / social democrats. According to Ben Wattenberg (1996), conservatives typically argue that social security provision encourages laziness and fraud, whilst liberals tend to disclaim this relationship and give other reasons for non-work (e.g. structural unemployment).

Can independent empirical evidence bring any light to the discussion as to whether benefit fraud and workshyness occur on a grand scale in Western welfare states? In Germany, comprehensive research on benefit fraud has been undertaken during the past two decades. From 1983 to 1989 the University of Bremen cooperated with the Centre for Social Policy (*Zentrum für Sozialpolitik*) to complete an extensive study on benefit abuse and poverty. Researchers examined the case of every tenth new claimant during the seven year period, conducted numerous interviews and analysed around 1,000 old files. They drew the following two conclusions. First, benefit abuse is a rare event as is the phenomenon of workshyness in claimants, most of whom were either close to pension age, ill or – at the time – without chances in the job market. Second, only a minority of 1.3 per cent of recipients slipped into long term dependency, i.e. stayed on benefits for more than ten years. Most people were confident and independent enough, according to research findings, to leave the rolls quickly (Leibfried et al., 1995).

In *Social Security – Myth and Reality* (1995 – my translation), Petra Buhr describes the provisional conclusions of an ongoing study at the Martin-Luther University in East Germany which began in 1994. According to Buhr, who is one of the participating researchers, this study shows that benefit fraud is restricted to a minority of cases. Most recipients are indeed not able to work either because of age, sickness or full time care obligations. She concludes that 'the reproach of abuse does not carry far: only a minority of benefit recipients is actually able to work ... 'abuse' and 'workshyness' are not really a topic' (ibid., p. 1067 – my translation). Rather than being an easy option for workshy fraudsters, welfare provision does, according to Buhr (ibid., p. 1068), fulfil its role in society as a temporary aid to self-help.

Although it could be argued that these research results have no explanatory power outside Germany, it must be noted that the 'work incentives' argument is based on an alleged anthropological constant – the desire for repose – and the specific design of the welfare state. This means that benefit fraud must be an unavoidable, general feature within all welfare states.

Based on the above studies, the existence of extensive benefit fraud could not be corroborated. On the contrary, fraud was shown to be minimal. Could it be that the fraud argument is right-wing rhetoric, i.e. a well maintained myth? This conclusion presents itself since the core statements cannot be squared with empirical data. To affirm this claim, developments in the German political debate will be analysed to see whether ideological elements can be detected.

The 'lazy scrounger' debate in Germany

In 1996 and 1997 allegations of widespread social security fraud by idle scroungers came to a halt in Germany. While former Chancellor Kohl (1995, p. 2 – my translation) earlier spoke of 'collective leisure parks' for the voluntarily unemployed which burdened the economy, he later directed his criticism towards other sections of the population, namely immigrants and women. However, unemployment and the resulting spiralling social security budget remained the major domestic problems in Germany. In the summer of 1998, 4.1 million people were registered as unemployed. What changed? Why did the 'lazy scrounger' rhetoric run out of steam in Kohl's last term of government?

In August 1995, German parliament passed a bill to target allegedly workshy individuals. Those who refused suitable work had their benefits reduced by 25 per cent. It was assumed that unemployment would fall significantly in the following periods. Estimates brought forward by conservatives suggested that at least 20 per cent of the unemployed could be brought back into work with this measure (ap / dpa, 1995, p. 1). The following chart shows the development of unemployment figures in Germany in the 1990s:

Figure 1
German unemployment 1991-1997

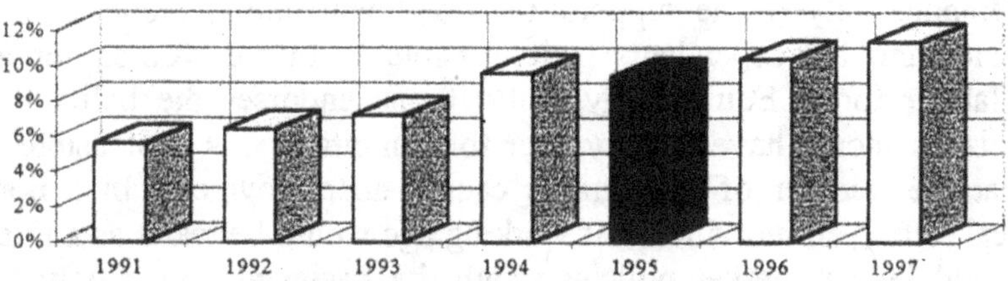

Source: Data from 'Bundesanstalt für Arbeit' (1998).

As can be seen, unemployment figures did not drop after 1995. On the contrary, a steady rise could – despite this measure – not be stopped. The assumption that unemployment is motivated by workshyness in approximately 20 per cent of cases was given up. Nobody argued that unemployment would have grown significantly more without the bill, that the workshy accepted a reduction in benefits in preference to working, or that the black economy has grown because of the bill. Rhetorical reference to the 'leisure park mentality' of voluntarily unemployed Germans simply vanished.

Instead, in a governmental statement in early 1997, Kohl (1997, p. 3) stated that the number of full time jobs has not fallen during the past twenty years. What has changed significantly is not the *demand* for, but the *supply* of, labour. First, women have taken up employment in huge numbers and second, Germany has experienced a large stream of immigrants in recent decades. To elucidate this point, Kohl stated that the country traditionally receptive to immigrants, the United States of America, allowed entry on a permanent basis to 720,000 individuals in 1995. During the same year, 1.1 million immigrants entered Germany. Horst Seehofer, the then German health minister, also tried to direct the public eye towards expenditure on immigrants. In a speech in 1996 (Seehofer, 1996, p. 14), he said that 32 per cent of all basic social security funds (*Sozialhilfe*) were paid to foreigners.

Rhetorical reference to the lazy (German) scrounger who causes deficits in the social security budget was hence not sustained after the new welfare bill was introduced. Although the German government now conceded that labour supply exceeded labour demand, no new measures to bring supply and demand into balance were proposed. Instead, new scapegoats were found, namely immigrants and women. The recognition that welfare provision does not cause major work disincentives must be applauded, but the appearance of another ideological explanation for unemployment is just as problematic. Only if one supports the traditional family model of one breadwinner and his dependants is it possible to blame women for an inflated labour force. Equivalently, only if one endorses the belief that native citizens should have priority over foreign citizens, is it plausible to argue that the number of immigrants causes unemployment. In a non-ideological setting all individuals of working age would be taken as a fixed constant and labour market policies would be designed accordingly (or unemployment be accepted as unsolvable). It can, however, be concluded that although one mode of right-wing rhetoric was replaced by another, the 'work incentives' argument suffered a silent defeat in the process.

Conclusion

'If you can have the good life anyway, why bother to work and strive?' Why? Because the good life in modern employment societies cannot be equated with subsistence on state benefits. Apart from income, 'working and striving' provide social contact, purpose and time structure. Often, they are the basis for self-respect, pride of accomplishment, happiness and identity and in some cases ensure prestige, respect and power. In contrast to the 'lazy scrounger' typology which paints the picture of a carefree malingerer enjoying plenty of agreeable leisure pursuits, studies on the effects of unemployment reveal a disquieting intensity of misery, hardship, illness, boredom and unhappiness. It is therefore not surprising that independent empirical research on benefit fraud showed it to be a rare event. Welfare provision does not foster a class of scrounging voluntary unemployed as libertarians and conservatives claim. Instead it fulfils its role in society as a safety net and temporary aid to self-help. In this respect it is a vehicle for basic social justice, understood as achieving a minimum standard of human well-being rather than a policy that provides a 'social hammock' for liars and cheats. In résumé, the work incentives argument must be unmasked as a myth which holds a dominant but unjustified position in the welfare state debate.

References

ap / dpa (1995), 'Sozialhilfe sinkt bei Arbeitsverweigerung', *Kölner Stadt Anzeiger*, 19/7/95, p. 1.

Ashdown, P. interviewed by Rogers, S. (1997), 'A Liberal dose of common sense', *The Big Issue in the North*, No.144, 03/03/97, p. 16.

Buhr, P. (1995), 'Sozialhilfe – Mythos und Realität', *Blätter für deutsche und internationale Politik*, Vol.40, No.9, pp. 1060-70.

Bundesanstalt für Arbeit (1998), Enquiry by telephone, 30/04/1998, 0049-911-1790.

Csikszentmihalyi, M. (1996) cf. Č.P. Šesin, 'Süsse Lust der Arbeit', *Die Woche Extra*, No.52, 20/12/96, p. 14.

Dex, S. (1989), cf. McLaughlin, E., Millar, J. and Cooke, K., p. 15.

Field, F. (1996), 'Making Welfare Work: The Underlying Principles', in Deacon, A. (ed.), *Stakeholder Welfare*, IEA Health and Welfare Unit, London, pp. 7-44.

Fisher, M. (1995), *After the Wall – Germany, the Germans and the Burdens of History*, Simon & Schuster, New York.

Franks, S. (1999) *Having None of It: Women, Men and the Future of Work*, Granta Books, London.

Freud, S. (1970; orig. 1930), 'Civilization and its Discontents', cited in Macarov, D., p. 89.

Fukuyama, F. (1992), *The End of History and the Last Man*, Penguin Books, Harmondsworth.

Galbraith, J.K. (1962), *The Affluent Society*, Penguin Books, Harmondsworth.

Grint, K. (1991), *The Sociology of Work*, Polity Press, Cambridge.

Handy, C. (1985), *The Future of Work*, Basil Blackwell, Oxford.

Jackson, P.R. (1994), 'Influences on commitment to employment and commitment to work', in: Bryson, A. and McKay, S. (eds), *Is It Worth Working? Factors affecting labour supply*, Policy Studies Institute, London, pp. 110-121.

Jahoda, M. et al. (1975), *Die Arbeitslosen von Marienthal*, Suhrkamp Verlag, Frankfurt.

Kohl, H. (1995), cf. Sussenburger, J., 'Es geht ans Eingemachte', *Kölner Stadt Anzeiger*, 19/7/95, p. 2.

Kohl, H. (1997), 'Eine gute Zukunft für Deutschland', *Das Parlament*, Vol.47, No.7/8, pp. 3-4.

Kühl, J. (1996), 'Warum schaffen zwei Millionen Betriebe und Verwaltungen nicht genügend gute Arbeitsplätze für alle?', *Aus Politik und Zeitgeschichte*, 12/1/1996, No.B3, pp. 26-39.

Kwiatkowski, G. et al. (1985), *Schülerduden – Philosophie*, Dudenverlag, Mannheim.

Leibfried, S. et al. (1995), *Zeit der Armut*, Suhrkamp Verlag, Frankfurt.

Lister, R. (1999) 'Reforming Welfare Around the Work Ethic: New Gendered and Ethical Perspectives on Work and Care', in: *Policy and Politics*, Vol.27, No.2, pp. 233-246.

Macarov, D. (1970), *Incentives to Work*, Jossey-Bass Inc. Publishers, San Francisco.

Macarov, D. (1980), *Work and Welfare – The Unholy Alliance*, Sage Publications, Beverly Hills.

Mazlish, B. (1975), *James and John Stuart Mill*, Hutchinson, London.

McLaughlin, E., Millar, J. and Cooke, K. (1989), *Work and Welfare Benefits*, Avebury, Aldershot.

Mead, L. (1986), *Beyond Entitlement*, Free Press / Macmillan, New York.

Minford, P. (1992) 'Gray on the Market', in J. Gray, *The Moral Foundations of Market Institutions*, IEA Health and Welfare Unit, London, pp. 115-118.

Muhr, G. (1994), 'Bekämpfung der neuen Armut erfordert Gegenmacht', in W. Beywl (ed.), *Soziale Sicherung*, Bundeszentrale für politische Bildung, Bonn, pp. 57-58.

Murray, C. (1996), 'The Emerging British Underclass', in R. Lister, (ed.), *Charles Murray and the Underclass – The Developing Debate*, IEA Health and Welfare Unit, London.

Negt, O. (1995), 'Die Krise der Arbeitsgesellschaft: Machtpolitischer Kampfplatz zweier "Ökonomien"', *Aus Politik und Zeitgeschichte*, 7/4/95, Vol.B15, pp. 3-9.

Pascall, G. (1986), *Social Policy – A Feminist Analysis*, Tavistock Publications: London.

Perkin, H. (1996), 'The Third Revolution and Stakeholder Capitalism: Convergence or Collapse', *The Political Quarterly*, Vol.67, No.3, pp. 198-208.

Rawls, J. (1995), 'Self-Respect, Excellences and Shame', in R.S. Dillon (ed.), *Dignity, Character and Self-Respect*, Routledge, London, pp. 125-132.

Rifkin, J. (1995), *The End of Work*, Jeremy P. Tarcher / Putnam Books, New York.

Robson, W. A. (1977), *Welfare State and Welfare Society*, George Allen & Unwin, London.

Rogers, D.T. (1978), *The Work Ethic in Industrial America 1850-1920*, The University of Chicago Press, Chicago.

Rosenstiel, L. von (1996), *Motivation im Betrieb – Mit Fallstudien aus der Praxis*, Rosenberger Fachverlag, Leonberg.

Seehofer, H. (1996), 'Mehr soziale Gerechtigkeit', *Das Parlament*, Vol.46, No.11, p. 14.

Shankland, G. (1980), *Our Secret Economy*, Anglo-German Foundation, London and Bonn.

Sharpe, S. (1986), cf. Pascall, G., p. 57.

Snower, D. J. (1994), 'Why people don't find work', in: Bryson, A. and McKay, S. (eds), *Is It Worth Working? Factors affecting labour supply*, Policy Studies Institute, London, pp. 39-59.

Speakman, A.J. (1951), *Work Study and Incentives*, Emmott & Co., Manchester.

Stiglitz, J.E. (1994), *Whither Socialism?*, MIT Press, Cambridge Massachusetts.

Telfer, E. (1995), 'Self-Respect', in: R.S. Dillon, (ed.), *Dignity, Character and Self-Respect*, Routledge, London, pp. 107-116

Warr, P. (1985), cf. Handy, C., p.165.

Wattenberg, B.J. (1996), *Welfare as seen by those who know*, on the Internet: http: //www.aei.org: 80/oti6829.htm, 08/1996.
Wilson, E. (1977), *Women & the Welfare State*, Tavistock Publications, London.

3 Liberalism and Social Justice: Voyaging between Conceptual Antipodes in the Good Ship Democracy

IAN DUNCANSON

(1) Australia and the 'new republics'

The title of our conference is 'The Liberal Order: The Future for Social Justice?'. Does the question mark suggest a questionable outlook for social justice in a liberal order, or does it nominate liberal ordering as social justice's future? The concepts of liberalism and social justice themselves are too large to define in a short paper and I must work with brief, largely implicit notions of them especially if, as I think, democracy belongs somewhere between them if they have any possibility of informing a stable political practice. Liberalism, transformed by substantive democracy might produce conditions of social justice, and we might call the citizen of this happy combination a free person. Whether liberalism so transformed would still be liberalism is another matter. Perhaps we should be more concerned with practices than with definitions, and not write as if concepts could be fixed, made unavailable for purposes not envisaged by earlier generations.

This paper was written in, and in part about, Australia, but some of the difficulties with the connection of liberalism and social justice faced by Australia are faced also by some of the newly independent countries of the east and south. Australia belongs to the Anglophone world, which the British and subsequently the US have made globally hegemonic. But Australians form perhaps 5 per cent of the population of that world and, like the new republics, are routinely expected to accept – and have applied to them by their governors – social, political and economic solutions worked out, often not well, in Britain or the United States. Neo- or market liberalism is being represented as the guarantor of freedom in both Australasia and the newly independent countries. I will explain why the doctrine threatens the opposite, but I want also to notice the imperialist cultural tradition from which it emerged. Market liberalism is the response of elites dismayed by the prospect that the containment of democracy by that earlier tradition was failing.

The high levels of foreign ownership in Australian production go together with the repatriation of profits, the location of basic research in overseas head offices and the pursuing of policies which have been formulated elsewhere. As in the new countries of the east and south, this gives Australian management, the 'organic intellectual' middle class (in Gramsci's sense; see 1971, chapter 1), some slight flavour of the third world comprador – the compliant middleman between overseas rentiers and an exploited local labour force (Colebatch, 1999) the recent attrition of whose trades union rights has attracted criticism from the International Labour Organization. The ease with which the practices of the rule of law, traditionally conceived, are dispensed with in Australia when government friends must be accommodated may also look familiar to easterners (Gough, 1999; Hayward, 1999). Finally, and there may be signs of change here, there is the question of the intellectual critic, and his or her role and effectiveness. Capitalist publishing and the willingness of a small country to perceive itself to be marginal reinforce each other in Australia in ways that may resonate elsewhere. To be an 'international scholar' in a world dominated by metropolitan publishing houses means to write for their, metropolitan, audiences, which are perceived as being uninterested in 'a faraway country of which we know little'.[1] Intellectuals who analyze their own, non-metropolitan society, may forfeit 'international scholarship' status and paradoxically lose legitimacy in their own country.[2]

(2) Liberalism, democracy and social justice

For the purposes of this paper I have taken liberalism to refer to two main ideas. First, that the deprivation of life, liberty and property are permissible only after affected parties have had a substantively equal opportunity to be heard by a tribunal with no vested interest in the outcome and which in its published reasons must demonstrate its impartiality. Where education and access to legal representation are rationed according to wealth, this requirement remains unsatisfied, and there are thus no fully liberal Anglophone societies. Second, I take liberalism to have inherited the requirement of its Whig antecedents that political authority should be subject to effective checks and balances. Liberalism, in this formulation, does not have much to say about who will check and balance whom and to what end, or about the desirable distribution of property. For this reason, it is unsafe to concede a discursive monopoly on freedom to philosophers who favor minimalist liberalism.

I have taken social justice to require respect for difference and the avoidance of major material inequalities, insofar as they become intergenerationally entrenched or produce major inequalities of life chances or well-being. But to move practically from liberalism to social justice without risking the disaster of authoritarian utopianism, one needs to place the abstractions about what social justice might mean into the context of the kind of democracy in which an informed, educated and politically active population has a voice in the institutions through which it is governed. The vitality of political debate and the existence of choice in the public arena (not just consumer choice in the market place) is where liberalism can commune with social justice, if it can do so at all. This situation is not unachievable and does not require an already perfected humanity, or involve fairy tale visions of eternal happiness. It will not be the end of history. So the point is that we will not agree about the ingredients of social justice either at any one time, or over time. The institutions of liberalism will not by themselves enable us to do so. Yet coupled with democracy, they can at least make it possible for us to live with disagreement. But then we need to pay some attention to the institutions which enable informed choices to be made. In an era of mass communication and mass higher education, the media and the universities are obviously of crucial significance.

(3) The media

The Australian media are currently treading gingerly around a new scandal. John Laws, one of Sydney's best-known 'shock-jocks' (Adams 1996), an influential radio talk-back host with populist conservative views, had been amplifying the prevailing conviction that Australian banks have become ruthless profiteers – closing rural branches, thus rendering local communities unviable, and treating staff and urban customers with contempt. His agent then approached the Australian Bankers' Association, proposing that Laws would cease his on-air attacks on their industry, if the Association paid him, according to ABA documents, $1,200,000. The money was paid, and Laws' listeners suddenly discovered from him that there were two sides to every story, and that there were, after all, reasons for the banks' policies (Melbourne *Age*, 24/7/99; http://www.abc.net.au/mediawatch/transcripts/990712).

The Laws case is perhaps just a logical extension of the idea of commercial intellectual property. Opinions are bought and used under conditions of commercial confidentiality. One does expect that commentators in certain media will reflect the strategic views of commercial employers, who are, or who are often linked to, large corporate interests. Thus while major social and personal crises exist in Australia because virtually all net job growth between 1985-1997 was in casual jobs with no recreation, sick leave or superannuation entitlements, to find serious discussion of this, one would need to tune into public or community rather than commercial radio, or read a newspaper not owned by a tycoon who is profiting from the process. However, governments do not want to fund media agencies which investigate their dealings with the corporate sector (Williams, 1996). Nor have they much interest in defending independent newspapers from predatory conglomerates, with whom governments often have cosy relations. Of concern here is the frailty of the independent press and the vulnerability of public broadcasting – not, nowadays, to a bureaucracy with parochial preoccupations about secrecy, morality and the national interest, but to a restructured and footloose capitalism often, in effect, masquerading as government.

Like his peers in Sydney, Perth and Adelaide radio and the right wing columnists in the tabloid and occasionally broadsheet press, Laws appeals to a no-nonsense individualism, suspicious of intellectuals, of complicated explanations for social problems, and of government and large organizations. Skilfully, these commentators have positioned themselves as spokespersons for a tactically useful new category of 'ordinary Australians'. Their skill has been useful to conservative politicians who give them interviews and reward their support with 'leaked' information about government intentions[3] (Toohey, 1994, pp. 221-2). Politicians have thus been able to appeal to 'ordinary Australians', or 'all Australians', whilst, for example, de-funding programs for Aborigines, new migrants or refugees, and pursuing regressive tax and labor relations strategies as part of the political economics of inequality.

Of course, the populations of all capitalist economies, whatever government they have voted for, have all had to manage the conflict between capital and labor by one means or another – usually in this century and during times of peace by recognizing it to be inevitable, but negotiating and skirmishing around it. All parties in the many other simultaneously occurring conflicts create their own myths, which may be appropriated by others. The ersatz Crocodile Dundee myth of mateship has functioned in Australian self-understanding[4] to displace urban struggles between privilege and its lack into a rural story in which all men in the outback help and acknowledge each other as equals, despite disparities of wealth and power (Ward, 1958; Trainor, 1996, ch. 6). Perhaps, once, as a narrative, 'imagining' a community in Benedict

Anderson's sense (Anderson, 1991), it helped the process of negotiation among men in the workplace in the absence of anything more substantial – certainly its principal analyst never claimed more than mythological status for it. But a progressive politics can perhaps learn from the critiques that its currency constituted a form of denial of the inequalities of ethnicity, class and gender in Australia (Pascoe, 1979; Kapferer, 1996). From the historian who has done most to recover the story of the Europeans' attempted genocide of Aboriginal people has come the agonized question about the denial of that issue, which most poignantly exposes the tawdry myth of mateship: '*Why weren't we told?*' (Reynolds, 1999).

Now that 'we have been told', the notions of 'all Australians' and 'ordinary Australians' seem yet more sinister than a story of inequality (and it has quickly led to the notion of 'un-Australian', a category whose overtones evoke unwelcome memories of recent US or European history.[5]) 'All Australians' were, according to the federal Attorney General, 'insulted' when the UN Committee on the Elimination of All Forms of Racial Discrimination found Australia in breach of its CERD obligations because of its treatment of Aboriginal people (Melbourne *Age*, 20.3.99) – an interpretation designed to undercut any Aboriginal claim to benefit from the mutual obligations of citizenship in a country which has ratified CERD. We may, if we are aware of the conflict of interest, be sceptical of stories about Aboriginal land rights told by media narrators whose employers run cattle on land they do not wish to be made subject to land claims. But the Laws episode leads us to suspect that even where there is no such visible conflict of interest, any editorializing may be the product of a sponsorship deal. The free market in ideas becomes the freedom of capital to create a fantasy world in which what it wants is good for everyone. In this world, to disagree is to be fractious and un-Australian.

Op-ed commentary, for long unwilling or unable to reflect on the use of some media to promote the other commercial enterprises of their owners, or on the permeation of 'lifestyle journalism' by advertising, seems, by its virtual silence on the Laws issue, to have developed a yet more refined myopia in order not to see the fundamental problem which covertly purchased opinion represents to democratic processes.[6] The conservatives' insistence that one has only to worry about instrumental distortion and propaganda in state-controlled media is wearing thin now that the Australian public broadcaster has become the only serious evaluator of government activity,[7] and the only one not owned by an organization which may expect government favors.[8] Perhaps the apologists will soon invoke the cynical possibility that the frothy quality of ever greater quantities of news and commentary, produced by ever fewer journalists (Tiffen, 1993), has led the public no longer to distinguish between information and entertainment – and to expect no more from 'this news up-date proudly brought to you by McDonald's family restaurants' than a reminder about burgers. So why, the question may be, give the viewers indigestion by confronting them with fare which has not been bought and processed with an eye to its profitability?

This corruption of good faith editorializing by commercial interests exposes the problem in the connection of liberalism to social justice, to the extent that the stability of the connection depends on informed democratic discussion and choice. On the one hand liberal freedoms are conventionally considered to depend in part and to involve a respect for property rights. On the other hand, the pursuit or defense of social justice in a liberal society – even the protection of the liberal polity itself – is thought to depend on there being an effective watchdog role for the media and its audience, because the opinion of an informed public is arguably the most effective influence over governments in office, and the precondition for effective choices between candidates for office. This is the rationale for the First Amendment to the US Constitution, in the world's first attempt at democratizing liberalism; and the Australian High Court has expressed the same sentiment in a case declaring unconstitutional a statute forbidding political advertising in the days immediately preceding a federal election (Australian Capital Television, 1992; Nationwide News v Wills, 1992). Where the subversion of the media's watchdog role is made possible by the political indulgence of corporate capitalism's preference for secrecy, near-monopoly or conglomerate media ownership, at best the achievement of greater social justice is likely to be limited, and at worst, liberal regimes may themselves not survive. Social justice has already suffered. In Australia, Brian Toohey has noted the complicity of journalists employed by corporate tycoons in justifying the regress (Toohey, 1994, p. 222).[9]

As to the demise of liberalism, we should not assume that authoritarianism, the erosion of citizenship, and the subversion of certain aspects of legality amid the practical destruction of free critical expression will announce their arrival suddenly or with military violence, as in the 1920s and 1930s, or in Chile in the 1970s. Nor, though, should we assume that the language of economics, through which the destruction of the twentieth century welfare state form of liberal government is being accomplished, is somehow not a form of authoritarian politics – whatever its users may say, or even think. The destructive potential of what is called in Australia 'economic rationalism' for both liberal freedoms and social justice is considerable;

and again one encounters the conflict between opinion which is held and expressed honestly and in good faith and that which corporate wealth has bought and which, in the vocabulary of corporate think tanks themselves, is used as 'propaganda' to 'bombard' 'enemy intellectuals' in educational texts, courses and seminars and in the news media. The intellectual odyssey of conservative political economy from think tanks to the political system and the corporately owned media has been well-documented. Making the world safe for corporate capital in the *fin de siecle* west is more likely to rely on the propagation of some ideas, the silencing of others and the co-optation and corruption of critical evaluation than on brownshirts.

(4) The universities

There is a belief often expressed by public commentators in Australia and elsewhere that ideas – especially those which form the currency of humanities scholars in universities – are a form of self-indulgence: 'hobbies' which are inconsequential, or worthy of attention and criticism only because they are seen to be publicly funded.[10] A decade ago, Stephen Knight wrote of the suspicion by business, the media and education bureaucrats in Australia of any research unlikely soon to make a profit (Knight, 1990) – and, one might add, of any education which is not simultaneously a form of job training. But 'universities must continue to adapt to the training needs of industry'[11] is the English mid-Victorian attitude so amusingly parodied by Matthew Arnold (Arnold, 1994; orig. 1869). Not only did the fixation at that time with the 'practical' and the vocational produce an intellectual rigidity associated by late nineteenth century writers with Britain's economic decline (Gamble, 1985, pp. 10-11), but Arnold believed that cultural sterility (self-imposed on the bourgeois, and imposed by them on the working class) had produced 'an upper class materialized, a middle class vulgarized and a lower class brutalized' (Arnold, 1994, p. 218).

Of course ideas are not inconsequential, and 'it would be deceptive to present the academy as a whole as marginal to the current socio-economic and political system' (LaCapra, 1997, p. 63). Much of the new theory in the academy which has attracted media scorn and bureaucratic ax-wielding, argues Threadgold (1997, p. 123),

> has been about challenging dominant narratives. This has meant that it has inevitably been about language, a struggle for meaning and for power ... Cultural theory in these terms has been threatening on several fronts at

> once: threatening to hegemonies, to those who prefer stasis to social change, threatening linguistically...

Both institutions of learning and some of the new intellectual developments have been the focus of the 'culture wars' (Reid, 1998).

In recent times, and not only in left wing paranoid fantasies, the CIA perfected a peculiarly illiberal defense of anti-Communism by the use of 'mercenary intellectuals'[12] – artists, writers, philosophers, orchestral conductors, ex-Nazis and middle of the road liberals – rhetorically conflating anti-Communism with liberalism and justifying bad faith by reference to supposedly lofty goals (Saunders, 1999). A secret 'entrepreneurial coalition of philanthropic foundations, business corporations and other institutions and individuals ... worked ... with the CIA to provide cover for its secret programs in Western Europe' (Saunders, 1999, p. 129). The CIA funded 'a seemingly limitless range of covert action programs affecting youth groups, labor unions, universities, publishing houses' and thoroughly penetrated the fund-giving foundations. The Ford Foundation 'had a record of close involvement in covert operations in Europe, working closely with Marshall Plan and CIA officials ... At times it seemed as if the Ford Foundation was simply an extension of government in the area of government propaganda' (Saunders, 1999, p. 139).

The ease with which the CIA was able to extract secret money from business corporations and use them as cover and accomplices in its operations, Saunders suggests, indicates a convergence of interests which need not surprise us between the Agency and multinational capital (see Wright, 1987, p. 369). The recurrence in the accounts of right wing think tank activities of some of the names on Saunders' lists of CIA-sponsored scholars and their promoters, and of most of the language, objectives and tactics of the CIA and its various front organizations such as the Congresses for Cultural Freedom, seems to confirm this (Carey, 1995). Just like that of the CIA, the cultural strategy of the Olin Foundation, the Heritage Foundation and countless others across at least the Anglophone world has been to pretend the existence of certain common values: a common culture from which some had unaccountably strayed, to which some could be converted, and in relation to which some would remain recalcitrant and have to be rendered ineffective – in the case of the environmentalists, for example, 'by pouring money into ad campaigns, lawsuits, elections, books and articles ... blaming the environmentalists for all the nation's ills, from the energy crisis to the sexual revolution' (Kirkpatrick Sale, quoted in Beder, 1997, p. 18). The CIA's purpose, according to Saunders, was to combat what it perceived to be a European preference for communism, and to combat it across the whole field of what anthropologists would conceive as culture: in formal political institutions, through covert intervention in elections and coups d'etat (http://www.seas.gwu.edu/nsarchive), in the institutions of civil society, in the arts, education and in scholarship and publishing. The overlaps in time, organizations and personnel and the isomorphism in political philosophy between the operation of the CIA depicted in Saunders' study and that of the think tanks in the studies of Carey (1995), Cockett (1995) and Kelsey (1995) suggest a continuity.

If the Ford Foundation could appear to Saunders' sources as at times a propaganda arm of the US government, certain key institutions in Anglophone governments in the last two decades have taken on the appearance of propaganda arms of corporate conservatism,[13] and this development is spreading to schools and universities whose independently administered funding was originally calculated to prevent this (Beder, 1997, p. 19):

> the Australian Chamber of Commerce and Enterprise Australia used surveys of school leavers to find 'deficiencies' in their attitudes to the free enterprise system and then circulated corrective materials through the schools.

Fund-starved public universities and university research centers are entering sponsorship arrangements with multinational corporations 'where the distinction between pedagogy, promotion and marketing is not clear' (Beder, 1997, p. 173). Not coincidentally, university managements are now promulgating 'codes of conduct' giving themselves the power to censor such expressions of academics which might offend the sponsors. Again, there is manifest an ironic parallel between corporate and Soviet politics.

(5) The context of Anglo-Australian liberalism

At the beginning of the paper I suggested some similarities between the developments and problems currently faced by Australia and by some newly independent countries. Clearly these can be overstated, and in the immediate postwar years, no similarities would have been apparent at all. Both the UK and Australia emerged from World War II with apparently intact representative democracies and an apparent commitment to some degree of equality and the collective sharing of risks of social harm. The conflict of interest between labor and capital had not been overcome, but in the broad social context, Keynesianism seemed to have allowed for constructive negotiations between the two. How was the political and cultural restructuring of the postwar changes possible, so that employment relations have once again become authoritarian and insecure, taxation is rapidly becoming more regressive, access to the legal system is becoming once again the sole preserve of the powerful, and citizens have been transformed into consumers? The economic determinist answer is not persuasive since not all successful socio-economic systems have adopted the Anglo/neo-liberal strategy (Hutton, 1995) (despite Australian financial journalists' attempts to demonstrate otherwise[14]), and since the 'economic' decisions made by elites in business and finance are simultaneously political. Hutton (quoted in Bell, 1997, p. 279) makes the same point slightly differently:

> policies that produce more output and stability of demand benefit ... labor ... and so directly constrain business power. From the elite's point of view, it may be preferable to run the economy more unstably and inefficiently if the alternative is any reduction in its autonomy of action.

What I want to suggest is a cultural answer. Liberalism without democracy would never go beyond a Whiggism of little use to most of us: a balanced constitution of elites – 'the managing committee of the bourgeoisie' in Marx's terms – and an arid equality of all before the law, which would ignore the problems of class and cost which beset litigation and legislation. Social justice without democracy would never contain the possibility of negotiation, compromise and change, without which it might amount to little more than an assumption that 'Father (or, less likely, Mother) knows best'. The future, and it is not a guaranteed future of justice, might be liberalism – but only, I suggested, in the presence of democracy, over which the culture wars have been fought. And the civic culture which forms the context of education in Anglo-Australia evolved over two centuries as a way of containing democracy.

This culture, in which the universities and the media developed, condensed around its current disciplinary assumptions during the building of an empire (not an egalitarian or democratic enterprise) and under the shadow of the French Revolution – the latter an event perceived by Britain's rulers as both democratic and an inevitable route to tyranny; and in turn, a threat to property. Race and class were not seen as exclusive categories in the nineteenth century (Thorne, 1997). The task of ordering the disordered by means of a gradual coalescence of culture and literature into Englishness was applied to natives, to middle and working class men and to women. In the process it seemed to define the national character, and, as Perry Anderson has noted of Britain, literature and criticism came to dominate the institutions of liberal learning in Britain (Anderson P., 1992, ch. 2) – to define the horizons of what is reasonable and possible. The East India Company, and later the Supreme Council of India, persuaded by Macaulay, determined to bind the natives to Britain through the use of English culture. A suitable class of Indians in blood and color, but English in aspiration and outlook, would be interpreters and intermediaries between the rulers and the millions (Viswanathan, 1997). The canon of English literature – the criteria and exemplification of excellence which came to define the discipline of English – began here, and, suggests Scholes (1998, pp. 105, 107)

> it is likely that the ready application of canes as weapons of punishment ... supported those dimensions of the meaning of kanon that connote severity and the imposition of power ... Many a native had Shakespeare as well as other canonical texts caned into him by the curricular arm of the British Raj.

India was, as Pennycook, writes 'a key site for the development of policies that then flowed back to England ... empire is ... a system that allowed culture and knowledge produced in the colonial encounter to flow back to the imperial center' (Pennycook, 1998, p. 69). In the early decades of the nineteenth century, Coleridge, revolting against both the failed promise of revolution and the inhumane prescriptions of Malthusian political economy, dreamt of a 'National Church', whose 'clerisy' would combine pastoral care and pedagogy to create a dutiful English subject, as well as add to the cultural stock of knowledge (Coleridge, 1817 and 1829, in Morrow, 1990). By 1847, Macaulay spoke in the House of Commons in favor of publicly funded elementary education (Macaulay, 1847, in Ellis, 1889) on the ground, among others, that a government with (necessary) rights to punish incivility had an obligation to teach civility. Not twenty years later, Matthew Arnold is comparing schools and prisons, as places both to confine potentially disorderly people and to teach them 'orderly, decent human behavior' (Baldick, 1983, p. 34). And, of course, to be taught one's duties, one required to have a teacher who had in turn learned – increasingly – *hers* (Eagleton, 1983, p. 27):

> the (male) working class was not the only oppressed layer at whom ... English was beamed. English literature, reflected a Royal Commission witness in 1877, might be ... a suitable subject for women and the second and third rate men who become schoolmasters.

I think Perry Anderson correctly identifies the persistence of this culture of placing (Anderson, P., 1992, chs. 2 & 5), remarking that whilst it produced admirable results in 1940, by the 1960s it was distinctly outmoded. Its erosion in an era of mass higher education, and when foreign ideas about democracy once more appeared likely to infect property rights and the conduct of business,[15] led to its transformation into something more effective. Neo-liberalism is the offspring. Among conservative intellectuals in both the US and the UK, the apparent collapse of the culture they espoused conjured all the demons it had been supposed to keep at bay: women, illiterate workers and black people, heavily armed with theories, would take over.

Conclusion

Culture is, of course, about placing, telling stories about who we are and why, but some examples of it are more liberating than others. Symptomatic of the imperatives permeating the culture I have described are the responses to the challenges to it, for example by the cultural theories to which Terry Threadgold refers (Threadgold, 1997). Democracy was perceived as French, and Anglophone culture was organized to preserve the world of the white gentleman from a fantasy in which radical theories would infect women, natives and workers and destroy civilization. 'Culture,' Matthew Arnold wrote, 'has but one great passion, the passion for sweetness and light. Yes, it has one greater! – the passion for making them prevail. It is not satisfied till we all come to be a perfect man' (Arnold, 1994, p. 460). This culture is not, in some naive accounts, theoretical, perhaps because theories may be evanescent or rejected in favor of other theories. Part of the reason for the failure of Australian universities, according to two authors, is that '(t)heory has become dominant in English and the other humanities. It is essentially French', as one would expect, and, it follows, also despotic: 'a graduate student who chose not to adopt a theoretical stance in his thesis would have to explain why' (Maslen and Slattery, 1994, Introduction). In Harold Bloom's lament for the demise of the old cultural story, the barbarians now within the humanities' academic gates are feminists, Marxists, Lacanian, Black Studies and New Historicist scholars (Bloom, 1995, ch. 23). The dominance of this coalition of black, left-wing, psychoanalytic women is a chimera, but one which neatly exposes the politics of the cultural story he is defending.

Neo-liberalism, which is offered to us by Anglophone missionaries as the savior of freedom, is, I have suggested, merely an updated model of the system of cultural beliefs espoused by Bloom, of which the British rulers were thoroughly convinced and the Americans at least found congenial and useful. Freedom seems to me much more likely as a result of a reflexive, self-conscious combination of liberalism, democracy and the permanent negotiation of social justice.

Notes

1 The description of Czechoslovakia popularly attributed to Neville Chamberlain after his 1938 pact with Adolf Hitler.
2 A culture which cannot take the analysis of itself as serious scholarship reminds us of the Marx Brothers joke that a club which would accept one's membership would not be worth joining.
3 Less influential Parliamentary journalists have been promised 'the high level drip' from government if they cooperate, and threatened with high level persuasion on their employers to sack them if they do not.
4 The current Australian Prime Minister wants to include the word 'mateship' in a new constitutional preamble.
5 Civil society organizations which a number of writers have seen as vital to democracy, and as distinguishing liberal or social democracy from Soviet-style communism (Keane, 1988) – organizations from free trades unions representing workers in particular industries, feminist groups and societies for the disabled, to ratepayers or the users of the local swimming pool – are re-labeled by the new conservatism as 'special interest groups'. They can then be contrasted with the abstraction of the ordinary Australian, and their claims translated into biased special pleading (Farrar and Inglis, 1996, Introduction). It is an interesting reversal of Thatcher's 'there is no such thing as society' into 'there is no such thing as the physical manifestation of democracy'. It is also one of many ironic resemblances between corporate and Soviet politics.
6 Concern has frequently been expressed, of course, but rarely in the media and media practice does not reflect much awareness of the problems raised in the literature (Curran et al, 1988; Baker, 1994; Bacon, 1995).
7 Conservatives' skepticism about government information is in any event very selective, as one saw during the recent NATO bombing of Serbia, 'smart' missiles which turned up in the Chinese Embassy or in Sofia, Bulgaria notwithstanding.
8 Recently, for example a TV station owner who was about to acquire a publicly owned asset from the state government on favorable terms, pulled a story investigating alleged insider dealing by the state premier.
9 See also McGregor (1997, p. 169) on the gushing tone adopted by the Business Review Weekly in 1987. Simon Marginson paraphrases von Hayek's message to the Economic Society of Australia and New Zealand thus: 'people must face uncertainty and stress, or they would not learn to prevail ... "To suffer disappointment, adversity and hardship is a discipline to which most in society must submit"' (Marginson, 1997, p. 67).
10 'Intellectual life is very vulnerable. If attitudes to it are not changed radically and quite quickly, Australia will find itself no longer the possessor of a .. lively and crucial cerebral component of the national culture' (Knight, 1990, p. 187). The essays in Bartolini, Lynch and Kendal (eds) (1997) respond to the

same (worsened) problem, which has now deteriorated further with the departure overseas of many leading scholars.

11 A quotation in The Australian Higher Education Supplement 7/4/99 from one Joanne Tylor in a new Green Paper on higher education.

12 The authors are actually describing the scholars sponsored by conservative think-tanks.

13 Notably, to begin with, Treasury departments (Kelsey, 1995, ch 2; Pusey, 1991). Subsequently, this process spreads, as the Westminster tradition of public service tenure erodes and corporate sector outsiders are employed to head departments as generic managers for whom education, ice cream and automobiles are fungible items (Alford and O'Neill, 1994; Gregory, 1997).

14 Toohey, 1994, p. 329 and elsewhere, quotes an attempt to demonstrate the failure of Sweden's economy in a graph comparing Australia's current account deficit with that of Sweden. The Swedish deficit was measured in kronor, the Australian in A$, and as A$1 was worth 4.86 kronor, the kronor number was bigger. Adjusting for the exchange rate made Sweden's deficit one third that of Australia.

15 The Bullock Report of 1977 recommended importing forms of industrial democracy familiar in Europe (Hutton, 1995, pp. 86-7). It was against the Wilson government which commissioned the report that Peter Wright alleged a coup was planned by a group of businessmen and MI5 operatives in 1974 (Wright, 1987, p. 369). Thatcher, beneficiary of the business abhorrence of Bullock, spent millions of British government money to have Wright's book suppressed, successfully in the UK, unsuccessfully in the US and Australia.

References

Adams, P. (1997), *Talkback*, ABC Publications, Sydney.

Alford, J. and O'Neill, D. (eds) (1994), *The Contract State: Public Management and the Kennett Government*, Deakin University Press, Geelong, Vic.

Anderson, B. (1991), *Imagined Communities* (2nd edn), Verso, London.

Anderson, P. (1992), *English Questions*, Verso, London

Arnold, M. (1994; orig, 1869) *Culture and Anarchy*, Yale University Press, New Haven, CT.

Australian Capital Television v Commonwealth (1992) 177 *Commonwealth Law Reports* 106.

Bacon, W. (1995), 'Market Control of the Media', in J. Rees and G. Rodley (eds), *The Human Costs of Management*, Pluto Press, Sydney.

Baker, E. (1994), *Advertising and a Democratic Press*, Princeton University Press, Princeton, NJ.

Baldick, C. (1983), *The Social Mission of English*, Oxford University Press, Oxford.

Bartoloni, P. Lynch, K. and Kendal, S. (eds) (1997), *Intellectuals and Publics: Essays on Cultural Theory and Practice*, La Trobe University School of English, Bundoora, Vic.

Beder, S. (1997), *The Global Spin: The Corporate Assault on Environmentalism*, Scribe, Melbourne.

Bloom, H. (1995), *The Western Canon*, Macmillan, London.

Bourdieu, P and Wacquant, L. (1999), 'On the Cunning of Imperialist Reason', *Theory, Culture and Society*, Vol. 16, No. 1, February.

Bowman, D. (1988), *The Captive Press*, Penguin, Melbourne.

Carey, A. (1995), *Taking the Risk Out of Democracy*, University of New South Wales Press, Kensington, NSW.

Cockett, R. (1995), *Thinking the Unthinkable: Think Tanks and the Economic Counter-Revolution 1931-1983*, Fontana, London.

Colebatch, T. (1999), 'Casual Jobs, Serious Crisis', Melbourne *Age*, 27 July.

Coleridge, S. T. (1990), 'Property and Responsibility: A Lay Sermon' (1817); 'On the Constitution of Law and State', in J. Morrow (ed.), *Coleridge's Writings on Politics and Society*, Macmillan, London.

Eagleton, T. (1983), *Literary Theory: An Introduction*, Blackwell, Oxford.

Farrar, A. and Inglis, J (eds) (1996), *Keeping it Together: State and Civil Society in Australia*, Pluto Press, Sydney.

Gamble, A. (1985), *Britain in Decline: Economic Policy, Political Strategy and the British State*, Macmillan, London.

Gramsci, A. (1971; orig. 1929-35), *Selections from the Prison Notebooks*, Q. Hoare, and G.N. Smith (eds), Lawrence and Wishart, London.

Gregory, R. (1997), 'The Peculiar Tasks of Public Management: Toward Conceptual Discrimination', in M. Considine, and M. Painter (eds), *Managerialism*, Melbourne University Press, Melbourne.

Gough, J. (1999), 'The Kennett Government and the Constitution: No Change?' in B. Costar and N. Economou (eds), *The Kennett Revolution: Victorian Politics in the 1990s*, University of New South Wales Press, Kensington, NSW.

Hayward, D (1999), 'We're on the move, but we're losing the race', Melbourne *Age*, 9 August.

Hutton, W. (1995), *The State We're In*, Jonathan Cape, London.

Kapferer, J (1996), *Being All Equal: Identity, Difference and Australian Cultural Practice*, Berg, Oxford.

Keane, J. (1996), *Democracy and Civil Society*, Verso, London.

Kelsey, J. (1995), *Economic Fundamentalism: The New Zealand Experiment*, Pluto Press, London.

Knight, S. (1990), *The Selling of the Australian Mind*, William Heinemann Australia, Melbourne.

LaCapra, D. (1997), 'Addressing the Politics of Research', in E.A. Kaplan and G. Levine (eds), *The Politics of Research*, Rutgers University Press, New Brunswick, NJ.

Macaulay, T.B. (1889), 'Speech to the House of Commons of 18/4/1847', in Ellis, T. (ed.), *The Miscellaneous Writings and Speeches of Lord Macaulay*, Longmans Green, London

Marginson, S. (1997), *Markets in Education*, Allen and Unwin, Sydney.

Maslen, G. and Slattery, L. (1994), *Why Our Universities Are Failing*, Wilkinson Books, Melbourne.

McGregor, C (1997), *Class in Australia*, Penguin, Melbourne.
Nationwide News v Wills (1992), 177 *Commonwealth Law Reports* 1.
Pascoe, R. (1979), *The Manufacture of Australian History*, Oxford University Press, Melbourne.
Pennycook. A. (1998), *English and the Discourses of Colonialism*, Routledge, London.
Pusey, M. (1991), *Economic Rationalism in Canberra*, Melbourne University Press, Melbourne.
Reid, I. (1998), *Higher Education, or Education for Hire? Language and Values in Australian Universities*, Central Queensland University Press, Rockhampton, Qld.
Reynolds, H. (1999), *Why Weren't We Told: A Personal Search for the Truth about our History*, Allen and Unwin, Sydney.
Saunders, F. (1999), *Who Paid the Piper? The CIA and the Cultural Cold War*, Granta, London.
Scholes, R. (1998), *The Rise and Fall of English*, Yale University Press, New Haven, CT.
Thorne, S. (1997), 'The Conversion of Englishmen and the Conversion of the World Inseparable: Imperialism and the Language of Class in Early Industrial Britain', in F. Cooper and E.A. Stoler, (eds), *Tensions of Empire: Colonial Cultures in a Bourgeois World*, University of California Press, Berkeley, CA.
Threadgold, T. (1997), 'Cultural Theory, Community Politics and the Media', in Bartolini, P. et.al, supra.
Tiffen, R (1993), 'The Press', in S. Cunningham and G. Turner (eds), *The Media in Australia*, Allen and Unwin, Sydney.
Toohey, B. (1994), *Tumbling Dice: The Story of Modern Economic Policy*, William Heinemann Australia, Melbourne.
Trainor, L. (1996), *British Imperialism and Australian Nationalism: Manipulation, Conflict and Compromise in the Late Nineteenth Century*, Cambridge University Press, Melbourne.
Viswanathan, G. (1997), 'Currying Favor: The Politics of British Educational Policy in India', in A. McClintock, A. Mufti, and E. Shoat (eds), *Dangerous Liaisons: Gender, Nation and Postcolonial Perspectives*, University of Minnesota Press, Minneapolis.
Ward, R. (1958), *The Australian Legend*, Oxford University Press, Melbourne.
Williams, R. (1996), *Normal Service Won't Be Resumed: The Future of Public Broadcasting*, Allen and Unwin, Sydney.

4 Why Pluralism?

ALISON ASSITER

Pluralism is assumed by many, liberals and communitarians alike, to be both factually inevitable in the contemporary world, and normatively desirable. John Rawls, for example, states the problem of justice as follows: 'how is it possible that there may exist over time a stable and just society of free and equal citizens profoundly divided by reasonable, though incompatible, religious, philosophical and moral doctrines?' (Rawls, 1993, p. xxv). Some contemporary liberals, indeed, see the toleration, or more strongly, the accommodation of a plurality of moral and religious viewpoints, to be of paramount importance. Tolerating and recognising difference becomes, on this view, a profoundly significant feature of what it means to treat another as a free citizen.

Pluralism is taken to be obviously true in the contemporary world, because what is often taken to be its contrary – universalism – is seen to be false. So, for example, it is said that universalism implies: (a) that we must develop a substantive conception of human nature, when all attempts to do that have been shown to be culturally specific; (b) improbably that one can consider the interests of the whole of humanity; and (c) some improbable way of looking at ideal political or moral outcomes as benefiting every individual in the same way. (This way of looking at some universalist arguments is usefully summarized by Calder, 1998, pp. 148-9.) The assumption underlying pluralism is that there can be no true conception of morality that all reasonable people would accept. I am not going to defend universalism in this paper, but I would like to look at some of the arguments that have been put and might be put in defence of pluralism, and to challenge some of them.

There may be some who would claim both to be pluralists and universalists. For example, Rawls might claim to be a universalist about justice and a pluralist about other values. However, it is questionable to what extent Rawls is a universalist. He certainly does not see himself this way in his recent work (Rawls, 1993). Rather he sees the task of political philosophy to be that of finding solutions to problems in a particular range of societies. He believes that there cannot be a 'true' moral theory. Several have argued that his conception of justice relies upon a particular institutional context (at the same time as it ignores some aspects of its institutional context; see for example Young, 1990).

I'd like to begin the paper by distinguishing types of pluralism, before going on to look at the kinds of argument that might be presented in favour of each type. The distinctions I am about to make are not necessarily either exhaustive or exclusive, but they may help to separate those pluralist clams that are legitimate from those that may not be.

Pluralism, in the literature, usually falls into the following categories: (i) cultural or national pluralism; (ii) moral or value pluralism; and a third category which is sometimes thought to underpin the first two – (iii) structural difference in such areas as class, ethnicity, sexual orientation, disability, gender and race. These structural differences are said to lead to pluralism of the first two types. In this characterisation of types of pluralism, I am specifically concerned with those categories that are of interest in political philosophy and political theory. (For a more general characterisation of pluralism, see McLennan, 1995.)

(1) Structural pluralism

I shall begin by discussing the third category. Feminists have argued that significant cultural, moral and political assumptions which in fact apply only to men have been presented as though they are universal truths. An example is the way in which classical liberal theory implicitly assumed the 'subject' – the free and equal citizen – to be the person who operated in the 'public' domain. This either explicitly or implicitly excluded women. Similar claims have been made by or on behalf of lesbians and of people of 'minority' cultures in some nations. The arguments either have been or could be extended, then, to apply to all the groupings listed. It is further argued that it is inevitable that the world is structured along lines of gender and race, if not all of the categories listed, and that therefore there can only be local or 'plural' cultural and moral assumptions. Both Rorty, and in recent years Rawls, have argued something like this.

Much emphasis, then, is placed here on the necessity of such divisions between genders, races and cultures. It might be possible to imagine a world that was not so divided: a world where there was, for example, only one gender and only one race. So long as there were some means by which the members of such a world could reproduce themselves, it would not be necessary to have the kinds of structured division we now know across the world. But it would be radically unlike the world we know – and in more than the sorts of ways customarily predicted by futurologists.

If, instead of beginning from the idea of the sort of human race one might imagine, we start from what is necessary to sustain a person's identity, which is the starting point of a lot of political theorists, then we reach a different kind of view. Many theorists have argued recently that it is the context of choice that makes it possible to have a freely choosing being, and, importantly, that this context includes the individual's identity. Gender and race, it is argued, are of crucial significance in identity formation, and it is wrong for one group, so defined, to impose its identity on another. But is gender identity crucial to making each person what she is? Is racial identity?

In order to make the pluralist point as strongly as possible, I would like to consider an argument that has been put by someone who wishes to challenge the scope of the pluralist claim. Keith Graham has argued that one constraint on the operation of autonomous choice is 'the constraint of necessity' (Graham, 1996, p. 139). There is, he has argued, a limit to how far a person can sensibly distance themselves from what they are. The limit is fixed by features over which the person has no control. These he calls 'constraints of necessity'.

However, it is possible to argue that although this point makes sense in theory, it is difficult to give examples of what actually constitutes a 'constraint of necessity'. Graham argues that 'my racial origin' falls into this category. Now, he might make this claim on the basis that one's race is a biological category and it is difficult to change one's biology. However, some transsexuals have argued that undergoing a difficult and complex and painful series of operations – to change their biological sex – is actually easier than identifying with the 'wrong' gender given a particular body. It is easier to undergo a complex and painful biological change than it is to go around identifying with the 'wrong' gender. So, the intuitive assumption that a biological alteration is more difficult to undergo than a social and cultural change is undermined. Moreover the changes undergone by Michael Jackson (the gradual lightening of his skin pigmentation) lead one to question the extent to which the 'look' of a person, which is part of the biological basis for categorising someone as belonging to a particular race, is unalterable. Secondly, the biological basis for racial identification is certainly not a sufficient condition for making a claim about someone's racialised identity and origin. The basis on which such claims to a particular racialised identity and origin are made include reference to country of origin, cultural identification and sometimes to a set of religious or moral beliefs. It would be difficult to say which of these constitutes, for each one of us, the constraint or constraints of necessity.

It is possible to argue, then, that race is an inappropriate example of a constraint of necessity but that there are clearly other characteristics of a person that are unalterable by them. So long as we are unable to travel in time, the date, the time and the location of our birth constitutes one such constraint. But the problem with listing this as a constraint of necessity on the ground that it is unalterable by me, is that what is important in identity-construction may not be the fact that this happened, but its significance for the individual. Is the person's place of birth significant for someone who was born in Australia, whose parents were Indian, and who spent most of her life in the UK? Is the nation of origin important for someone who was born in Israel, and who lived all her life in the US? For someone who wishes to obtain a UK passport, the fact that he or she happened to be born in the UK is highly significant. For someone who wants to get the free bus pass available only to individuals over a certain age then their date of birth is important. But if these things ceased to have that significance, then so would that fact about the person.

One might categorise a constraint of necessity differently and suggest that such a constraint would be one that is relatively difficult to change because so doing would require complex psychic and deep alterations to the individual's personality, altering ways of life that are deeply entrenched in the individual. However, it is very difficult to offer a general categorisation of this kind of thing. What constitutes a deep psychic change for one person, may mean little in psychic terms to another. For me to undergo what Michael Jackson has undertaken would be deeply traumatic. Maybe it has been for him too, but he has continued to function. For one person, having a sex change is what enables them to live a fulfilled life, whilst for another it would, no doubt, cause them to have a breakdown. It may also be the case that, for one person, a social and cultural change, like, for example, a move of job or house is deeply traumatic and deeply affects the person's sense of identity whilst those things are insignificant for another.

An alternative model of identity looks, then, not at general and necessary features of all of us, but at what is psychically significant for each one of us. The particular psychic, social, biological and cultural context in which each of us grew up, is what, on this view, is of deep and ongoing significance for each of us, for our identity. What is significant for each of us, moreover, is structurally determined by the economic, social and cultural assumptions into which we are born and under which we live out our lives. Debbie Epstein, for example (Epstein, 1999), has argued that the education system, certainly in the UK, educates children into compulsory heterosexuality. Some children of 'mixed race' parents (this is itself a contested category, since we are all, to different degrees, of 'mixed race') argue that they are categorised by others by the way that they appear to those others. The 'look' of the individual becomes deeply significant in identity-construction. For example, an English woman whose partner is of Indian origin has two children. One 'looks' Indian and is so categorized by others in the UK. The other 'looks' Mediterranean and is categorised as Italian or Greek by others in the UK. For these children, the way that they are categorised by others is of deep significance in their identity construction. Another case is of the woman who, when asked at a conference to identify herself either as black or as white, said that she was both. She was both because she was usually seen as black by white people and white by black people. So it is not even obvious that each one of us is either black or white. A further point that would need to be established here is this: just because something is very difficult to alter, does it mean that I have a right to hang on to it? In extremis, it might be very difficult for me to get rid of my Nazi beliefs, but that doesn't by itself give me the right to hang on to them.

It is not obvious, then, that we can distinguish degrees of constraint and categorise individuals on that basis. Does pluralism therefore follow? I suggest that it does not for two reasons. One is that the sorts of constraint outlined earlier, in most cases, represent structural features of most societies, where one grouping is in a position of relative power over another. To say that pluralism and toleration represents a partial solution to this problem is problematic. Kymlicka (1995), for example, assumes that a 'minority' grouping can be identified, its culture outlined, and its members protected by being 'accommodated' or 'tolerated'. However, in the case of the gender example mentioned earlier, the members of the female sex were not in a position to identify what was 'their' point of view, and thereby to have it 'accommodated' and 'tolerated', (a) because it took years of education and experience to arrive at the viewpoint, and (b) because the 'female' point of view actually challenged the legitimacy of the 'male' point of view. Just 'accommodating' and 'tolerating' it was therefore not sufficient. Indeed, feminism poses a challenge to the idea that a range of beliefs and cultures simply exist alongside one another, tolerating and accommodating one another. In fact, many values represent challenges to each other and one will be right and the other wrong. The feminist 'point of view' challenged the outlook of the liberal male. It showed him to be wrong both factually and morally in some of his assumptions.

But there is another reason why pluralism is open to question. There are some clear examples of 'constraints of necessity'. There are material constraints that affect all of us. Each one of us has to have our basic needs satisfied in order to survive at all. Any value system that prevents vast numbers of people's needs from being satisfied, should not be tolerated. These arguments need to be developed. I will go some way towards doing so in the following sections of the paper.

(2) Cultural pluralism

Let us move on, now, to look at the second type of pluralism – cultural pluralism.

An argument put by cultural pluralists is that upheld by communitarians and now accepted by many liberals, against the 'atomistic' view of the self. It is said, as we have seen, that it is impossible to make moral choices, except from within a given cultural context. Both Rawls and Dworkin propose a version of this thesis (Rawls, 1993; Dworkin, 1977). Kymlicka has put a version of the argument in a critique of what is possible in a communist society (Kymlicka, 1995). It is nonsensical, he argues, to postulate 'free creativity', since creativity only makes sense in a context. One cannot pursue 'freedom' for its own sake; rather it is the context of moral choices that gives freedom its meaning. Once this is accepted, pluralism follows. Cultures, and the contexts of moral choice that give them meaning, must be plural for freedom to flourish.

But one is free to the extent of not being constrained, quite independently of any context. I am free to stretch my arms and adopt the yogic 'dog' posture, just so long as I am 'fit' enough to be able to do so, and no-one is preventing me from so doing. I can do so in whatever moral and cultural context I like. All I need by way of 'context' is some knowledge of yoga. There may be circumstances where so doing would be deemed inappropriate behaviour or rude or odd, but its being so regarded is not a constraint on my freedom to do it. Similarly, I am free, if so disposed, to express critical views on the Blair government in the UK in whatever context I like, unless someone prevents me from so doing.

The Rawls/Kymlicka argument is sometimes expanded in the following way: one's identity is tied up with one's belonging to a particular culture; to one's espousing a particular set of values. The preservation of this culture is important for one's sense of self, for one's being a certain kind of person. Kymlicka has proposed a version of this argument. The modern world, he claims, is divided up into 'societal cultures' that are 'typically' associated with nations. Rawls, too, has argued in his later work that it is difficult to leave one's 'societal culture' because one's 'societal culture' is crucial to one's sense of well being, and to one's self-identity. Kymlicka believes that there are many 'societal cultures'; that being part of one of these things is, no doubt, 'deep in the human condition' (Kymlicka, 1995). Kymlicka stresses the importance of 'societal cultures' to self identity, at the same time as denying the communitarian thesis that values are constitutive of one's identity. By contrast, he believes that values are revisable.

Here, then, are two distinct arguments against the atomistic view of the self. Communitarians argue that values emerge from one's social and cultural context, and are tied up with identity. Cultural contexts and contexts of value are plural. Kymlicka, by contrast, hangs on to what he sees as a crucial component of liberalism, namely that each one of us must be able to revise the values we hold dear; yet he holds that our identities are embedded in cultures and contexts, which are plural.

On one interpretation, this is an argument about individual self-identity. Being part of a societal culture is said to be essential to an individual's sense of identity. If we identify 'societal culture' with nation, however, as Kymlicka sometimes appears to do, then there are a number of difficulties that arise. There are a plenty of cases where culture and nation part company. Is there a Scottish culture, for example? Did the Jews have a culture before the creation of the state of Israel? Is there a Kurdish culture? Do the Celts fail to qualify as a distinct cultural grouping because of their geographical dispersal and different languages? The first of these is a grouping who identify with a region that did, at one time, qualify as a separate nation. The Kurds today, and the Jews throughout history, have experienced degrees of discrimination and oppression – and degrees of identification with the grouping that have been partly to do, historically, with their lack of a nation state (see, for example, Bauman, 1989). Is there a British culture? If there is, are the features that encourage individuals to identify with it – it has been recently argued that one of the significant features of 'Britishness' is the summer series of Proms concerts at the Albert Hall in London – the same as the features that cause individuals to self-identify as Canadian, or French, or Czech? If they are not the same, then what sense can be given to the idea that national identity is significant for all of us, because it is formative of our identity?

But another set of problems concerns the division between, on the one hand, 'societal culture' which is supposed to be formative of identity, and on the other hand, the possible revisability of value. A deeply religious Catholic, of Irish origin, who has lived in London for some of her life, would no doubt argue that her nationality is revisable, but her values are not, because the latter are formative of her identity in the way that the former is not. For the woman of Indian origin, who moved with her family, along with many 'Ugandan Asians', to Uganda, only to be uprooted from there by Idi Amin's policies and forced to come to Britain, her leftist values may be more significant to her sense of who she is than her particular set of national identities. For the girl of Peruvian origin, who has grown up in Boston with her two lesbian mothers, and who has been provided with a particular set of values that derive from that experience, her identity is tied up, in complex ways, with lots of things other than her nationality. One more case: the woman of Israeli origin, who has lived for much of her life in Britain, for part of it in the USA, and who is deeply critical of the policies of the Israeli state, has a set of values that, for her, are constitutive of who she is, but they certainly do not derive from her country of origin. That these are not, in fact, just hypothetical cases is borne out by the fact that each of these descriptions is of a person I know.

The pluralist may argue, now, that these cases constitute the exceptions to the rule. Civic nationalism, the liberal pluralist may argue, is a necessary background condition for the operation of liberal tolerance and liberal autonomy and freedom. Historically, there are four components of the western model of the nation: historical territory, rule-governed legal political community, legal-political equality of members and a common civic culture (see, for example, Smith, 1991, p. 11). Rawls and Dworkin have argued that, providing that such societies conform to objective principles of justice, then they provide the only foundations that liberalism requires (Rawls, 1973, Dworkin, 1977). Taylor also makes the point that 'our' capacity to be free agents requires a context in which the rule of law operates (Taylor, 1985). This is a different interpretation of the Kymlicka argument, however. Whilst this argument might have some plausibility in relation to the requisite framework for liberal principles, it does not establish either cultural or moral pluralism. Rather, the argument is about the constitutional framework necessary for the operation of liberal principles. This is significantly different from the arguments about identity. It is about the set of rules that everyone must follow in order to live equitably with one another in a broadly liberal and tolerant manner.

Underlying the pluralist point is a very general claim to the effect that, whatever I choose to do, in whatever context, that affects others (and the way in which it affects others) contributes to shaping the context in which that choice is made. But this claim can be made without accepting any of the forms of pluralism I have distinguished.

The argument for pluralist cultures comes up against what we might call the Cartesian objection. Descartes argued that culture and tradition were dispensable in the search for truth. One could make a parallel point that they are dispensable when it comes to establishing what is the right thing to do. Descartes believed that culture hampered one, that it caused one to hang on to implausible claims just because they had been handed down by culture and habit. An illustrative example might be provided by a friend of mine who used to recount the story of his mother reading from the Koran to him as a child, and twisting her hair through her fingers as she did so. For years, he believed that this was part of the ritual, and desperately tried to do it himself – wondering, in his difficulty, if it was morally wrong to have short hair.

The communitarians would no doubt argue that Descartes comes up against the 'empty self' argument. Yet they would be wrong. Descartes did cut himself off from the Thirty Years War, from friends, contemporaries, from his 'culture'. Yet he did not cut himself off from himself. He was left with a room, a stove, food, and doubtless pen and paper. He was left, in other words, with the necessities of life. More should be made of the significance, for moral choice to be possible, of these bare necessities. They were what enabled him to produce his arguments, and not either his 'bare' transcendent self or his cultural context. He was able to make choices within that very limited, and solitary, cultural context. Arguably, therefore, it is the material context that provides the set of constraints that are minimally necessary for any choice to be made. This kind of context is not plural but common to everyone. Indeed, it is arguable that Descartes actually attributed too much of his own situation to that of everyone else, since he not only supposed that everyone had access to the bare necessities, which as a matter of fact they did not (some did not have the freedom to write as they wished), but he also generalised a formal, minimal notion of reasoning that might not have been appropriate to all outside that context.

One might argue that the choices Descartes made were odd; arguably his individualism was his downfall, in so far as it deprived him of the sorts of critical commentary on his work that could have benefited the argument.

But there is a different kind of argument that might be made. It could be argued that my culture, however defined, is constitutive of my identity because I have worked on it, because I have mixed my labour with it, and it has therefore become mine. I have laboured to maintain my religion, my language, my ethnicity. It is therefore mine; it forms the context within which I make my choices, and I am therefore entitled to hang on to it. Whatever this context is, it is mine, and forms the basis on which I make choices of all sorts.

I think that this argument carries greater force than one which says that my culture and my nationality are 'deeply part of the human condition' (as Kymlicka puts it). But once more it encounters the Cartesian objection: that the effects of culture and habit are merely peripheral when it comes to our identity as rational beings.

Let us move, then, to look at moral pluralism.

(3) Moral pluralism

A weak argument in favour of the moral pluralist view is simply that it is a fact of life – moral pluralism is an inevitable feature of a large, complex, highly populated world. Unless we are to have a population of identikit Martians, which no-one would want, moral pluralism is inevitable. The pluralist thesis is said to be desirable, then, on the ground that its contrary – a world of identical moral clones – is highly undesirable. This begs the question, often put by proponents of equality, of whether a lack of moral pluralism implies sameness. Equality, it used often to be said, does not imply sameness. Similarly, the moral monist might argue that his thesis does not imply sameness, even in respect of moral claims. The view of the moral monist might be that this perspective on the world is one of whose truth and moral correctness he hopes eventually to be able to persuade others. The moral monist might believe, however, that the process of deciding on the correctness of moral claims would involve majority voting, and would not therefore imply that everyone held the same moral views. Moral monism, then, is compatible with difference in respect of moral ideals, and is certainly compatible with differences between people in all sorts of other respects – circumstances, abilities, wealth and ways of realising the ideal. So a moral monist world need not be a world of clones.

There is an important point that the pluralist 'toleration of moral difference' leaves out of account. Liberal advocates of pluralism stress the importance of agreeing principles of justice that would be perceived as fair and impartial by all adherents in a society that is characterised, as one commentator has put it, by 'a deep and enduring pluralism of views about human excellence' (de Wijze, 2000, p. 70). Most liberals of such a persuasion stress how difficult, if not impossible, it is to agree on one view of what human flourishing should consist in. Yet most of them rule out some views as unacceptable. This particular thinker stresses that there are two broad categories of moral thought that are 'unreasonable' and that should therefore be ruled out of the scope of recognition and toleration. One category is the set of bizarre beliefs about the world – for example a doctrine that insists that the world is made of cream cheese and consequently pink elephants, not human beings. The second is a doctrine that is 'evil' – a doctrine that seeks, for example, the unlimited domination or destruction of others. The Nazis stand as the paradigm case. Very few liberals would want to tolerate the Nazis.

Such liberals also object that it is wrong to impose one view of what is right or acceptable on another group. I agree. I don't, however, think that you have to be a moral pluralist to agree with this view.

Let us spend a few moments discussing the case of 'madness'. It is interesting that beliefs commonly classified as 'mad' are exemplary of the kind that Descartes ruled out in his discussion of possible counter-examples to his Cogito. He ruled out of account, without any argument, the views of the 'madman'. In his early work, *Madness and Civilisation*, Michel Foucault analyses the historical coincidence of the emergence of the Cartesian Cogito, the birth of the Enlightenment, which splits reason and its others, with the beginnings of the internment of the insane. Prior to this, madness was seen to be a moment in reason; in Mediaeval times in Europe, for instance, the 'fool' epitomised the fate of humanity in dreams and illusions. Madness was imbued with moral significance. Up until the Renaissance, mad people were listened to. Renaissance people recognised the limitations of reason.

Descartes, however, splits reason and its others – the latter symbolised by madness – within his method of sceptical doubt. All that might threaten reason's certainty is banished: dreams, errors, the senses, madness. For Foucault, the Cogito implies an ethical stand against reason's others. Reason is affirmed over against unreason, and the self-reflective subject is thereby constituted. In the process of doubting Descartes considers, in order to reject, various possible sources of knowledge: he might, he suggests, gain knowledge through the senses. But his senses sometimes deceive him. Therefore they constitute an unreliable source of knowledge. He considers the possibility that he whatever he is experiencing might be the product of a dream: it is possible that he is dreaming that he sees the fire in front of his eyes. In all such cases of possible deception except that of madness, Descartes sets up an hypothesis to refute. But madness is simply ruled out of account. As Descartes puts it, in the first Meditation: 'And how could I deny that these hands and this body belong to me, unless perhaps I were to assimilate myself to those insane persons whose minds are so troubled and clouded by the black vapours of the bile that they constantly assert that they are kings, when they are very poor; that they are wearing gold and purple, when they are quite naked; or who imagine that they are pitchers or that they have a body of glass?' (Descartes, 1972, p.62).

Foucault stresses that whereas dreaming is contained in Descartes' method, as a possible subject for rational discussion, madness is excluded a priori; madness both demarcates the individual's domains of irresponsibility, and constitutes the banished 'other', excluded from the civil community, from the domain of subjecthood. The subject who doubts excludes madness. If Descartes were to take seriously the hypotheses of mad people, that would indicate that he himself were mad. In the case of potential errors of thinking occurring in dreams or through the senses, the object of thought is analysed. With madness, however, it is the subject of thought himself that is at issue. The subject as intellect cannot be mad. This Cartesian subject of reason becomes the subject of the post-Renaissance world.

When reason defines the scope of what is acceptable, then, madness, – as the negation of reason – has to be ruled out without argument. But what if the arguments of the 'mad' person challenged the liberal pluralist tolerator of a range of points of view? It was not difficult for the arguments of early feminists to be represented as those of 'mad' people. Those who challenge received wisdom – Galileo, for example, Wittgenstein, as another – are more easily dismissed if they are characterised as stark raving bonkers. But don't we give a stronger message to those who might otherwise consider or take seriously the argument of the 'mad' person, if we explain, with careful argument, and backing up with good reasons, that this person's premises are false – that he is wrong?

Doesn't the same point apply in the case of those whose doctrines are rejected because they are 'evil'? Don't we give them less credence if we show carefully and painstakingly, once again, that they are wrong? Doing this of course offers a challenge to pluralism. We would have to accept that there are some moral views that should not be tolerated, not because they are unreasonable, but simply because they are wrong. A parallel point arises in the following example. At a recent conference I was involved in a discussion of liberalism. A good liberal was putting the pluralist case for the importance of tolerating a range of moral viewpoints. Not tolerating difference and difference in respect of moral outlook, he was arguing, has unacceptable consequences – it has led to wars and to one set of values being imposed on another. He gave an example. He said: 'A friend of mine believes that homosexuality is unnatural. This friend is a deeply religious Catholic.' At that point I became upset. I said later that I had once been in love with a woman, and that this was in part, I thought, why I had become upset. In reality I did not quite know what exactly had upset me. Perhaps, though, I believed that this view of his friend should not have been tolerated. Why not? It should not, I believe, for the same sorts of reason that the classical liberal view of women I outlined earlier should not have been tolerated. It should not be tolerated because it supposes that one group of human beings is unnatural. Homosexuality is deeply part of the identity of many 'out' gay men and women, and to describe it as unnatural is to describe them as unnatural. Similarly, I believe, the views of Nazis should not be tolerated not because they are unreasonable, but because they are wrong. They are wrong partly because they involve denying the humanity of certain groups of people – Jews, gypsies, black people and whoever else individual Nazis might have included into their particular categorisations.

Elsewhere I have tried to defend the view that there is a set of values that represents a 'true' set. I use the concept of an 'emancipatory value' (Assiter, 1996 and 2000). I use the concept 'emancipatory' in the following sense: a value will be emancipatory if it contributes to removing oppressive power relations. The most fundamental emancipatory values will be those that ensure life. It may be argued, however, that this claim is not uncontroversial. One such kind of argument is that of Rawls. Rawls argues that, however long reasonable people spend discussing which values to accept, they will never reach agreement. All moral views, then, should be upheld with a degree of caution. For Rawls, anyone who upholds the kind of view that I am advocating is illiberal in so far as she is not admitting the possibility that she could be wrong. The believer in true moral values, then, is characterised as a kind of fanatic. Since it is never possible to reach agreement on the set of fundamental moral values, anyone who tries to persuade someone else of the rightness of their view will be imposing it on the other, and that, of course, is illiberal and the wrong thing to do.

However, I see no good reason for supposing that arbitration between moral viewpoints, in the case of a set of ultimate values, is impossible. I have argued elsewhere that it is possible to specify the conditions under which knowledge claims are more likely to be able to be made. Making a knowledge claim requires that the person making the claim should be credible and that she should be recognised as such (see Fricker, 1999 for this idea). I suggest (see Assiter, 2000) that it is possible to describe the sort of community in which the individual is most likely to be able to make such claims. Knowledge claims that are able to be accepted as true are more likely to be made in communities that are relatively free from oppression, because, in oppressive regimes, at least one person's credibility on at least one subject is thrown into question. Similarly, true moral claims will be those that are made in communities that are relatively non-oppressive. This idea involves spelling out what constitutes a non-oppressive regime.

The basic value of a non-oppressive regime, I have argued, is a commitment to life – to the value of the material life of all. Can this claim be upheld? Gayatri Chakravorty Spivak (1988) has written of the difficulty of judging whether white liberal colonial values were emancipatory for Indian women even in the extreme case of their disallowing suttee – self-immolation on the funeral pyre. Paul Gilroy (1993) has advanced the case that for some black American slaves, death was actually a preferable alternative to continuing in the kind of extreme subjugation that denied them entirely their freedom as human agents. The question can be asked, though: for whom is the choice of death preferable to the option of enslavement? It is hard to argue that it is actually preferable for the enslaved person, since he or she would be no longer there to make any kind of choice at all. Is death the best option in order to provide a symbol for others; to point out to them that it is possible to reject the fundamentally dehumanising role of the slave? Perhaps, but death is clearly a tragic and drastic option to be forced to take. As a symbol of the potential emancipation of slaves, no doubt death (and imprisonment in the case of many black Africans over the years) is valuable. But is it not the perspective of the believer in the possibility of emancipation, that allows us to see such deaths as symbolic in this way? Don't we need the perspective of a universal humanity, in order to see it in this light? Isn't it the notion of a scale of types of emancipatory value – with the preservation of life as the ultimate one – that allows us to see things this way?

One aspect to the claim I am making is particularly important, I think. It is only possible to claim that I am wrong about the value of life if the person making the claim is living. Unless we are all committed to the truth of the moral claim that each one of the reasonable people whose doctrines we should tolerate deserves to live and to have his or her basic needs satisfied, then there is no point in tolerating that person's views. Those who deny that there are moral truths might say: 'Oh if *that* is all you mean, then I accept that.' But it is important to note that accepting this is tantamount to believing a moral truth, and therefore rejecting the view that there are no moral truths.

I accept that there are many cases of conflicts of moral value that will be very difficult to resolve. An example would be that between those who believe in abortion and those who think that abortion is both morally wrong and detrimental to the future of a cultural grouping. I do not think that it is necessary for me to argue that every moral claim must be able to be resolvable in the way that I suggested the earlier examples could be resolved. Suffice it to say that I am committed to believing that there is a possible ultimate resolution to that kind of disagreement. In the meantime, I think, dialogue between the parties and discussion of the issues, is the best way to go about conflict-resolution.

References

Assiter, A. (1996), *Enlightened Women*, Routledge, London.

Assiter, A. (2000), 'Feminist Epistemology and Value', forthcoming in *Feminist Theory*.

Bauman, Z. (1989), *Modernity and the Holocaust*, Polity Press, Cambridge.

Butler, J. (1990), *Gender Trouble: Feminism and the Subversion of Identity*, Routledge, London.

Calder, G. (1998), 'Liberalism Without Universalism?', in B. Brecher, J. Halliday and K. Kolinská (eds), *Nationalism and Racism in the Liberal Order*, Ashgate, Aldershot.

Descartes, R. (1972), *Meditations* and *Discourse*, trans. E. Anscombe and P. Geach, Nelson's University Paperbacks, Norwich.

de Wijze, S. (2000), 'Reasonableness, Pluralism and Justice: A Pragmatic Approach', in G. Calder, E. Garrett, and J. Shannon (eds), *Liberalism and Social Justice: International Perspectives*, Ashgate, Aldershot.

Dworkin, R. (1977), *Taking Rights Seriously*, Duckworth, London.

Epstein, D. (1999), 'Structurally Adjusting for Sexuality: Globalisation, Education and the Regulation of Gender'. Presentation to National Women's Conference, University of Warwick.

Foucault, M. (1965), *Madness and Civilisation: a History of Insanity in the Age of Reason*, abridged and translated by Richard Howard, Pantheon, New York.

Graham, K. (1996), 'Coping with the Many Coloured Dome: Pluralism and Practical Reason', in D. Archard (ed.), *Philosophy and Pluralism*, Cambridge University Press, Cambridge.

Kymlicka, W. (1995), *Multicultural Citizenship*, Oxford University Press, Oxford.

McLennan, G. (1995), *Pluralism*, Open University Press, Buckingham.

Rawls, J. (1973), *A Theory of Justice*, Oxford University Press, Oxford.

Rawls, J. (1993), *Political Liberalism*, Columbia University Press, New York.

Smith, A. (1991), *National Identity*, Penguin, Harmondsworth.

Stoller, R. (1984) *Sex and Gender: the Development of Masculinity and Feminity*, London, Maresfield Reprints.

Taylor, C. (1985), *Philosophical Papers, Volume 2: Philosophy and the Human Sciences*, Cambridge University Press, Cambridge.

Young, I.M. (1990), *Justice and the Politics of Difference*, Princeton University Press, New Jersey.

5 Reasonableness, Pluralism and Democracy: A Pragmatic Approach

STEPHEN DE WIJZE

The concept of 'the reasonable'[1] fundamentally underwrites all conceptions of justice which seek to justify their claims without relying on either a notion of *mutual advantage* or *reciprocity*.[2] 'Justice as impartiality' (as such theories have come to be labelled) cover a variety of different approaches, from John Rawls' political liberalism to the universalistic approaches of Brian Barry and Jürgen Habermas.[3] The deep motivation for pursuing this approach lies in a desire to find inclusive principles of justice which can be willingly endorsed by free persons 'on a footing of equality' (Barry, 1995, p. 52). Furthermore, once the condition of pluralism is acknowledged as an enduring and inevitable feature of contemporary democratic societies, then a workable notion of 'the reasonable' is indispensable for developing just and stable principles which will obtain the requisite political legitimacy.

Yet 'the reasonable' remains an opaque and somewhat controversial notion. The central concern of this short paper is to outline a particular pragmatic approach to understanding 'the reasonable', one which performs three essential functions within a particular context; firstly as a criterion of exclusion and inclusion, secondly, as a justificatory yardstick to replace divisive and conflicting claims to the truth and, thirdly, as the moral basis for citizens to engage in social cooperation, so that there can be civility within conflict. This approach to understanding the notion of reasonableness gives rise to a version of political liberalism, one that differs from the well known Rawlsian articulation, but offers the best chance of achieving maximum inclusivity within democratic pluralist societies despite some inevitable exclusions. My account of 'the reasonable', then, is one that seeks to gain acceptance in a multicultural/pluralist society and provide the alternative to an appeal to truth as the basis for developing an inclusive conception of justice. However, such a notion cannot have universal appeal. In order to achieve a widespread agreement on political principles of justice, despite deep differences between different moral, religious and philosophical conceptions of the good, it must be based on shared values that are latent in a democratic public political culture. Consequently, the requisite understanding of 'the reasonable' cannot be neutral between all moral doctrines. Inevitably for those moral doctrines that reject the ideal of democracy as the right and proper form of governance, 'the reasonable' will be perceived as a sectarian attempt to impose modernist values based on the glorification of Reason, despite its claim to be fair to all.

The structure of the paper is as follows. I begin by outlining the deep motivation and constraints that face those who advocate a form of 'justice as impartiality'. I then raise two doubts about the very possibility of finding a widely accepted notion of 'the reasonable'. The remainder of the paper attempts to circumvent these problems by locating such a notion in a particular context with three specific roles. I conclude by acknowledging the limits and advantages of this account of reasonableness.

(1) Impartiality and reasonable pluralism

Justice as impartiality, whether it be Rawls' version of political liberalism or Barry's attempt to argue for universally valid liberal egalitarian principles (Barry, 1995. p. 3), or Habermas' 'Discourse Ethics', all seek to establish principles of justice that could be willingly endorsed by free and equal persons who would perceive them as fair and impartial. To this end, Rawls evokes his device of the 'original position', Barry uses Scanlon's notion of 'reasonable rejection' and Habermas postulates an 'ideal speech situation'. However, achieving a wide ranging agreement on principles of justice that would be perceived as fair and impartial by all adherents faces a particular difficulty in a society characterised by a deep and enduring pluralism of views about human excellence. Any appeal to a particular view of the truth for motivational or justificatory purposes will face strong opposition from moral doctrines that hold different and conflicting views. What is needed is a notion that is flexible enough to provide a basis for justification and motivation without appealing to one sectarian view of the truth.

Put another way, the problem for those who advocate justice as impartiality is to find a way to accommodate *reasonable pluralism.*[4] In order to take pluralism seriously, it is not sufficient for a liberal conception of justice to tolerate those who disagree with fundamental liberal values such as autonomy and individuality. Rather, to achieve maximum inclusivity based on principles all free and equal persons would willingly endorse it is necessary to restrict their scope and offer a freestanding justification. This is the strategy of political liberalism. It utilises a notion of 'the reasonable' as a substitute for the truth so that illiberal moral doctrines which do not accept the substantive liberal concepts of autonomy and individuality can be incorporated as equal partners in the process of developing a political consensus. This is done by building on values all parties can endorse as true from within their own comprehensive moral doctrines even if they believe that other comprehensive moral doctrines are wrong or misleading.

(2) Two concerns about defining reasonableness

Given the fundamental importance of a concept of 'the reasonable' for the success of any political liberal approach, a clear and rigorous definition of 'the reasonable' must be ascertained. However, there is considerable scepticism that such a definition can indeed be found on both theoretical and empirical grounds.[5] The theoretical concern is this. If we find persuasive the claim that contemporary societies will always be characterised by significant and deep disagreements about what constitutes human excellence and the good life (the fact of reasonable pluralism), then it seems that we ought to expect a similar pluralism of views on a notion of 'the reasonable'. The empirical grounds for scepticism arise from the fact that despite many attempts by political theorists, no one as yet has managed to come up with a definitive and widely accepted definition.

Both these concerns have force but I believe that a notion of 'the reasonable' can be developed which could achieve a very widespread consensus in societies with a democratic public political culture. The theoretical worry is overcome by seeking a notion of reasonableness that is grounded in the *shared* values of those who endorse the ideal of democratic governance. The empirical concern is addressed in this paper by demonstrating how a new approach promises to develop a notion of the 'the reasonable' that has eluded us so far. However, such a definition cannot (and must not) strive to be universal and ahistorical in its appeal. Some moral doctrines, specifically those which reject the ideal of democracy, will reject the imposition and use of any such notion as sectarian and unjust. Such moral doctrines will unfortunately have to be tolerated rather than incorporated within a political liberal society. What is more, despite the irenic nature of political liberalism, should such doctrines seek to destroy or seriously undermine it, there may be no alternative but the use of force to suppress or eliminate their ability to do damage.

(3) 'The reasonable' in a political liberal context

Political liberal doctrines offer a distinct and unique approach to the problem of political power in the face of reasonable pluralism. Such doctrines share a number of defining characteristics which arise from their aim of establishing *political justice* as the end result of an overlapping consensus between reasonable comprehensive moral doctrines. They strive to develop a minimum moral conception that occupies the middle ground between a comprehensive view of the good and an amoral *modus vivendi* based on entirely prudential strategic considerations. The cardinal virtue of the political liberal approach lies in its ability to achieve that which eludes the other two options: justice with stability.[6] To this end, all versions of political liberalism strenuously avoid embedding political principles in any single comprehensive moral doctrine by seeking overlapping normative political commitments which are justifiable to both liberals and non-liberals. This necessitates three distinct departures from standard conceptions of justice. The first concerns the *scope* or *subject* of justice which is now restricted to the political domain. Secondly, political liberalism adopts a particular *strategy* for justifying the principles derived, that of 'public reason',[7] which demands that the reasons offered in support of a set of principles must be those that no free and equal citizen could reasonably reject. Thirdly, the *source of shared substantive values* upon which to build a conception of justice cannot be based on any particular comprehensive moral doctrine but must arise from the common public political culture that has developed in the society. Furthermore, political liberalism sees public/political life as a sphere where citizens are united by deep ties of mutual respect regulated by principles all can endorse from within their own world views. Arising from this is the recognition that sectarian principles are inappropriate for deciding public issues and so it rejects the imposition of any one particular view as unreasonable and contrary to achieving the goal of a just political community. However, as its name makes clear, political liberalism is a *liberal* doctrine in so far as it adheres to a liberal notion of legitimacy[8] and individual rights for citizens *qua* citizens. Its appeal to non-liberal doctrines rests on both its ability to find just principles they can endorse from within their own comprehensive moral doctrine and its guarantee that the liberal commitments will only legitimately extend into the personal spheres of citizens' lives when it is necessary to protect their abilities to act as free and equal political agents. It is in this sense that the principles of justice will be fair and neutral between differing conceptions of the good and allow the greatest degree of inclusivity possible in a pluralist society.

The very possibility of a political liberal doctrine requires a notion of 'the reasonable' to facilitate an appreciation of the independent validity of the other people's claims. It is a higher order concept (it has a specific kind of moral content) and although complementary is not derived from 'the rational'. Rational conduct has two important aspects to it: the issue of choosing certain ends given certain preferences and the issue of how such ends are to be achieved. I am rational if when choosing certain *ends* or *projects* I am aware of the nature of those ends, and the effects they will have on myself and others. These choices must be guided by past experiences, future expectations and, when necessary, the advice of relevant experts so that they are not based substantially or entirely on emotional concerns. A second dimension to rational action concerns the question of choosing the most effective *means* (all things considered) to attain a selected end. In short, 'the rational' focuses on the link between preferences and choice and then the connection between those choices and action. What 'the rational' lacks, however, is a 'particular form of moral sensibility that underlies the desire to engage in fair cooperation as such, and to do so on terms that others as equals might reasonably be expected to endorse'(Rawls, 1993, p 51).

The normative dimension of 'the reasonable' is captured by saying that such an action is one that, from an impersonal point of view, is fair and takes into account the interests of others. Here we find a willingness to realise and accept that our actions may be harmful to others *from their point of view* and that this stands as a possible valid objection to them. Reasonableness requires that we enter the world of others as equals and be prepared to propose and accept fair terms of cooperation with them provided they reciprocate in kind. A person, then, is being reasonable when she is prepared to justify her actions in terms of principles, arguments and claims which all concerned parties could reason about in common. Consequently, 'the reasonable', contains a public dimension in a way that 'the rational' does not. In organising our social relations, reasonableness requires that we publicly work out the framework in a manner that everyone can be expected to endorse and act upon provided others can be relied on to do the same.

So although we might not be able to define a universal ahistorical and neutral account of 'the reasonable', we can develop a notion that can be used to derive and justify an inclusive set of overlapping principles of justice for liberals and non-liberals in a democratic society. Outside of this context the meaning of reasonableness varies dramatically. What counts as consistent, relevant, and appropriate (all essential aspects of what it is to be reasonable) will vary considerably across an indefinite variety of different contexts and conceptions of the good. So outside a carefully defined context, we have no reason to believe that in a pluralist or multicultural society we will find a universally acceptable definition.[9]

How then do we formulate the problem of political order in the face of pluralism? Rawls presents the context in the form of a question:

> How is it possible that there may exist over time a stable and just society of free and equal citizens profoundly divided by reasonable though incompatible religious, philosophical and moral doctrines? (Rawls, 1993, p. xviii).

In order to find an answer to this question, 'the reasonable' must enable the possibility of several theoretical manoeuvres so that political liberalism can develop its overlapping consensus on principles of justice. To this end it must:

- underwrite a principle central to political liberal conceptions, namely that the *Right* is prior to the *Good*.[10] Political liberalism is especially reliant on a process of procedural justice, set up as either a hypothetical contract position, neutral dialogue or general discourse. The rationale of using this approach is that if certain procedures are accepted as fair by all reasonable citizens, then the outcome of this process will deliver principles that can be taken to be fair and binding. A notion of 'the reasonable' is meant to offer a plausible explanation of why the value of political principles derived in this way have priority (in the all but exceptional cases) over the particular values held by different reasonable conceptions of the good.
- enable the notion of publicity to be automatically built into the process of establishing inclusive principles of justice. Political liberals are committed to using public reason in order to develop political principles that are acceptable to citizens from a wide range of comprehensive moral doctrines. Since these principles will be affirmed by all citizens they must have a common *public* basis of justification.
- offer a shared motivation in order to seek an overlapping consensus on normative principles, that is, to treat other free and equal citizens with mutual respect and civility in the search for common ground.
- be freestanding. There is a need for an impartial notion to replace the use of a sectarian and divisive appeal to 'the truth'.

The possibility and effectiveness of 'the reasonable' being able to fulfill the roles outlined above and still find a widespread acceptance among a large range of conflicting world views lie in the contingent fact that it exists as a central part of all moral doctrines that have integrated and cherish the values and importance of *democratic* governance. Democracy offers an adversarial procedure to ensure civility within conflict by electing leaders and providing institutions that enable serious political and social conflict to be resolved by an agreed set of rules. The *concept* of democracy 'can be identified by the particular source of legitimate authority it establishes' (Leader, 1994, p. 49), one where political power always remains a derived authority given by way of delegation from the citizens. If this is correct, then the ideal of a concept of democracy entails both a recognised procedure and a set of substantive values in its *preconditions*, *implications* and *rationale*.[11] As democrats, citizens affirm the obligation to be reasonable in public life and justify this reasonableness in a variety of different ways internal to their particular comprehensive moral doctrines.[12] A reasonable person is someone who holds a reasonable moral doctrine. What this means is that such a person seeks to cooperate, compromise, and shows tolerance and civility towards those with whom she has deep disagreements about the good life provided others do likewise. A reasonable person does not seek to impose her views on others using force (she is committed to the view that the coercive force of the state is legitimate only when its use cannot be reasonably rejected by those subject to it) nor does she deny basic civil rights to other citizens. In short, she exhibits a desire to live in a just society and has a commitment to develop just social principles for political community in the face of ineliminable pluralism.

(4) The three specific functions of 'the reasonable'

Let us turn to the three specific functions required of 'the reasonable'. By closely examining its role in developing a political conception of justice we are able to extract a clearer sense of what this notion demands of people in a democratic society.

i) Criterion of inclusion and exclusion

A notion of 'the reasonable' is required to serve as a *criterion of inclusion and exclusion*. In seeking the most inclusive principles of justice possible in a pluralist society there will always be some moral doctrines that will have to be excluded. There are two broad categories of unreasonable moral doctrines that make a political liberal project unworkable. The first are those kinds which make cooperation and compromise impossible due to their bizarre beliefs and/or outright rejection of tolerance and civility. Such doctrines are generally perceived to be based on insane beliefs about the world and/or espouse evil world views. A doctrine which is based on psychotic beliefs about the world cannot be accommodated if only for the reason that it would make demands of others that would be impossible to satisfy. For example, a doctrine that insists that the world is made of cream cheese and consequently pink elephants, not human beings, ought to be given political office clearly cannot be incorporated into a political liberal society.[13] Evil doctrines are those which seek the unlimited domination or destruction of others and recognise no other possibility. The Nazis stand as the paradigm case. There is no need to try to accommodate such views and here the overriding concern is how to neutralise and/or eliminate such doctrines from the body politic.

The second broad category of unreasonable doctrines are those that claim privileged access to the truth and insist that they would lose their meaning and identity if they made any significant compromises in the search for political community. Religious doctrines that rigidly assert that *extra ecclesiam nulla salus* and insist that the state enforce religious beliefs and practices on everyone in the society exclude themselves as reasonable participants in the political liberal project. The troubling aspect of this exclusion is that, unlike the previous category, it is possible to recognise that proponents of these views are motivated by 'a certain kind of moral vision' (Moon, 1993, p. 11) which must be excluded due to its uncompromising aim to impose itself on others.

'The reasonable', then, substitutes for the criterion of truth as a criterion for inclusion, here understood as the willingness to seek shared political principles while allowing considerable latitude for other citizens to pursue their own visions of human flourishing. This does raise the question of whether it is possible to avoid a reference to the truth. Doesn't the use of 'the reasonable' conceal a sectarian notion of the truth albeit one that champions world views that encourage tolerance, compromise and so on?

This concern, however, is misplaced. This notion of 'the reasonable' does not evoke truth claims because it need not do so. The test for whether certain principles are acceptable is determined by their political *legitimacy* among persons who wish to find a conception of justice despite their disagreements about human excellence and the good life. Legitimacy in turn is established by the acceptance of the principles of justice by all those who will be subject to their force. Undoubtedly, each person will endorse these principles as part of their own true moral doctrine. However, they will also accept that such values will be endorsed by others in terms of a different moral doctrine. Each will view the other as endorsing the correct political principles even if they do so for what they consider to be the wrong reasons. Ultimately, what matters is that these principles will serve to provide the basis for a stable and just society despite the fact of pluralism.

ii) Basis of Moral Motivation

A notion of reasonableness is required to provide the requisite normative motivational drive for citizens to seek a just political community. This motivation translates into a desire to develop and live in a just society with the allied commitment of mutuality and respect for others. This normative dimension is important for political liberalism's long term stability and is what distinguishes it from a political accommodation of pluralism based on a mere *modus vivendi*. Although pragmatic and strategic considerations will motivate citizens to seek political association, more is required if a stable and just solution is to be found.

Two questions now arise concerning the usefulness of 'the reasonable' as a motivational notion. Firstly, is this form of motivation compatible with alternative motivational assumptions held by the different moral doctrines? Secondly, does a notion of 'the reasonable' serve as a *non-sectarian* form of motivation? To respond to both questions: 'The reasonable' understood as a motivational force does not insist that moral doctrines must accept an *external* standard of reasonableness whatever their own motivational assumptions. The desire to be reasonable is something that emanates from the values constitutive of those moral doctrines. There is no clash between a desire to be reasonable and the specific internal motivational assumptions of specific moral doctrines. Political liberalism, with its use of 'the reasonable' engages in the hermeneutic task of articulating a common normative moral motivational element for all moral doctrines concerned with developing a just community based on a deep commitment to mutuality and respect for others. It is a shared normative motivation found embedded in the public political culture of a democratic society and it expresses the view that even though we may disagree with others and reject what they say as false, *political legitimacy* requires that the use of state power is proper only if it is used in accordance with political principles agreed to by all reasonable citizens who would be subject to them.

There are at least three reasons that support the widespread existence of this notion of reasonableness as a motivational source for liberal and illiberal moral doctrines alike.

a) The desire to be reasonable, that is the desire to justify our public behaviour in terms which others could not reasonably reject, is a deep intuition found in moral doctrines (liberal or otherwise) committed to values that encourage fair procedures, decency and civility as goods worth pursuing. In fact, the desire to be able to justify our actions (and institutions) on grounds that others find acceptable (or at least could not reasonably reject) is very widespread. People are willing to go to considerable lengths, involving quite heavy sacrifices, in order to avoid admitting the unjustifiability of their actions and institutions (see Scanlon, 1982, p. 117). This claim does not serve to elevate 'the reasonable' to an universal or a natural property constitutive of all groups in society. Rather, this desire, as Scanlon rightly points out, is formed through a process of moral education found in most cultures and societies which teach that social justice is a great political virtue, one which stresses the importance of justification as fundamental to decency and civilised behaviour.

b) The desire to be reasonable arises out of the ability to see the world from an impartial perspective which nearly all moral viewpoints demand. Ethical reasoning in general (with the exception of Egoism) demands that a principle of what is right or wrong be universalizable despite the fact that each person has primary attachments to their own personal interests, projects and commitments. All moral doctrines share 'the moral point of view' which provides the groundwork from within which the desire to be reasonable takes root.

c) Persons living as willing participants in a democratic society, acknowledge the fact (for a variety of reasons internal to their own moral doctrines) that disagreement is endemic to human coexistence and requires institutions and procedures which can contain and mediate hostilities in a civilised manner. Since democrats acknowledge that reasonable disagreement is possible and inevitable, they reject (as both practically ineffective and morally inadmissible) attempts to maintain political legitimacy through the use of coercion.[14] Democratic structures, institutions and practices seek to accommodate a diversity of opinion and provide a formal adversarial procedure which can resolve deep seated differences without resorting to violence.

The desire to be reasonable is, therefore, found as a deeply held conviction within the vast majority of moral doctrines. Since it does not arise from one particular moral doctrine but is contained within the vast majority of them, it provides an attractive (and probably the only) alternative to evoking the 'true doctrine' as the motivational basis for citizens to engage in the political liberal project. Reasonable citizens, then, can agree to seek common principles knowing that there is a non-sectarian widely shared motivational impetus to make this project succeed.

iii) *Non-sectarian justification*

In a pluralist society, political principles must avoid appealing to any controversial sectarian religious, moral or philosophical commitments. To avoid this problem, principles are justified by appealing to their reasonableness rather than their truth. Rawls, for example, insists that the idea of reasonable justification is 'a practical and not an epistemological problem' (Rawls, 1993, p. 44). Consequently, being reasonable is not 'an epistemological idea (though it has epistemological elements)' and is 'part of a political ideal of democratic citizenship that includes the idea of public reason' (Rawls, 1993, p. 62). Political liberal principles are justified in terms of their reasonableness, that is, as a political value rooted in all reasonable moral doctrines where the adherents of those doctrines take such a notion to be integrally part of the true comprehensive moral doctrine. So even if adherents of one particular moral doctrine think that another doctrine is false, they will, at least, agree that this false doctrine supports the correct political principles. So, as a great and correct political value, reasonableness is upheld, often for different reasons, by a wide variety of comprehensive moral doctrines for their own internal reasons.

But without truth isn't the notion of reasonableness and the justification it provides contingent and fragile? However, contingency need not mean fragility and lack of foundations. Reasonableness is a strong value embedded in the public political culture of democracies and it has a political sophistication and gravity arising from the conviction, born out of a long history of brutality and suffering in the name of *the* truth, that peaceful coexistence in a pluralist society cannot be organised using coercion to enforce one particular conception of the good. This conviction is not likely to be swayed by the vicissitudes of day to day changes in superficial social values. The virtue of reasonableness was forged in the heat of civil wars and great social tragedies and it would require events as momentous for it to suddenly lose its attraction.

(5) Reasonableness and neutrality

I now return to the question of what can be said to those moral doctrines that perceive the notion of 'the reasonable' outlined above as sectarian. What ought to be said to moral doctrines that entirely reject the liberal problematic and the strategy for dealing with difference? Any notion of 'the reasonable' that can perform the roles outlined above and seeks to justify a set of robust values must inevitably be, to some degree, exclusionary. Recognising this is to acknowledge 'a tragic view of political life and its possibilities' (Moon, 1993, p. 10) where even the best attempts to achieve political community sometimes fail and the resolution of some deep conflicts requires coercion and the imposition of principles on those who disagree with them. There can be no social life without cost.[15] Cases such as these occur when we recognise that certain moral doctrines have coherent, consistent, stable and much cherished visions of human excellence which are irreconcilable with a political liberal doctrine. Certain peaceful fundamentalist religious conceptions of human excellence spring to mind as doctrines which reject the political liberal assumption that all citizens will endorse and support a democratic society. Some moral doctrines, for example, vigorously reject any suggestion that it is possible to separate political and personal values. A notion of reasonableness for them would not necessarily allow for compromise and tolerance of others in order to build a just political community. There are also those moral doctrines which reject the axiomatic subjectivist and historicist perspective on beliefs that is engendered by 'critical-objective' modes of thought dominant in contemporary western political philosophy.[16] Political liberalism, with its attendant notion of 'the reasonable' is wedded to the central idea that belief systems are subjective creations of the human mind, which might or might not be adopted. This is strenuously opposed by fundamentalist religious doctrines who see the principles of tolerance and accommodation of difference, with their method of public reason as an unacceptable surrender to the false values of secular humanism.

All that can be done with these difficult cases is to set up the problem in a way which makes the proposed solution difficult for anyone to reject. Strenuous attempts must be made to find some common ground (perhaps in common practices or common historical events) and, from this basis, seek to build the framework where political liberal values are not seen as an unjust imposition. If this fails, the hope is that the number of such doctrines are so small that they can be marginalised and their destabilising potential easily curtailed. However, I believe that the political liberal problematic with its use of 'the reasonable' is one which a significant number of persons from a very wide range of moral doctrines (liberal and otherwise) living in a democratic society would find intuitively plausible. To be committed to the democratic ideal is to have already accepted values that provide a workable definition of reasonableness which in turn underpins a political liberal conception of justice.[17] Although the notion of reasonableness used is neither universal in its appeal nor neutral between all possible moral doctrines, it does strive to be neutral between committed democrats and in this context the hope is that such a definition will achieve a very widespread appeal.

These points may still not satisfy the trenchant critic. After all, it seems to be a neutrality that is achieved by defining pluralism and reasonableness very narrowly. Political liberalism and its notion of 'the reasonable' excludes non-democrats along with religious fundamentalists and all those who are unwilling to accept that reasonableness rather than truth must be the focus of the political domain in order to achieve an overlapping consensus on political principles. However, we must not overlook the huge step forward that could be achieved by a political liberal society. No conception of justice can accommodate every moral doctrine but political liberalism, with its pragmatic notion of reasonableness, provides perhaps the most inclusive and viable alternative to 'both politics as holy war and politics as the embrace of nonjudgmental, unqualified pluralism' (Macedo, 1995, p. 470).

Notes

1 I am grateful to the following persons for their helpful comments on earlier drafts of this paper. Alison Assiter, David Archard, Sorin Baiasu, Jeremy Barris, Bob Brecher, Peter Carruthers, Ian Chowcat, Phillip Cole, Alistair Edwards, Edward Garrett, Attracta Ingram, Harry Lesser, Geraint Parry, Maurizio Passerin d'Entreves, Susan Mendus, Jenny Saul, Bob Stern, Ursula Vogel and Leif Wenar.

2 Gibbard (1991) describes three kinds of theories of justice each based on different assumptions about human motivation. *Justice as Mutual Advantage* is premised on the assumption that society consists of rationally self-interested individuals seeking social cooperation to attain desired goals which are impossible without such cooperation. *Justice as Reciprocity* agrees that egoistic motives play a part in motivation but importantly there is also the desire to conform to the rules of the social structure because they are fair and proper. *Justice as impartiality* rejects any appeal to the motive of self-interest and locates the motive solely in the notion of reasonableness, 'the desire to act in ways that can be defended to oneself and others without appealing to personal advantage'.

3 Those theorists that offer a version of 'justice as impartiality' are Barry, (1995), Beitz, (1989), Larmore, (1987) and (1996), Moon, (1993), and Rawls, (1993). Advocates of Deliberative Democracy and a Discourse Ethics such as Cohen, (1993), Fishkin (1992), Gutmann, and Thompson, (1996) and Habermas, (1981) and (1990) also evoke a notion of 'the reasonable' albeit using a different terminology.

4 It is important to distinguish between the simple fact of pluralism and the fact of reasonable pluralism. The former concerns the brute existence of moral disagreement which can arise in any society for a number of historical, social

and political reasons.

5 See Buffachi (1998) for an account of why the very approach to finding a definition of 'the reasonable' leads to three errors in our theorising about justice.

6 A *modus vivendi* jettisons the normative dimension essential to a notion of *justice* and is unstable due to its vulnerability to the vicissitudes of fortune. Political association based on amoral self-interest alone dictates that the compliance with the terms of a *modus vivendi* are rational if, and only if, one's enemy is too strong to vanquish. On the other hand, normative principles of justice based on a comprehensive conception of the good generates instability as those citizens who hold different values would experience an incongruity between the *status quo's* conception of justice and their conceptions of the good.

7 For an excellent and extensive account of public reason see Rawls (1997).

8 *Liberal* political legitimacy is not identical with political legitimacy *per se*. The latter refers to the question of whether those who rule have the right pedigree, that they have assumed the mantle of power in accordance with established rules and traditions in the society. A typical case of non-liberal legitimacy arises in some societies from a notion that the monarch has a divine right to rule. The liberal notion of legitimacy can be stated as follows: The exercise of political power is legitimate if, and only if, it is exercised in accordance with a constitution which citizens cannot reasonably reject.

9 Consider the different meanings and uses for *reasonableness* in the following contexts: a poker hand; a story for children under two years old; a second hand car; a discussion between enemies; and a period of recovery in the stock market, deciding on moral principles of justice.

10 I follow Rawls' definition: 'A conception of right is a set of principles, general in form and universal in application, that is to be publicly recognised as a final court of appeal for ordering conflicting claims of moral persons'. See Rawls (1971, p.135). For a discussion on the confusions between the relationship between the Right and the Good see Kymlicka (1989, ch. 3).

11 See Cohen (1994). The ideal of democracy implies the values of *political equality* (the recognition of the universal right to expression) and *equal opportunity and fair distribution* (the public recognition of every citizen's equal standing and worth). It also requires *political freedom* coupled to *rights of suffrage*. Democracy also encourages the creation of a public political culture informed by the values of *tolerance*, *rule of law*, and *freedoms of conscience, association and speech* (to some minimal degree at least). David Archard and Attracta Ingram have suggested to me that the ideal of democracy for which I argue might be understood as a specifically liberal account. If this is so, the non-sectarian appeal basis in which the notion of reasonableness is grounded becomes unable to appeal to non-liberals in a way that this paper suggests. However, it seems to me that the notion of democracy I have outlined with its substantive values and recognised procedure, does not imply any particular conception of democracy, be it liberal, communitarian, republican, post-

modernist etc. Rather it lays down the minimum political values and institutional structures required for citizens to be able to freely and equally exercise their choices of who should exercise political power over them. For a more extensive discussion of this issue see my 'Political Liberalism: A consolidation, reconstruction and defence', PhD Thesis, University of Sheffield, 1998, chapter 3.

12 These justifications may legitimately take many different forms. For example, some may arise out of i) religious beliefs about fairness and equity or ii) from pragmatic justifications rooted in experiences of the futility of past conflicts, or iii) where doctrines hold fairness and tolerance as widely shared deep intuitions, or iv) where moral doctrines hold that certain political virtues are good in themselves and need no further justification.

13 The bizarre nature of the 'pink elephant' example ought not to obscure a very difficult issue here of *who* decides that a world view is psychotic and on *what* basis. A belief in an invisible all powerful deity could be deemed psychotic and delusional by an atheistic hardline evidentialist but is considered perfectly sane, proper and essential to the good life by a religious person. There is no hard and fast rule here and each case needs to be judged individually after considering several salient questions. Firstly, does the doctrine pose a significant threat to the holder and to others due to the actions that flow from it? Secondly, does the doctrine contradict a significant amount of generally accepted knowledge consistent with the basic canons of scientific reason, logic and common sense available at the present time? Thirdly, does such a doctrine exhibit a high degree of inconsistency and incoherence? Fourthly, are those expounding the doctrine suffering from a severe psychological trauma and/or not functioning to full capacity due to injury or intoxicants?

14 Rawls refers to this as acknowledging the 'fact of oppression'. See Rawls (1993).

15 This point is made by Berlin (1990, pp. 11-15) and echoed by Rawls. (1993, p. 197).

16 See Stolzenberg (1993, p. 665). Stolzenberg's article offers a searching and sympathetic account of fundamentalist complaints against liberal forms of education. It seems to me that she identifies one of the deep reasons why all politics will have an unavoidably tragic dimension to it.

17 Lack of space prevents me from defending this assertion in more detail. See my 'Political Liberalism: a consolidation, reconstruction and defence' PhD Thesis, University of Sheffield (1998).

References

Barry, B. (1995), *Justice as Impartiality*, Clarendon Press, Oxford.

Beitz, C. (1989), *Political Equality*, Princeton University Press, Princeton.

Berlin, I. (1990), *The Crooked Timber of Humanity*, H. Hardy (ed.), John Murray Publishers Ltd, London.

Buffachi, V. (1998), 'Reasonable Agreement: A Defence' in *Imprints*, Vol. 2, No.3, pp. 223-240.

Cohen, J. (1993), 'Moral pluralism and political consensus' in D. Copp, J. Hampton and J.Roemer (eds) *The Idea of Democracy*, Cambridge University Press, Cambridge.

Cohen, J. (1994), 'Pluralism's Proceduralism', *Chicago-Kent Law Review*, Vol. 69, pp. 589-618.

Estlund, D. (1996), 'The Survival of Egalitarian Justice in John Rawls's *Political Liberalism*', *The Journal of Political Philosophy*, Vol. 4, pp. 68-78.

Fishkin, J.S. (1992), *The Dialogue of Justice*, Yale University Press, New Haven.

Galston, W.A. (1991), *Liberal Purposes: Goods, Virtues, and Diversity in the Liberal State*, Cambridge University Press, Cambridge.

Gaus, G.F. (1995), 'The Rational, the Reasonable and Justification', *The Journal of Political Philosophy*, Vol. 3, pp. 234-258.

Gibbard, A. (1991), 'Constructing Justice', *Philosophy & Public Affairs*, Vol.20, pp. 264-279.

Gutmann, A. & Thompson, D. (1996) *Democracy and Disagreement* Harvard University Press, Cambridge (Mass.).

Habermas, J. (1981), *The Theory of Communicative Action*, Beacon Press, Boston.

Habermas, J. (1990), *Moral Consciousness and Communicative Action*, MIT Press, Cambridge Massachusetts.

Hampshire, S. (1989), *Innocence and Experience*, Harvard University Press, Cambridge, Massachusetts.

Kymlicka, W. (1989), *Liberalism, Community and Culture*, Clarendon Press Oxford.

Larmore, C. (1987), *Patterns of Moral Complexity*, Cambridge University Press, Cambridge.

Larmore, C. (1996), *The Morals of Modernity*, Cambridge University Press Cambridge.

Leader, S. (1996), 'Three Faces of Toleration in a Democracy', *The Journal of Political Philosophy*, Vol. 4, pp. 45-67.

Macedo, S. (1995), 'Liberal Civic Education and Religious Fundamentalism: The Case of God v. John Rawls?', *Ethics*, Vol. 105, pp. 468-496

Moon, J.D. (1993), *Constructing Community: Moral Pluralism and Tragic Conflicts*, Princeton University Press, Princeton.

Moore, M. (1996), ' On Reasonableness', in *Journal of Applied Philosophy*, Vol. 13, No. 2, pp. 167-178.

Nagel, T. (1991), *Equality and Partiality*, Oxford University Press, Oxford.

Rawls, J. (1971), *A Theory of Justice*, Oxford University Press, Oxford.

Rawls, J. (1993), *Political Liberalism*, Columbia University Press, New York.

Rawls, J. (1997),.'The Idea of Public Reason Revisited', *The University of Chicago Law Review*, 64, No.3, pp. 765-808.

Raz, J. (1986), *The Morality of Freedom*, Clarendon Press, Oxford.

Raz, J. (1990), 'Facing Diversity: The Case of Epistemic Abstinence', *Philosophy & Public Affairs*, Vol. 19, pp. 3-46.

Scanlon, T.M. (1982), 'Contractualism and utilitarianism' in A. Sen and B. Williams (eds) *Utilitarianism and Beyond*, Cambridge University Press, Cambridge.

Stolzenberg, N.M. (1993), '"He Drew A Circle That Shut Me Out": Assimilation, Indoctrination, and the Paradox of a Liberal Education', *Harvard Law Review*, Vol.106, pp. 581-667.

6 The Freeman and his Doubles: Reading Mill's *On Liberty*

JUDITH GRBICH

You will remember, lady, how the morn
Came slow above the Isle of Athelney,
And all the flat lands lying to the sky
Were shrouded sea-like in a veil of grey,
As, standing on a little rounded hill,
We placed our hands upon the Holy Thorn.

Do you remember in what hopeful fear
We gazed behind us, thinking we might see
Arthur come striding through the high, bright corn,
Or Alfred resting on a Saxon spear?
And as the cold mists melted from the fields
We seemed to hear the winding of a horn.

You will remember how we walked the Vale
Through Meare and Westhay unto Godney End;
And how we said: 'time is an endless lane
And Life a little mile without a bend...
Behind us what? Before us, if we ran,
Might we not be in time to see the Grail?'
(H.V.Morton, *In Search of England, 1927*)

Liberalism's blend of the priceless worth of each individual in the pursuit of his own life plan is one that each person in a western culture would find difficult to forego. Liberty of thought, action and feelings of worthfulness are linked in such a way that supporters of both left and right politics would reach consensus on these practices as being uncontested. The identity, or humanness of the western citizen in the twentieth century is built upon these humanist beliefs. In the words of Mill, 'In proportion to the development of his individuality, each person becomes more valuable to himself, and is therefore capable of being more valuable to others. There is a greater fullness of life about his existence, and when there is more life in the units there is more in the mass which is composed of them'(Mill, 1975, p. 78).

My paper seeks to question who pays for these particular practices? It asks at what price to the non-western citizen, at what price to third world nations, do western practices of liberal politics depend? Not all of the units in whose life enhancement Mill rejoices are human. In liberal politics each person, whether human or the artificial legal person of the corporation, is entitled to equal treatment before the law. Within my questions are the assumptions that the tenets of liberalism's focus on the worth of the individual were the tenets also of a British nationalism and imperialism intent upon fostering a new politics for securing global markets for British products, including financial products – such as the loan of British capital. I am arguing that the focus in Mill's classic text *On Liberty* on the worth of the individual, and the rights of the freeman against interference from the state, was part of a practice of grounding the sensibilities of the western citizen in freedom and rights, part of a politics of monetary colonization, and part of a cultural habitus in which the western citizen's sense of being – the tying of self-worth to individuality of thought – was made contingent upon financial degradation of others. In Mill's text the 'sovereign individual' is both the 'freeborn Englishman' and the personification of domestic and external monetary practices by which the pound sterling was maintained. In Mill's text the sovereign individual is more than the human individual, more than the coin embossed with the head of the sovereign – an aesthetics of monetary colonization has been instituted. How one reads the signs of 'life', as it were, in the working capacities of non-human financial actors and their legal entitlements to revenues proportionate to the quality of their work, and aspirations, can be understood as a cultural habitus, or way of being.

I propose to sketch some aspects of this cultural habitus or way of being, and have positioned the Morton poem at the beginning of my essay as a sign post to the cultural poetics or poiesis, for how this habitus was created and is maintained. In these lines of remembrance and hope, one's sensibilities move through time as if at a human walking pace; life itself is a portion of time, characters of national inspiration and national becoming lie within sight of where we started, and ahead we hope to sight the Grail. Perhaps we have touched the thorns adorning Christ's brow on the cross, the sign of his kingliness and the suffering endured for us, perhaps we will see the mystery of the fulfilment of our good works which Christ has laid out for us in the form of the Grail. In this poem are interwoven remembrance and our hopes, Christianity and the traditions of British sovereignty, and a relationship of life itself to the distance each life travels in a spiritual journey – a relationship which perfectly matches the relationship of each monetary unit of a physical or 'intrinsically' worthful kind, such as a gold sovereign, to the possibilities for imaginary or national monetary units of account. Mill's sovereign individual has many doubles.

He is the English freeman, of Arthurian times and of the present; he is also a portion of the sum total of the British pound sterling.

In a longer paper I would focus on how the legal doctrines of income taxation link these two varieties of the sovereign individual. Here I can only assert that they have been linked in legal doctrinal practices of British income taxation (and every other legislature which followed the British model) and continue so,[1] and to point out that taxation laws form an implicit but central thread in Mill's text (Mill, 1975, pp. 115-141). Mill's text was written in 1854-55, following a period of intense political struggle in England around various kinds of taxation (Woodward, 1962, pp. 113-125, 162-172). Should import duties be lifted and free trade be installed? Should these indirect methods of taxation be phased out in place of the introduction of more direct methods and more extensive implementation of older direct taxes – income taxes upon earned income and real property? In his essay Mill considered the appropriateness of active interference 'of mankind' in the expression of opinions on corn laws and corn profiteers, 'An opinion that corn-dealers are starvers of the poor, or that private property is robbery, ought to be unmolested when simply circulated through the press, but may justly incur punishment when delivered orally to an excited mob assembled before the house of a corn-dealer, or when handed about among the same mob in the form of a placard' (Mill, 1975, p. 69). Mill's text *On Liberty* was completed before any settlement of these struggles on import duties on corn and the introduction of free trade was reached, before the landed aristocracy was 'compensated' for their loss of protectionism for home grown foodstuffs by the installation of direct taxes on the middle classes – who it was reasoned would also benefit from the expected drop in food prices.

Mill envisaged his text as a 'mental pemmican' for taking on a long journey, a pemmican being a condensed form of food. He wrote, in 1854, of the need to work the text 'into a fit state for printing – if not in the best form for popular effect, yet in the state of concentrated thought – a sort of mental pemmican, which thinkers, when there are any after us, may nourish themselves with and then dilute for other people' (Mill, 1972, p.141).[2] My essay will ask, have we carried it for too long, or can it be melted down and reworked into something of a different kind? I am assuming that this task is one of 'deconstruction' – a working with the meanings which Mill's expression of his ideas create in another generation of readers, and my methods are those of a critical jurisprudence[3] in which the frames of authority are noticed as having origins in legal theory and that their modes of interpretation lie in the cultural commitments of western classical and Enlightenment philosophies.

(1) Liberalism and judgement

Mill's *On Liberty* can be read as a text in which the reader sits in the judgement seat of the holder of permanent interests and is confronted by his power of judgement. Should he act in self-interest and preserve the interests he holds even if this is a matter of inaction which will harm others? That is, should he act or 'judge' in such a way that self-interest and harm to others is evenly balanced? (Should a holder of permanent interests be content to balance his own against the life interests of others?) Should he in effect judge as a political being, one interested in both a stable order and a progressive practice of social and economic reform?

But the power of judgement contains within it a capacity not to exercise judgement in this way. He may read not as a political being, but as an ethical or moral being, one for whom self-interest has a real moral quality in its practice but which may fall short of a higher good which can be imagined. *On Liberty* can be read with sensibilities in which an ethics exceeds those posited by legislative bodies – the moralities of law, legislation and judicial sanctions. The power of judgement contains an ethics, a use of conscience in Mill's words. It is being a person who would, 'step into the vacant judgement seat, and protect those interests of others which have no external protection, judging himself all the more rigidly, because the case does not admit of his being made accountable to the judgement of his fellow creatures' (Mill, 1975, p. 17). Mill has woven a text in which 'liberty of thought', or judgement, or freedom, is balanced against practices which are posed as the very grounds of its existence and grounds which are contradictory and oppositional – in the same way that the judgment involved in interpretation of his text, the relation between the reader's sensibilities and capacities and the meanings of *On Liberty* are also balanced.

Does one read this text as a politics, in which the liberties of thought have already been coded as a form of work – a code which legitimises the complex financial arrangements of an advanced capitalist society and in which the liberty or originality of thought confirms a financial code of authorship, and the efficacy of complex tax planning paper schemes – all built upon the work of thought being a male activity which validates maleness as originary, life-giving, and worthful (Grbich, 1997c). Or does one read this text as an ethics, in which it is noticed that the 'liberties of thought' have been built upon the backs of the unfree within a nation, the unfree dwell in a code of feminized existence, and upon the backs of the unfree outside that nation. Whole peoples are racialized in the codes for reading the poetic meanings in documents of income tax law and financial planning – to the extent they depend for their standard of life upon a monetary system subject to that of the British pound.

(2) Reading Mill's politics

As a description of a just politics, as a text describing a politics in which freedom and fairness can be achieved, Mill's text fails. He has balanced two modes of politics, the modes of 'a party of order or stability, and a party of progress or reform', both 'necessary elements of a healthy state of political life; until the one or the other shall have so enlarged its mental grasp as to be a party equally of order and of progress, knowing and distinguishing what is fit to be preserved from what ought to be swept away' (Mill, 1975, p. 59). He has balanced two modes of politics, naming them 'modes of thinking', in such a way that reform can only ever confirm that order of a stable politics which Mill lays out with his account of the relations of the freeman, the state, and the relatives spheres of each.

If his text is read for the plain meaning of its words, for the reasonableness of its arguments, for its rationality, its conservative privileging of wealth holding is confirmed. It remains a text for the 1850s and 1860s in which wealth holding in any form is validated; whether held in land by the aristocratic families of Britain, whether 'unearned income' in the form of rents or shares, it is protected from unwarranted invasions of revenue taking by the state. It is also a text in which the 'earned income' of the business proprietor, the holder of earnings from a small business is given a sympathetic focus in his rights to retain wealth. To those who have in the 1850s and 1860s *On Liberty* is a comfortable form of liberty. To the unfree, the employee whose Will is regarded as directed by the Will of another – the employer, it is as if the text has nothing to say. He is, as in Kant's metaphysics of morals (Kant, 1991, p. 126), not yet fit to have his desires measured against those with a free Will.

Mill's reference to the oppositional qualities of the party of order or stability, and that of progress or reform (Mill, 1975, p. 59), to the newly emerging conservatives-come-liberals and the reform proposals of the aristocratic Whigs, glosses over the extent to which it was difficult for the players themselves in these parliamentary alliances of the 1840s and 50s to decide whether they were in fact 'conservative-liberals' or 'liberal-conservatives'. While the landed aristocracy and its concern to protect locally grown corn with the import duties of the corn-laws appeared to be in opposition to rich manufacturers who wanted import duties lowered (so that local manufactured goods would be more widely accepted by other external buyers, a protectionism vs free-trade axis), it was just as plausible to place anyone who opposed free trade as being on the side of the manufacturers, on the ground that cheaper food would allow them to lower wage rates to workers. In this second scenario the landed aristocracy and the manufacturers seemed to be one, against the interests of the small business man, and even the labourer if his interests were ever considered.

Mill's two opposing parties are alike in their holding of permanent interests – landed wealth and commercial interests, one realty and the other incorporeal property of various kinds. Each part of the interests Mill describes as oppositional is a kind of domestic, or internal wealth; whether real or incorporeal, its value lay within the geographical boundaries of England.

It is possible to read these holders of permanent or perpetual interests as in opposition to other interests, interests largely unacknowleged in party political terms in 1852-55, but growing in strength – the holders of those with 'life' or 'limited' interests, both the holders of interests in their lives in trusts governing the distribution of incomes of both landed estates and businesses, and the life interests of those of the middle classes – the professionals dependent upon their skilled labour or intelligence to maintain a level of income, a skill which had a finite term in the life of the professional. Each of the holders of a 'life interest' is comparable in the precariousness of their separate means of livelihood, and to the extent each interest is fungible – able to be translated or transformed into money – each is dependent upon the extrinsic worth of the national currency. To the extent the value of the British pound varied in relation to other currencies, and internal prices of imported commodities similarly varied, the person who lived by the exchange of labour for money – whether intellectual or manual, was hostage to the policies of free trade or protectionism of those with more permanent interests.

(3) A narrative of the coming of modern politics

However, there are many reasons to believe that Mill did not intend his text to be read only for its plain meaning, and regardless of his intentions his text has a meaning which lies beyond the historical context of the 1850s and 60s. It can be read for the utility it has for the reader in the 1990s. Mill does not disown a connection between the inherent worth of thought, and the use to which this might be put, notwithstanding his structuring of thought as a liberty of the individual ultimately connected to a character's sense of self-worth, a worth intrinsic to that character.

There are many reasons for suggesting that Mill's text can be positioned within a postmodern reading of how liberty is to be achieved, and that Mill has himself laid out these methods for going beyond the self-interested frame of nineteenth century liberalism to a more ethical practice of a communitarian politics. Mill's text presents an allegory of historical materialism to a reader for whom the ethics of law cannot be separated from the politics of how law's authority is maintained. I am arguing that Mill's text is not a description of a just politics, or even a description. It provides a narrative of a modern politics – the struggle between Liberty and Authority – in which reference is made to a pre-existing or older form of politics. *On Liberty* can be read as a narrative of a political becoming, a narrative which structures the characters and plots in such a way that only some particulars or attributes of its characters have survived over the course of time, much in the same way – as argued by Mill (Mill, 1975, p. 60) – that present texts of Christian morality are survivals of older writings within the Church or even are survivals of reactions to the pagan philosophies of the Greeks and Romans.

The characters of Mill's narrative of the coming into being of modern politics are, like Mill's own description of the precepts of Christian morality (Mill, 1975, p. 60), presented in general terms, terms of 'wide or broad generality', 'impossible to be interpreted literally' and 'possessing rather the impressiveness of poetry or eloquence than the precision of legislation'. Instances of older forms are used as both survivals and forms which have been transformed into the character of the modern practice. As in the case of the formation of theological morality described by Mill in the essay itself, the modern forms of politics in Mill's narrative are the product of the ideas and feelings over time which, in the light of modern practices, 'are not sanctioned by it' (Mill, 1975, p. 61).

(4) Philological traditions for interpretation

Mill's account of the struggle between Liberty and Authority as a narrative of the coming into being of a modern politics must be set in the context of the shift in approaches to language, or philology, in England in the 1840s and 50s. The philological traditions of the German theorists, such as Grimm and Bopp, were being taken up in England with a revival of interest in the existing texts of Anglo-Saxon 'english'. Kemble published a two volume work in 1849 on Saxon philology. Its purpose was to discover in the earlier Saxon words, and their arrangements in composition, traces of the authentic spirit of each inner self, which when arranged cumulatively would reveal an authentic spirit of the nation. Kemble repeats the combination of philology, romantic aesthetics, and a decidedly modernist historiography, which had been assembled by Herder, Schlegel and Humboldt. His analysis of the Saxon terminology in documents of 'grants of kings and bishops, settlements of private persons, the conventions of landlords and tenants, the technical forms of judicial proceedings' (Kemble, 1849, vol. I, p. vii), combined with latinate versions of similar documents permitted him to infer that it was on the basis of the use of these terms that Queen Victoria was safe from the current political upheavals in France. In Kemble's words, 'the exalted lady who wields the sceptre of these realms, sits safe upon her throne, and fearless in the holy circle of her domestic happiness, secure in the affections of a people whose institutions have given to them all the blessings of an equal law' (Kemble, 1849, vol. I, p. v).

Kemble was able to confirm for an anxious English readership that the political unrest within France was not for England. The principles of constitutional settlement in England and nations of Germanic blood rested, he argued, upon two main foundations. 'First, the possession of land; second, the distinction of rank, and the public law of every Teutonic tribe implies the dependence of one upon the other principle, to a greater or less extent, even as he who is not free can, at first, hold no land within the limits of the community, so is he who holds no land therein, not fully free, whatever his personal rank or character may be' (Kemble, 1849, vol. I, p. 35).

While not all of the documents used by Kemble were in Saxon words, he was nevertheless able to confirm that survivals of Saxon words for the freeman in the nineteenth century, in Germanic nations, were evidence of the organic nature of the relation of land possession and rank to the freeman. The spirit of freedom began by each language user attaching the name of 'freeman' to the idea of a relation between land possession and rank. In Kemble's words, 'originally the Freeman is he who possesses at least as much land as, being tilled, will feed him, strength and skill to labour, and arms to defend his possession. Married to one free woman who shares his toil, soothes his cares, and orders his household, he becomes the founder of the family – the first unit in the state ... The union of a greater or less number of free heads of houses upon a district sufficient for their support, in a mutual guarantee of equal civil rights, is the state itself' (Kemble, 1849, vol. I, p. 129).

It is worth presenting more of Kemble on the freeman, as it is a class of persons out of whom Mill appears to have drawn both his characters of Liberty and of Authority. The class of freemen includes the nobles, who are 'the representatives of the general sovereignty'. The tendency of the power of these representatives of general sovereignty is, 'continually to increase, while that of the mere freeman is continually to diminish, falling in the scale in exact proportion as that of the noble class arises' (Kemble, 1849, vol. I, p. 135). The freeman can be distinguished from the unfree, the stranger, the serf or the freedman, by having a 'proper measure and value ... the price of a man'. This is the 'proper measure' 'by which his social position is ascertained and defended'. The freeman has the 'proper measure and value' of the price of a man, no more no less in price. This is a certain price for his rank, it is above the stranger, the serf, or the freedman, though 'not rated so highly as the noble'. Kemble says of the freeman, 'His life, his limbs, the injuries which may be done to himself, his dependants and his property, are all duly assessed' (Kemble, 1849, vol. I, p. 134).

In Kemble's schema the king of Saxon times is also a freeman, though more `judge like' in his kingly powers of assessing the harm done to others for whom compensation is payable, and exacting monetary dues from others for both the purpose of fighting invaders and as compensation for disturbing the peace. In Kemble's schema a freeman is a finite portion of general sovereignty. Authority or kingly powers is that practice of being entitled to extract the 'liberties' of the freeman. In this schema 'liberties' are fungible and also stand as the meaning of both what belongs inherently to the rank of freeman, and to what is within the power of the sovereign to grant or collect – a franchise, a tax, seignorial rights. 'Liberties' are the things possessed by the freeman's body, harms which are compensable by the wrongdoer and in which place of judgement of harm done or liberties owed stands the sovereign. In a fungible sense the Saxon king is the sum of the price of each freeman, just as each freeman is a portion or fungible part of that sovereign sum. The freeman is to Authority as Authority is to the freeman. Liberties are what each is and each has, and the relation of each to the other.

The freeman and Authority form a kind of hermeneutic or interpretive framework, of a somewhat stable kind, fixed as it were in an earlier time, as an earlier form of politics. The relation between them is one of 'the liberties', a quality of both having of, and being of, an indeterminate fungible quality constituting both freeman and lordship. Kemble was at some pains to deny that this meant any centralised form of authority. In his reading of the Saxon documents he could find no signs of a centralised authority. He argued that modern sovereignty was the effect of 'the introduction of Christianity and the progressive consolidation and extension of the kingly power' (Kemble, 1849, vol. II, p. 2). In Kemble's words, 'Taking all the facts of the case into account, we cannot but believe that the introduction of Christianity, which not only taught the necessity of obedience to lawful authority, but accustomed men to a more central and combined exercise of authority through the very spectacle of the episcopal system itself, tended in no slight degree to perpetuate the new order which was gradually undermining and superceding the old Mark-organization, and thus finally brought England into the royal circle of European families' (Kemble, 1849, vol. II, p. 27).

In Kemble's schema Arthurian freemen are travelling a road of a more modern form of authority, a road travelled by the spirit of a people evidenced in their words naming inner feelings and ideas of freedom. But at what kind of ethics of reading have they arrived, and where do we place the 'writer' who produces further signs of how freedom can be achieved? My questions are not so much ones of author and text, but the relations between them of 'writing' and reading, and the extent to which beliefs about them in the twentieth century are so real that they form the basis of Truth itself. In the language of the City, the 'writer' is a character who originates financial script – novel, and not so new, forms of financial transactions whose viability often rests upon a faith in the future rather than any sign of their having underwritten the lives of living beings. A quick loss of faith by a western culture in these forms has the ability to demolish a national economy elsewhere.

(5) In search of an ethics of the translation of fungibles

If Mill's text *On Liberty* fails as a description of a just politics, can his text be read as an ethics of law, as a morality which can be understood as surviving its failure as a prescriptive politics? Can a reader stand at the aporia, or ambiguity of judgement, and bring a conscience to a reading of its politics – in such a way that both an ethics and a politics are visible?

It is in the context of the renewal of interest in philology as a history of national character and as the method for an evolutionary constitutionalism, that Mill's concerns in *On Liberty* with the having of liberty of thought and his one principle can be read as pivoting around his structuring narrative of the coming into being of a modern politics. Liberty of thought had been the assumption underlying Kemble's historical philology; because the Saxons possessed land and named the possessor the 'freeman', a characteristic of freedom can be said to have remained inherent in this form, in Kemble's arguments. Liberty is the name which has been given to the ideas which has survived into the modern age. It is an idea which can be linked to any new thing, any thing can be named liberty and be true, provided all kinds of people are able to use the language as they please. The truth of liberty is, in Kant's a priori sense, what is named a liberty. Being responsible for, or owning oneself, can be named liberty, and in this sense can be true. The judgement of the truth of 'being free', lies upon a philological style and a liberty of thought, in the sense that it is true by definition, at least if you follow Kemble's style of historiography of being English.

Mill stated that the object of his essay was to assert 'one very simple principle', as entitled to govern absolutely the dealing of society with the individual. 'That principle is, that the sole end for which mankind are warranted, individually or collectively, in interfering with the liberty of action of any of their member, is self-protection. That the only purpose for which power can be rightfully exercised over any member of a civilized community, against his will, is to prevent harm to others' (Mill, 1975, p. 15). This principle remains paradoxical unless interference with liberty of action is read in Kemble's sense of something fungible, a 'libertie', capable of being both the action of the collective such as a tax exaction or the action of an individual which harms or diminishes the body of a person. Interference is a tax due from the person's wealth, or a compensable harm to the person's body. Mill imagines individuals, I would argue, as sovereigns, as fungible, and interference as a diminishing of monetary assets. Interference by the collective is the monetary taking. The object taken or harmed has an ambiguous character as perhaps real or personal property in a fungible form, or perhaps the human body or the holding of such an asset by its owner. One can conclude that Mill's description of liberalism in the 1850s was a barely disguised apologia for the protection of the aristocrats and the newly wealthy. A plain reading of his text gives an all encompassing account of those propertied interests who held parliamentary and social power.

But Mill's narrative can be read as more than the coming into being of a fiscal politics in which all but the English propertied classes are held hostage to global monetary developments. Mill's 'vital question of the future', the one which 'has divided mankind, almost from the remotest ages' (Mill, 1975, p. 5) and which 'presents itself under new conditions' is whether the question of liberty of thought, and his essay on the tenets of liberty, can be read differently. Where the self-protection of the liberties of the social (Mill, 1975, p. 5) have become questions of British and other western national monetary formations being validated in their extraction of monies due from nations with weaker currencies – in the names of freedom and individuality, Mill's principle for the translation of monetary or fungible entities into things with human aspirations needs rethinking. The poetic tropes which we use to liken the 'work' of monetary entities to the work of human beings are fundamental to the intelligibility of modern financial systems of western nations. Upon the sensibilities of the western citizen's sense of self and freedom of thought and expression have been created financial practices which diminish the life chances of peoples elsewhere, and deprive some human beings of the possibilities of ever sharing in emancipatory politics.

Is understanding of the truth of a text, such as Mill's text, structured or made contingent upon some practices of how truth itself is to be understood? This is the focus of Kant's work on the metaphysics of morals (Kant, 1991). Is there a difference or discretion in our capacities to make judgements about truth itself, which governs how each judgement of truth is made? Such a question puts the liberty or freedom of each person's judgement within a cultural frame; thought ceases to be solely an expression of an inner self or the product of an inner sense of worthiness. It also puts under scrutiny the extent to which the sense of self-worth of each individual in a western culture is contingent upon those practices of a cultural kind which stand for truth itself.

If there is a difference or discretion in our judgement of the truth, what rule governs the truth status of the difference we exercise in judgement? It is here that Kant opted for an aesthetics of judgement, a bringing in of questions, of feelings and imagination to the regularities of how a moral judgment is made. I would argue that Mill has similarly instituted an aesthetics in which the sovereign individual stands before an image of the general will of the nation, pictured as the sovereign writ large, whether a kingly sovereign or a monetary sovereign – both are positioned at the horizon of sight as the holy grail.

Mill was part of, admittedly indirectly, the reestablishment of medieval narratives of noble travels and Arthurian iconology in the mid-nineteenth century in England, at least to the extent his characters follow a quest modelled on the travels of a Christian saviour and biblical icons. Mill has grafted his narrative of the survival of forms of an older political order, an older arrangement of liberty and authority, onto the similarly told sagas of the commercial and trust lawyers of the 1840s and 50s who were weaving stories of the survival of Roman forms of life in modern commercial law documents. At stake for the commercial lawyers was to find a new stable home for movable money, stable in ideological terms, able to be transferred and protected as if it were realty. In the reading traditions of the equity lawyers the monies produced by debts or mortgages over land, and held on trust, were spoken of poetically as like the offspring of the body which bore them, alive and able to generate new offspring – whether that birthing body was Roman law language of the equity doctrines or the Italian customs of the double-entry accounting books. These monies were held within female like forms, forms capable of generating new monies. This reading tradition coded the acts of reading as an invention, a making and the reader and his materials were variously arranged as father and mother, author and text, akin to a godly son of the author of nature (Grbich, 1997c).

New monetary arrangements of the commercial lawyers, where there were initial doubts about the efficacy of 'paper work', could be blended imperceptibly within these readings of the signs of creation. Doubt was resolved in the sensibilities of the reader by an understanding that the judgement of both commercial morality and legality about a new arrangement was more akin to a discovery than an invention. In biblical exegesis a sudden awareness or discovery of understanding revealed to oneself that spiritual wisdom dwelled within and one became as if the first Son. Thinking itself, in the equity tradition, was that skill passed down by the barristers on reading the writing of monetary arrangements as if they were scripture. Mill followed the precepts of Kemble in picturing authority, 'through the very spectacle of the episcopal system itself' (Kemble, 1849, vol. II, p. 27). Mill's picture of the individual kind of sovereign both repeats scriptural reading traditions and institutes a pre-history and a future for financial scrip – commercial paper – the work of thought reified and propertised within the poetics of equity texts.

The western reader is presented with an ambiguity of judgement. It is true that commercial paper – promissory notes, derivatives, futures, financial scrip – is a legal kind, upon which the self-interest of the western subject has been made dependent, and upon which practices of morality western nations have posited conformity. And it is also true that commercial paper can present to readers trained in legal interpretation a judgement of an ambiguous kind, in which the real and contingent foundations of these posited laws – these politics of monetary globalization – are subject to a truth or justice which lies beyond present conventional moralities. The certainties of commercial paper can melt away into thin air. Western legal ethics can appear as a white mythology, a mythology in which those unlike the heroes of this parable of the holy grail have become the bearers of its truth.

Notes

1 See, for a longer discussion of the forms and politics of national and personal developmental paradigms replicated in taxation law practices: Grbich (1997a); Grbich (1997b); Grbich (1996); Grbich (1993).

2 See Himmelfarb's discussion of Mill's hopes for his text, at Himmelfarb (1974,

p. 21).

3 See Duncanson's early critical jurisprudence: Duncanson (1978); Duncanson (1979); Duncanson (1982); Goodrich has produced some early texts on this approach to the study and meaning of law, in Goodrich (1987, 1988).

References

Duncanson, I. (1978), 'Legal Positivism as Ideology', *City of London Law Review*, pp.20-42.

Duncanson, I. (1979), 'The Strange World of English Jurisprudence', *Northern Ireland Legal Quarterly*, pp.207-224.

Duncanson, I. (1982), 'Jurisprudence and Politics', *Northern Ireland Legal Quarterly*, pp.1-20.

Goodrich, P. (1986), *Reading the Law: A Critical Introduction to Legal Method and Techniques*, Basil Blackwell, Oxford.

Goodrich, P. (1987), *Legal Discourse: Studies in Linguistics, Rhetoric and Legal Analysis*, Macmillan, Basingstoke.

Grbich, J. (1993), 'Writing Histories of Revenue Law: The New Productivity Research', *Law in Context*, Vol.11, No.1.

Grbich, J. (1996), 'The Taxpayer's Body: Genealogies of Exertion' in P. Cheah, D. Fraser, and J. Grbich (eds), *Thinking through the Body of the Law*, New York University Press, New York; and Allen & Unwin, Sydney.

Grbich, J. (1997a), 'Taxation narratives of Economic Gain: Reading Bodies Transgressively', *Feminist Legal Studies*, Vol.5, No.2, August, pp.131-168.

Grbich, J. (1997b), 'The Form of the Tax Reform Story: Marshall, Ordinary Meanings and the City Men', *Griffith Law Review*, Vol.5, pp.40-76.

Grbich, J. (1997c), 'Reading the Phantom: Taxation Law, Psychoanalysis, and Apparitions', *Australian Feminist Law Journal*, Vol.8, pp.81-109.

Himmelfarb, G. (1974), 'Editor's Introduction' in *John Stuart Mill: On Liberty*, Penguin, London.

Kant, I. (1991), *The Metaphysics of Morals*, Cambridge University Press, Cambridge.

Kant, I. (1993), *Critique of Pure Reason*, V. Politis (ed.), Everyman, London.

Kemble, J.M.(1849), *The Saxons in England: A History of the English Commonwealth till the Period of the Norman Conquest*, Vols, I, II, Longman, Brown, Green and Longmans, London.

Mill, J.S. (1972), *The Later Letters of John Stuart Mill, 1849-1873*, F.E. Mineka and D.N. Lindley (eds), Vols. XIV-XVII of *Collected Works*, Toronto

Mill, J.S. (1975), *Three Essays: On Liberty; Representative Government; The Subjection of Women*, Oxford University Press, London.

Woodward, L. (1962), *The Age of Reform, 1815-1870*, Oxford University Press, London.

7 The Liberalist 'Esprit analytique' as a Hindrance to Social Justice

KALLE PIHLAINEN

Questions of social justice are often in everyday practices seen to belong to a sphere other than the political. In our liberalist societies, the distance existing between the political and the cultural appears to be one major contributor to this state of affairs: since political activity is primarily aimed at ensuring that individuals receive their allotted share of rights, the need to positively support individual projects of self-determination is easily neglected. The support and development of individual talents (as in fact of the ability to exercise individual rights) is left largely to the whims of educational and cultural institutions as well as to the initiative of non-governmental organisations. In a liberalist society this is, perhaps, just as it should be. Where values are tied to a system of free exchange, social justice is not a question of 'fairness' but one of rights, resulting in the loss of the critical role that culture could otherwise assume; the function of culture is reduced to its ability to entertain (see e.g. Karkama, 1998, p. 205).

This shift in emphasis from fairness to rights becomes more understandable when we realize that social justice is no longer seen as the direct outcome of a respect for the essential 'humanness' of others but, rather, as a question of legislation and 'equal opportunities'. We no longer speak of respecting others but only of finding a workable system. Leaning on intuition, the desire motivating this system needs, of course, to be something other than an appeal to its practical applicability. Yet talk of any fixed human essence or 'human nature' is obviously out of bounds when *social* justice becomes reduced to the *political* question of pragmatic arbitration between competing rights claims.

Even explicitly pragmatist modern-day liberals such as Richard Rorty do, in the end however, appeal to something that we need to respect – be it the actual suffering of others or their susceptibility to humiliation – rather than relying merely on the idea of contract (Rorty, 1989). Ultimately this appeal is to something quite private and personal – to an empathy on our part toward the plight of others whom we see in situations in which we would not wish to find ourselves. At the individual level, this position was well summarized by Jean-Paul Sartre in his emphasis on humans as situated beings: it follows from this that the political responsibilities that we have result from our sharing what Sartre terms the 'human condition' (see e.g. Sartre, 1995, pp. 54, 60; 1949, p. 24).

To overcome the determinism that we easily succumb to is, for Sartre, to exercise our freedom and simultaneously to take significant political action. We take charge of our lives by accepting responsibility for our actions both in how they affect us and in how they affect others. For Sartre, the move from private actions to the public sphere occurs in our recognition that others share this same freedom (ultimately to self-determination). Although often termed a philosophical sleight-of-hand, Sartre's argument for the mutual recognition of freedoms is quite appealing.[1] Finding the starting point for his argument in the nature of prose literature, he claims that the writer-reader relationship does not permit the objectification of the other but, rather, forces both participants to recognize the freedom and uniqueness of the other, suggesting that mutual respect and equality in all social encounters will follow from this understanding. The generosity that is involved in this 'recognition of freedoms' is a pledge to respect (and in fact to further) the freedom of others (Sartre, 1949, pp. 48-54). What is more, it is also a commitment to respect the particularity of the other since, according to Sartre, 'what the writer requires of the reader is not the application of an abstract freedom but the gift of his whole person, with his passions, his prepossessions, his sympathies, his sexual temperament, and his scale of values' (Sartre, 1949, p. 51).

Following from such a position, socially responsible action would then be more a question of generosity – or in Humean terms, benevolence – than of justice. While perhaps providing a suitable base for some forms of liberalism, it is more often today argued that such a reliance on a standard of generosity is not enough when compared to the standard of justice. This is so because generosity is based on an expectation of what the other wants or desires, yet our perceptions of that other's needs are always unreliable and insufficient – even when not obviously 'distortive'. As Michael J. Sandel formulates this argument: 'Where for Hume, we need justice because we do not *love* each other well enough, for Rawls we need justice because we cannot *know* each other well enough for even love to serve alone' (Sandel, 1984b, p. 167).[2]

Extending the idea of generosity from the specific case of the writer-reader relationship to society and social interactions at large does indeed expose certain weaknesses: not being able to achieve a 'true understanding' of another's desires leads to problems in the application of generosity. Making a somewhat unnerving epistemological claim, Sartre later takes, however, a bold stand in favour of the possibility of reaching a full understanding of another human being. As he says of his last work, *The Family Idiot*, its 'underlying project ... is that of showing that ultimately everything is communicable and that one can succeed, without being God, whilst being a man like any other, to understand perfectly – if one has the necessary facts – a man' (Howells' translation – see Howells, 1988, pp. 172, 266).

Obsessed throughout his life with the idea of describing a human situation fully, Sartre was often at odds in trying to rehabilitate this aim with a respect for the autonomy of others. As he writes in his *Anti-Semite and Jew* (Sartre, 1995, p. 90) concerning authenticity:

> If it is agreed that man may be defined as a being having freedom within the limits of a situation, then it is easy to see that the exercise of this freedom may be considered as *authentic* or *inauthentic* according to the choices made in the situation. Authenticity, it is almost needless to say, consists in having a true and lucid consciousness of the situation, in assuming the responsibilities and risks that it involves, in accepting it in pride or humiliation, sometimes in horror and hate.

Precarious as it already is, maintaining 'a true and lucid consciousness' of one's situation is even more difficult when attempts at conveying it become involved. The appropriation that takes place in linguistic figuration seems in itself enough to make for serious distortions in such a communication. For the receiver, this 'true and lucid consciousness' is easily (though not, claims Sartre, necessarily) destroyed since the experience has to be viewed from the outside – another's subjective understanding obviously being difficult (even if not impossible) to reach. Carrying such an understanding over into political and social matters is of course even more problematic since the focus then is primarily on groups, differences between individuals being lost in the process of their being taken as representatives of some given group.

(1)

Coming to terms with the question of adequate (authentic) representation of others while admitting the necessity of a certain level of abstraction is obviously a problem for any political theory. For Sartre, 'liberalism' and the analytic generalizations it utilizes do a great deal of harm in obscuring reality and thus in hindering understanding of the situatedness of humans. When no longer seen as a heuristic tool toward a comprehension of particular situations, emphasizing 'rights' (though a significant step from relying on a general human nature) is a very misleading abstraction.

Explaining this in his *Anti-Semite and Jew*, Sartre writes somewhat disparagingly of the liberal democrat: 'The Jews have one friend, however, the democrat. But he is a feeble protector. No doubt he proclaims that all men have equal rights ... but his own declarations show the weakness of his position. In the eighteenth century, once and for all, he made his choice: the analytic spirit' (Sartre, 1995, p. 55). This 'democrat' (and later even 'the most liberal democrat') 'recognizes neither Jew, nor Arab, nor Negro, nor bourgeois, nor worker, but only man – man always the same in all times and places' (Sartre, 1995, p. 55). Recognizing only universal traits rather than culturally bound characteristics, this ideologue is thus unequipped to understand social problems; problems which are always results of a concrete historical situation. As Sartre argues, it therefore 'follows that his defense of the Jew saves the latter as man and annihilates him as Jew' (Sartre, 1995, p. 56).[3]

Conversely, this same criticism (directed at utilitarianism) is, of course, repeated by many liberals today. Indeed, as Michael Sandel (1984a, p. 3), writes:

> Contemporary liberals extend Kant's argument with the claim that utilitarianism fails to take seriously the distinction between persons. In seeking above all to maximize the general welfare, the utilitarian treats society as a whole as if it were a single person; it conflates our many, diverse desires into a single system of desires, and tries to maximize ... [T]his fails to respect our plurality and distinctness. It uses some as means to the happiness of all, and so fails to respect each as an end in himself.

Or, as John Rawls states this: 'It is customary to think of utilitarianism as individualistic. ... Yet utilitarianism is not individualistic ... in that, by conflating all systems of desires, it applies to society the principle of choice for one man', thus overlooking 'the plurality of distinct persons with separate systems of ends' (Rawls, 1984, p. 40).

Like Sartre, most contemporary liberals would, then, also deny such an approach based on an idea of 'the good', advancing the familiar maxim that no preferred way of life should be imposed on others. All individuals should be free to choose and pursue their own life projects. For rights-based liberals like Rawls this amounts to the construction of a (minimal) set of rules within which each individual is free to choose a course of action that she finds personally appealing. Attempting not to evaluate particular beliefs, this brand of liberalism thus attempts to promote social justice by providing a framework in which the realization of individual eccentricities is protected against more established (institutionalized and socially reinforced) patterns of behaviour.

While such an emphasis on rights comes, admittedly, close to Sartre's somewhat ambiguous use of the idea of freedom, Sartre's criticism regarding the abstraction involved in the idea of rights themselves remains valid. Recognizing only 'man' ('always the same in all times and places'), the liberal takes it upon himself to define the needs and desires of others. Even accepting that Sartre's use of the goal 'freedom' is on a par with a broader discussion of rights, it is difficult to fully agree with Michael Walzer, who – in his introduction to the *Anti-Semite and Jew*, terms Sartre a liberal, 'for all his Marxizing sociology' (Walzer, 1995, p. xix). Although Sartre may indeed be 'a liberal', the definition of the nature of his liberalism that Walzer provides seems a little simplistic. Let me explain. Walzer continues by stating that Sartre is definitely *not* 'a pluralist liberal'. This, apparently, is because Sartre sees social groupings as to be valued only as long as they remain oppressed as groups. Otherwise (in the utopian future that Sartre envisions), argues Walzer, it is only the rights of individuals that he would have us defend (Walzer, 1995, p. xviii).

Quite rightly viewing Sartre as hoping for an end to social pluralism in the long term, Walzer (see Walzer, 1995, pp. xx-xxi) does not, to my mind, sufficiently emphasize the significance of the argument regarding the 'analytic spirit' that drives the liberalist to generalizations. Although seeing pluralism as a major cause of social problems, Sartre would not, in my opinion, be willing to endorse the ideal of a society where 'man' would indeed be 'always the same'. Valuing individual differences, Sartre rather urges us to abandon the overly rational 'analytic spirit' in favour of what he terms a '*concrete liberalism*'.

Following Walzer's interpretation, this would mean – for now – an understanding and taking into account of social differences and – in the utopia of a 'non-pluralistic' society – the understanding and taking into account of individual differences. To me, this is only a difference in quantity. The point is that Sartre defines his concrete liberalism as simply a matter of giving 'the full rights of citizens' to all those who are involved actively in the development of their country. Emphasizing that rights are given to people as what they are, '*as* Jews, Negroes, or Arabs – that is, as concrete persons' (Sartre, 1995, p. 146), Sartre also draws our attention to the way in which even the need for 'rights' and the ability to exercise them, varies with the concrete situation of a given individual.

(2)

Sartre's argument serves well to remind us that a great many things in life are completely value-neutral. There are differences between people which need to be understood (and which indeed could not even be eradicated) only because they are constitutive for certain concrete persons in who they are. Recognizing differences of background does not, in itself, however, lead to a stance of relativism with regard to such political and social questions as could be termed moral.

An appeal to rights in this sense, then, is a way of denying the 'anything goes' stance that is easily associated with a liberalist ideology. Since there obviously exist practices that we do not wish to condone, the rubric of 'justice' provides a good means of resisting them. Yet this justice and the appeal to rights is a consensual matter, or, to be more accurate, a matter decided by majority vote. While – or perhaps because – Sartre seems to fully have perceived the difficulties that his earlier stand of absolute freedom led him to, we see him later approaching communitarian ideals, rather than being satisfied with the abstractions of (even a rights-based) liberalism.[4] Advocating thus an ontological freedom that allows for individual fulfilment while taking into account the freedom of others through his ideas of commitment and generosity, he brings the situational context to the fore in his investigations.[5]

This clearly fits in well with the communitarian criticism of the rights-based ethic: our freedom to choose – and indeed the very fact of who we are – is determined to a great extent by our situation. We are 'situated selves', implicated in a prior course of action by our very existence. Fitting in well with Sartre's critique of the 'analytic spirit' which leads the liberal to treat everyone equally – conflating distinct desires and giving no mind to differences in situation as noted earlier – Alasdair MacIntyre has provided us with a stronger, more substantive conception of the self, as Sandel (1984a, p. 9) describes:

> In contrast to the liberal's unencumbered self, MacIntyre proposes a narrative conception of the self, a self constituted in part by a life story with a certain *telos*, or point. As the *telos* is not fixed or fully identifiable in advance, the unity of a life is the unity of a narrative quest, a quest whose object is a fuller and more adequate grasp of a good only intimated at the outset. On the narrative view, my identity is not independent of my aims and attachments, but partly constituted by them; I am situated from the

> start, embedded in a history which locates me among others, and implicates my good in the good of the communities whose stories I share.

For Sartre, this telos is, of course, the individual's 'life project'. But as MacIntyre makes the point, this moral particularity to my own life is inseparable from those factors – comprising the various 'debts, inheritances, rightful expectations and obligations' which 'I inherit from the past of my family, my city, my tribe, my nation' – which constitute 'the given of my life, my moral starting point' (MacIntyre, 1985, p. 220).

In this sense, it is obvious that the abstract conception of an absolute freedom to make choices is, at the very least, unrealistic. As Walzer nicely puts this in the preface to *Anti-Semite and Jew*, while people do, for Sartre, indeed choose, it is 'clear that they make their choices under duress' (Walzer 1995, p. viii). Constructed by their environment and also by the particular choices they have already made, humans are – although still free – first of all 'situated', unable to fully ignore the set of concrete limitations that they share or the expectations that they themselves (as well as others) have regarding who they are and how this will lead them to behave.[6]

Moving in this manner from the level of abstract rights to the choices of particular individuals, it is clear that we can no longer speak only of justice-as-rights or even of justice-as-fairness (this amounts to what, returning to my opening remarks, can be termed *political* justice). There is a further sense of justice which incorporates, or rather allows for, the very important goal of self-determination (what I see as the essence of *social* justice). As Walzer again interprets Sartre: 'The aim of a concrete liberalism, one would think, is to design situations from which an honorable escape is possible – but where it is also possible to feel at home, to live with friends and relatives, chosen and inherited, not only in traditional but also in innovative ways, in peace' (Walzer, 1995, p. xxv).

Since individual autonomy is so resistant to governance, these situations cannot be brought about through the general application of rules but require, rather, quite localized decision-making. This would, to me, again suggest that Sartre's critique of liberalism is still quite valid and proceeds along what are today termed communitarian lines. Note Sandel's observation: 'More generally, where the liberal regards the expansion of individual rights and entitlements as unqualified moral and political progress, the communitarian is troubled by the tendency of liberal programmes to displace politics from smaller forms of association to more comprehensive ones' (Sandel 1984a, p. 6).

In implementing the ideal of equality, freedom – even of the mutually respectful kind that Sartre advocates – is, then, not enough. Parallel to this freedom must exist an equality in what Agnes Heller and Ferenc Fehér term 'life-chances', a conception which makes allowances for differences in the situations of individuals. As they argue, a demand for equal freedom is a claim for political justice, whereas the demand for equal life-chances is specifically a claim for *social justice* (see e.g. Heller and Fehér, 1988, p. 125). The political framework provided by equal freedom and rights is, then, a practical requirement for the realization of social justice 'via negotiation and discourse' (Heller and Fehér, 1988, p. 127) but does not by itself necessarily lead to practical changes.

As noted, to view someone's personal idiosyncracies or 'constitutive attachments' (a term Sandel uses for the values that a person holds due to being who she is) in the 'analytic spirit' as insignificant for their choices would lead to an incapacity to empathize with and understand them. For, like me, they are indeed tied to their respective situations (they have a character in 'the constitutive sense' – see Sandel 1984b, p. 173). As I experience this fact whenever I share an insight with a friend, or when I find something touching or amusing in a television programme or a novel, or – simplified to the extreme – when I attribute an emotion to an experience, so do they. Even if we do not go so far as to say that language speaks through us, we can agree with Sartre when he expresses the experience that, in speaking, 'the meanings of the very words in my mouth are changed by others' (Sartre, 1991, p. 98).[7] While accepting that my rights may be abstractly dealt with, I, as a member of society and constituted by my situation, want my unique desires and abilities to be taken into consideration when my needs are discussed. Indeed, I have a 'right' to expect this. Just as no-one can justify their behaviour by pointing to external conditions while still remaining authentic, 'no-one has,' argue Heller and Fehér, 'the right to ascribe [the needs of others] to false consciousness, to arbitrariness, or to mere fancy' (Heller and Fehér, 1988, p. 26).

Yet this argument is easily turned around and a similar move often made in veiled defences of the status quo. Let me explain. As Heller and Fehér argue (1988, p. 58), an acceptance of the diversity of beliefs and values as well as of practices is an essential aspect of modern experience:

> Particular moral worlds are different in kind, whether they are religious, communal, co-operative, political or whatever. To create 'harmony' among the heterogeneity of *Sittlichkeit*, or even to make the different kinds of *Sittlichkeit* equally dense or equally loose, is an enterprise which is doomed to failure in the contemporary world. ... The modern individual (the

> singular) is contingent in every *Sittlichkeit*, yet he/she can choose himself or herself as well as he/she can fall short of choosing, can be a person of conscience as much as not, can be authentic as much as inauthentic within the framework of each and every particular world.

Emphasizing that in addition to supporting such freedom to difference we should be concerned with attending to the 'common business' of public life, Heller and Fehér deny the stance of moral relativism that this fashionable insistence upon difference as a prime value in itself often leads to. Indeed, as Honi Fern Haber, for example, has pointed out, even in the work of Rorty, with its strong separation of public from private matters, a 'universalization of difference' takes place which makes oppositional politics ineffective (see Haber 1994, pp. 49-50). After all, if all human practices are equally ungrounded, how could we argue in favour of or against any particular ones? How are we to oppose those practices we find unjust?

As Heller and Fehér state, '[t]olerance is a traditional value in liberalism and, as such, one of the preconditions of negative liberty which all democratic politics must preserve'. Yet, as they go on to point out, tolerance as a universal credo (seen, that is, in a mind-set guided by 'the analytic spirit') is only another name for relativism: 'when applied to the coexistence of different ways of life, liberal tolerance simply means that I pursue my happiness in my own way, you do it in your own way, and the one is of no concern to the other' (Heller & Fehér, 1988, p. 83). Jettisoning principles of charity or generosity of understanding in favour of the universalization of difference in this way obviously leads to difficulties for concerted efforts aimed at change.

(3)

Though we may often be very sensitive to the excuses that we ourselves make to escape the demands of authenticity, any attempt to point out such behaviour in the actions of others is doomed to fail since self-understanding and self-determination cannot be imposed. As Heller and Fehér remind us, 'initiators of projects of self-determination ... must always resist the idea that people can be forced to be free' (Heller & Fehér, 1988, p. 38).

The 'analytic spirit' which, I have argued, Sartre attributes especially to liberalism, is, however, also closely linked to what Heller and Fehér characterize as 'rhetorical discussion'. This denotes a situation where the participants no longer (or do not yet) 'stand in a symmetrically reciprocal relationship' but where, rather, one party attempts to influence others in a way that we would in most (other) contexts term dishonest. The adoption of the rhetorical stance leads easily to distortions of the substance of the discussion, permitting 'the manipulation of facts, the withholding of certain items of information and the overemphasizing of others, it appeals to non-rational emotions (envy, vanity, aggression) and the like' (Heller and Fehér, 1988, p. 38).

Although not perhaps intentionally rhetorical, the analytic spirit lends itself to similar distortions, thus contributing to such rhetorical discussion and to assumptions that 'I know better', giving the speaker justification for attempting to 'instruct' others. Effectively blocking any realization of self-determination, even well-intentioned classifications and attempts at understanding may thus lead to oppression.

For Sartre, any such totalizations need to be avoided since they are imposed on experiences that cannot be totalized (or as it is often put today, 'colonized'). Although the possibility of understanding remains, we should not aspire to 'knowledge' of the 'lived experience' of others, since this experience 'remains necessarily opaque to itself ... [as] a constant totalization, and a totalization *which cannot be conscious of what it is*' (cited in Howells, 1988, p. 258 – her translation). Sartre's 'concrete liberalism' would, then, first of all recognize that authentic behaviour *eludes* description (cf. McBride, 1991, pp. 49-50) whereas inauthentic behaviour yields easily to description since it is, by itself, already an attempt to (re)present a category or an instance of something *in-itself*. Such descriptions are, of course, in 'bad faith', in that they assume that human beings might have a determined nature or role in any finally describable sense.

At work in each action, claims Sartre, is a dialectical relationship between the situation and the individual's choices. Understanding this leads to a practical recognition of, and respect for, an individual's right to autonomy – and consequently, a prohibition of all actions that infringe on that autonomy. Each person 'forms a synthetic whole with his situation – biological, economic, political, cultural, etc. He cannot be distinguished from his situation, for it forms him and decides his possibilities; but, inversely, it is he who gives it meaning by making his choices within it and by it' (Sartre, cited in McBride, 1991, p. 50 – his translation). An autonomous individual thus embraces her contingency happily, and takes responsibility for her actions within the boundaries that it places. As McBride argues, it is for this reason that Sartre feels 'the abstractly universal way of conceiving of "the Jewish question" that characterizes the liberal democrat is unacceptable' (McBride, 1991, p. 50). Indeed, such abstractions only serve to prolong inauthentic existence on the part of the subjects described through being incorporated into their self-images.

In order to avoid these problems of abstraction, what is needed, says Sartre, is 'a concrete community engaged in a particular fight having nothing to do with universalist abstractions of legality' (Sartre, 1995, p. 153). This, on my view, should be simultaneously taken as a definition of self-determination at the level of the community – a community that is working toward concrete, local self-determination, or, should we say, self-government. Admittedly, to read Sartre in this way is somewhat problematic. Arguing that change toward increased self-determination cannot be brought about through education or legislation, Sartre sees the answer to problems of social inequality to be found only through the kind of solidarity that can be realized in a 'classless society'. Using the specific case of anti-Semitism, he feels he has successfully demonstrated how such injustice 'can exist only in a society where a rather loose solidarity unites strongly structured pluralities; it is a phenomenon of social pluralism' (Sartre, 1995, p. 149). A plurality of group identities is thus not, for Sartre, conducive to social justice. Yet I think we would be foolish to conclude – as he himself sometimes suggests – that a firmly entrenched solidarity at the level of the nation-state could really provide a solution to the problems of injustice through displacing plurality at the level of groups and individuals.[8]

Rather, Sartre's 'concrete liberalism' should be seen as valuing group identities inasmuch as these are constructive of individual differences, and thus as ultimately challenging us to see beyond such groupings. In this way, his emphasis on individual differences and the consequent avoidance of the reductive totalizations performed in the analytic spirit offers an alternative route by which to approach problems of social justice. A route that – as I hope to have shown – also avoids the dangers of a purely individualistic conception of justice or authenticity.

In speaking of the resolution of these problems at the level of the individual, Sartre claims that 'the choice of authenticity appears to be a moral decision, bringing certainty to the Jew on the ethical level but in no way serving as a solution on the social or political level' (Sartre, 1995, p. 141). In saying this he is not, however, altogether true to his more committed stance. Invoking Heller and Fehér's argument that achieving self-determination presupposes a respect for and practical commitment to the self-determination of others (cf. Heller and Fehér, 1988, pp. 36-37), it could better be said that authenticity as a moral choice points us (at least theoretically) toward practical social and political solutions. Which is – as we have seen – what Sartre argued with regard to respecting the freedom of others through the extension of the writer-reader relationship: his 'pact of generosity'.[9]

Notes

1 For a critique of Sartre's argument, see e.g. Howells (1988, p. 132).

2 Obviously, the existence of a fixed human essence or nature is firmly denied in such thinking; we cannot know another well enough because there is no such essence. Sartre too, makes this point quite clear: '*we do not believe in "human nature"* ... we believe that it is necessary to consider biological, psychical, and social phenomena in a spirit of synthesis' (Sartre, 1995, p. 59, emphasis mine).

3 For the Jew, Sartre similarly terms such an espousal of rationalism as 'an escape into the universal'. An escape from the historical irrationalities, the 'ensemble' of values and beliefs, that plague his self-creation (Sartre, 1995, p. 112).

4 Indeed, William L. McBride sees *Anti-Semite and Jew* as the work where Sartre first demonstrates an, at least partial, realization of the necessity of an understanding of history for constructing a social theory (McBride, 1991, p. 49).

5 Cf. Steven Wall, who makes a good argument for the benefits of an increased amount of options to the realization of autonomy; especially for the need of options that provide a person with 'the opportunity to develop his talents and capacities' (Wall, 1998, p.142).

6 Cf. Sandel (1948b, p. 173): 'When I act out of more or less enduring qualities of character, by contrast, my choice of ends is not arbitrary in the same way. In consulting my preferences, I have not only to weigh their intensity but also to assess their suitability to the person I (already) am. I ask, as I deliberate, not only what I really want but who I really am, and this last question takes me beyond an attention to my desires alone to reflect on my identity itself'.

7 As one commentator puts it, language, for Sartre, 'is the supreme example of those institutions, norms, and conventions which are the "congealed" praxis of others and which mitigate against the subject's own freedom and praxis' (Wolfe, 1991, p. 79).

8 As Walzer notes, Sartre does not wish the 'disappearance of historical peoples, like the French ... and so he must imagine a future international society of distinct nations' (Walzer, 1995, p. xix).

9 Yet for Sartre this might not be a point to ponder now, since it is only once a truly classless society is achieved and social injustices thus removed, that the time to return to metaphysical questions comes: 'when men are liberated, it [metaphysics] will become again an essential concern of mankind' (Sartre, 1995, p. 133). Before that time we must, however, find practical solutions to

our problems. 'Here and now,' then, as Walzer points out, 'difference must be accepted: there is no honest alternative' (Walzer, 1995, p. xix).

References

Haber, H.F. (1994), *Beyond Postmodern Politics: Lyotard, Rorty, Foucault*, Routledge, New York and London.

Heller, A. and Fehér, F. (1988), *The Postmodern Political Condition*, Polity Press, Cambridge.

Howells, C. (1988), *Sartre: The Necessity of Freedom*, Cambridge University Press, Cambridge.

Karkama, P. (1998), *Kulttuuri ja demokratia. Kirjoituksia kulttuurin nykytilasta* [*Culture and Democracy. Essays on the Condition of Contemporary Culture*], SKS, Helsinki.

MacIntyre, A. (1985), *After Virtue: A Study in Moral Theory* (2nd edn), Duckworth, London.

McBride, W. (1991), *Sartre's Political Theory*, Indiana University Press, Bloomington and Indianapolis.

Rawls, J. (1984), 'The Right and the Good Contrasted', reprinted in M.J. Sandel, (ed.), *Liberalism and its Critics*, Blackwell, Oxford.

Rorty, R. (1989), *Contingency, Irony, and Solidarity*, Cambridge University Press, Cambridge.

Sandel, M.J. (1984a), 'Introduction', in his (ed.), *Liberalism and Its Critics*, Blackwell, Oxford.

Sandel, M.J. (1984b), 'Justice and the Good', reprinted in his (ed.), *Liberalism and Its Critics*, Blackwell, Oxford .

Sartre, J.-P. (1949), *What is Literature?*, trans. B. Frechtman, Philosophical Library, New York.

Sartre, J.-P. (1991; orig. 1960), *Critique of Dialectical Reason, Vol. 1: Theory of Practical Ensembles*, trans. A. Sheridan-Smith, ed. J. Rée, Verso, London and New York.

Sartre, J.-P. (1995; orig. 1948), *Anti-Semite and Jew*, trans. G.J. Becker, Schocken Books, New York.

Wall, S. (1998), *Liberalism, Perfectionism and Restraint*, Cambridge University Press, Cambridge.

Walzer, M. (1995), 'Preface' to Sartre's *Anti-Semite and Jew*, trans. G.J. Becker, Schocken Books, New York.

Wolfe, C. (1991), 'Rethinking Commitment: Ontology, Genre, and Sartre's Mallarmé', *Diacritics*, Vol. 21, No. 4.

8 From Metaphysics to Pragmatism: Rorty on Liberalism and Social Justice

JUSTIN CRUICKSHANK

(1) Politics without metaphysics: introductory remarks

In his essay on 'Postmodernist Bourgeois Liberalism' (in Rorty, 1991; orig. 1983), Richard Rorty draws a distinction between 'Kantians' and 'Hegelians'.[1] He argues that Kantians (such as Dworkin) are definable in terms of their acceptance of the Enlightenment justification for liberalism, which turns on the notion of a metaphysical subject that is separate from, and transcends its socio-historical environment. The Hegelians, by contrast, make no such distinction between the self and its socio-historical environment. For the Hegelians, the identity of the subject is constituted by its socio-historical location. As Rorty (1991, p. 197) puts it,

> They [the Kantians] are opposed by people who say that 'humanity' is a biological rather than a moral notion, that there is no human dignity that is not derivative from the dignity of some specific community, and no appeal beyond the relative merits of various actual or proposed communities to impartial criteria which will help us weigh up those merits.

This leads some Hegelians (such as communitarians like MacIntyre and Unger) to reject liberalism, Rorty notes, because they maintain that liberal political *institutions* cannot be accepted if (amongst other reasons) their *philosophical justification* is untenable. To reject the Kantian justification for liberalism is to reject liberalism.

Other Hegelians, however – such as Dewey and Oakeshott – accept liberalism, whilst recognising that there can be no appeal to a transcendental subject. In this case, then, the legitimacy of liberal institutions is separated from the philosophical attempt to justify these institutions in Kantian terms. Rorty agrees with such a view, and in doing so he describes himself as a 'postmodernist bourgeois liberal'. He says his position is 'postmodern' because it rejects the 'metanarrative' about a transcendental subject, or Kantian 'noumenal' self, and it is 'bourgeois' because he accepts the Marxist view that liberal institutions can only exist in certain socio-economic conditions (Rorty, 1991, p. 198-9).

In other words, we have to recognise that liberalism is contingent upon certain historical-material conditions, and that the self is contingent upon its socio-historical location for its constitution. In which case, the defence of liberalism has to be in terms of what Rorty (1991) refers to as 'ethnocentrism'. What this means is that given the recognition of such contingency, any defence of liberalism will have to be internal to the norms of liberalism, with liberalism being regarded as good for those socialised into liberal norms. There can be no appeal to anything other than such norms. Of course this defence is circular, but the circularity is virtuous rather than vicious, in this case, because it simply recognises that there are no neutral standpoints outside the norms and practices of different communities, from which to judge those communities. We cannot defend liberalism by saying it is in accord with some universal atemporal and asocial essence for the self, and nor can we say that liberalism is to be defended as the necessary outcome of some teleological historical process.

Rejecting teleological arguments about history is in accord with the postmodern aspect of Rorty's postmodernist bourgeois liberalism, because such conceptions of history are seen as objectionable metanarratives which seek a totalistic explanation. Consequently, Rorty rejects Hegel's teleological philosophy of history, along with the Marxist view that history will lead to communism. Rorty regards arguments which explain political systems as the necessary outcome of historical forces as 'romantic'. Such arguments are romantic because they believe that something beyond us gives our lives meaning, as we are part of 'something bigger'. As Rorty (1998a, p. 235) puts it

> By inventing 'History' as the name of an object that could be conceptually grasped, Hegel and Marx made it possible to keep the romance of the Christian story about the Incarnate Logos, and the Christian sense of solidarity against injustice, even after we lost religious faith.

Rorty uses this argument to criticise Fukuyama's view that liberal democracy is the end of history, with all other grand political ideologies (i.e. socialism and fascism) having been defeated and discredited (Fukuyama, 1992). Fukuyama recognises that there will be problems to solve but he is worried about boredom and depression setting in, with the loss of grand belief systems offering challenges to liberalism. According to Rorty (1998a, p. 231), though, what Fukuyama is really

> ... worried about is not the end of history, but the end of the philosophy, and thus the romance, of history. What bothers him is our diminished ability to

> use History as an object around which we intellectuals wrap our fantasies.

So, romantic conceptions of history, along with the transcendental self, must be rejected.

Rorty may say he is postmodern because he rejects metanarratives, but it is misleading to think of Rorty as a postmodernist. When Rorty refers to himself as postmodern there is an element of irony in this, because he also, in the same article, describes himself as an 'Hegelian'. To be sure, he rejects the philosophy of history, which would be a metanarrative. However, simply to align oneself with a philosopher such as Hegel who, along with Marx, is often regarded as building metanarratives for totalistic explanations, would be antithetical to many who apply the 'postmodern' rubric to their work. This use of irony signals some conceptual distance from postmodernism, manifested also in Rorty's pragmatic acceptance of science, against the postmodern view that scientific values form a technocratic metanarrative.

Rorty (1980) rejects the view that a philosophy of mind can explain how beliefs directly represent non-beliefs, but despite rejecting the view that knowledge mirrors 'reality-in-itself', Rorty still accepts that 'science works'. As a pragmatist, he accepts that the practices of natural science help us go on in the world, whilst rejecting the view that philosophy (in the form of epistemology) could explain this. This distance between Rorty and postmodernism has widened in more recent works, where he criticises postmodernism for replacing a romantic conception of history with a romantic conception of the 'other'.

Rorty (1998a) argues that the works of authors such as Marx, Bentham and Foucault ought to be read as attempts to 'do the right thing', rather than criticised for conceptual inadequacies, with another theory being sought to overcome the perceived inadequacies. That is, we should move from the level of abstract theory to the practical consequences of particular arguments (1998a, p. 242):

> We might then stop trying to find a successor to 'the working class' – for example, 'Difference' or 'Otherness' - as a name for the latest incarnation of the Logos. [... This will help us avoid] the idea that a materialism and a sense of historicity more radical than even Marx's will some how provide a brand-new, still bigger, albeit still blurrier, object – an object called, perhaps, 'Language' or 'Discourse' – around which to weave our fantasies.

Instead of a romantic conception of history, therefore, Rorty points here to a romantic conception of the other, or difference, or language, as something beyond our concrete practices, which gives meaning to those practices and which is some form of 'moving force'.

So, Rorty's pragmatism rejects metanarratives about the self, history and the other. This pragmatic position may, I would suggest, be re-titled as 'modern bourgeois liberalism'. This does not mean that 'modern' is simply a default position for thinkers who are not postmodern. Rather, it means that Rorty's pragmatism may be read as a realisation of what modernity really ought to be, in intellectual terms. We can say that Rorty is modern because he agrees with Kant's definition of the Enlightenment as 'man's [*sic*] emergence from his self-imposed immaturity' (1989, p. 54). To be immature is, for Kant, to rely on dogma and prejudice for one's (putative) knowledge, instead of having the courage to use one's own understanding, to explore matters for oneself. Rorty's pragmatism is in accord with the sprit of this, as it accepts those modern advances of science which have challenged the worldly remit of religious dogma.

However, given such a pragmatic approach, we would have to regard Kant's Enlightenment philosophy, along with Hegel's and Marx's post-Enlightenment philosophies (not to mention postmodernism), as being 'immature', and therefore unmodern. This is because such philosophies were *metaphysical appeals to something beyond concrete practices*, whether this was an appeal to a transcendental subject constituted prior to its involvement in community, or a romantic conception of history (or the other). This unmodern use of metaphysics is akin to relying on religion in worldly matters, because a dogma is posited as an ultimate explanation or metanarrative. So, with Rorty's pragmatism, we are to escape from our self-imposed immaturity by focusing on practices rather than appealing to metaphysics. In terms of Kant's definition, then, to be modern for Rorty is precisely to reject all recourse to the Enlightenment's metaphysical philosophy of the subject (including, of course, Kant's transcendental model) – and indeed all metaphysics. It is, in a sense, to carry through on Kant's own logic. Therefore instead of applying the term postmodern to Rorty because he rejects metanarratives, it is better to focus on the rejection of metaphysics, and to regard pragmatism as an attempt to move from references about 'something beyond' practices to practices in themselves. In which case, I would argue, Rorty is trying to tell us how to be modern, by escaping our self-imposed immaturity which stemmed from appeals to metaphysics.

So, to be modern is to be mature, which means taking responsibility for our practices by seeking practical solutions to practical problems. Conversely, to be unmodern is to be immature, in that we appeal to something beyond us to give meaning to what we do, and seek a metanarrative to furnish some form of definitive explanation. With the former we have to face the insecurity of contingency, given the removal of metaphysics, and with the latter, a (specious) security against contingency is sought in a realm away from our practices, or ways of going on. This means that, as regards politics, one ought to adopt the position of ethnocentrism, because there are no criteria to assess a political system other than its own norms: without metaphysics the evaluation of a political system will be internal to the norms of particular communities and their political systems.

Evaluation of politics concerns social justice in a twofold sense. Firstly, there are abstract arguments about a particular political philosophy as an adequate model of the 'good society'. Secondly, we can assess issues of social justice in terms of the actual practices within a political system. Rorty deals with both types of social justice in his evaluation of liberalism. As we will see though, his arguments that liberalism provides social justice not only violate his stated position of ethnocentrism, but further, his arguments are 'immature', in the sense noted above, because they preclude the critical distance necessary to 'stand back' and analyse issues of social justice. Rorty actually rules out possibilities for applying our own understanding, and does so by using arguments which seek to be definitive and thus beyond question.

(2) The good society

Rorty's defence of liberalism, as a political philosophy which posits a model of the good society, rests upon linking Nietzsche's arguments about the self and poetry, to the liberal defence of freedom and prevention of harm. Rorty writes (1992, pp. 27-8; emphasis in the original) that Nietzsche

> saw self-knowledge as self-creation. The process of coming to know oneself, confronting one's contingency, tracking one's causes home, is identical with the process of inventing a new language – that is, of thinking up new metaphors. For any *literal* description of one's individuality, which is to say any use of an inherited language-game for this purpose, will necessarily fail. One will not have traced that idiosyncrasy home but will merely have managed to see it as not idiosyncratic at all, as a specimen of a type, a copy or replica of something which has already been identified. To fail as a poet – and thus, for Nietzsche, to fail as a human being – is to accept somebody else's description of oneself, to execute a previously prepared program.

Having accepted the Nietzschean view of the self as a poet, Rorty goes on to argue that liberalism will furnish the good society because it allows individuals the freedom to recreate their identity, or 'final vocabularies' (1989, p. 73) in private, whilst protecting individuals from the harm of humiliation, in the public sphere. To create a final vocabulary is a 'poetic achievement' (1989, p. 77), but if one poetically created a new identity for another, and imposed this upon them, then one would be humiliating, i.e. harming, that individual (1989, p. 91). This recognition of the potential for harm, rather than a fixed human essence, is the basis of solidarity in liberal societies. As Rorty puts it, '[h]er [the ironist's/pragmatist's] sense of human solidarity is based on a sense of common danger, not on a common possession or a shared power' (1989, p. 91). Yet this is not just applicable to liberals, for Rorty also says that what unites the human species is a susceptibility to a special sort of pain which animals cannot experience, *viz.* the pain of humiliation, or redescription (1989, p. 92). So, liberalism is justified because the liberal distinction between the private and public spheres allows individuals the freedom to recreate themselves, whilst preventing others being harmed. Hence Rorty's 'liberal utopia' – his view of the good society – would be one wherein the individual was a Nietzschean poet in the private sphere and a liberal following J.S. Mill in the public sphere (see Rorty, 1989, especially chapter 4).

In the literature on Rorty, this argument about liberalism meets with three main criticisms. The first is that Rorty does make appeal to a theory of human nature, or a transcendent essence for the self, because he believes that people are distressed by witnessing humiliation. Such potential for distress is a trans-cultural human universal (Critchley, 1996; Dews, 1990; Geras, 1995; Warren 1990). So, contrary to the argument which rejected any metanarrative about a transcendental subject, in favour of holding that the self was a socio-historical contingency, Rorty does posit a human universal. Rorty thus ends up giving us a metanarrative, which explains that all individuals, whatever their socio-historical location, find humiliation distressing.

The second criticism is that the private/public distinction is an empty abstraction, devoid of any socio-historical substance – the upshot being that a definition of liberalism is used as a defence: the conceptual distinction alone is used to justify liberalism's claims to protect freedom, and prevent harm (Ball, 1990; Bhaskar, 1991; Laclau, 1996; Warren, 1990). So, instead of, for example, analysing how public matters, such as the existence of pornography, may affect relations in the private sphere; or how the public/private boundary is an historical contingency with, for example, the state now intervening to prevent domestic violence, when previously it was regarded as a 'private' matter and not for the state to deal with, we are simply told that the public/private divide provides social justice. That is, we are told that the public/private divide protects freedom and prevents harm, giving us the good individualist society, but we are not told anything about substantive social relations.

The third criticism is that there is a tension between liberalism and poetry. What this means is that the poet may resent the liberal who tries to restrict the use of poetry (Bhaskar, 1991; Fraser, 1990). It may well be that the poetic are more Nietzschean than liberal, and that they would want an elitist society, believing that liberalism would debase civilisation and culture. Restricting poetry to the private sphere would be seen as an illegitimate limitation upon the freedom of the poet.

Now whilst it is correct to maintain that Rorty does actually posit an essence for the self, in terms of the capacity to feel distressed by harm, it should be recognised that he also has a more active/positive conception of the self. Rorty (1989, pp. 23-43; 1991, pp. 113-25, 175-202) describes the self as a de-centred contingency, meaning that the self has no defining features which are separate from the norms or rules of the prevailing language game, and this is taken to be compatible with the Nietzschean emphasis on poetic self-creation. As the self has no defining essence it can be poetically re-created, by fashioning new 'private language'.[2] However, these two views are mutually exclusive. For if the self were a de-centred contingency which was solely constituted by the prevailing rules of the language game, then the self would be a passive automaton. As there was nothing to the self other than the said rules, there could be no self capable of poetically using those rules to recreate an identity which was separate from the prevailing rules. In this case, we could remove any reference to a self and adopt a behaviouristic approach which held that the agent had their behaviour determined by the rules *qua* positive and negative reinforcement stimuli.[3]

Conversely, if the self is a poet, then the self has the capacity for free will, which can be exercised by fashioning a new identity – or final vocabulary – via the poetic reworking of a language game. In this case, instead of a behaviouristic determinism which produces conformity to any prevailing political system, we have an argument for liberalism which rests upon some conception of a transcendent human essence. The self transcends its socio-historical environment because the self has the poetic ability to separate itself from the prevailing norms, in order to rework those norms. If the self did not transcend its social milieu then it would be a passively determined epiphenomenon. Further, the self is to be understood not just in terms of a potential to exercise free will in such a fashion, but to benefit from it. The self does not just have the capacity to be poetic; moreover, in being poetic the self is enriching itself. *Therefore liberal institutions, which allow individuals the freedom to be poetic, and which protect this freedom by preventing humiliation, constitute the good society for all human beings, contra* ethnocentrism, because liberalism is in accord with a transcendent human essence.

As regards the criticisms concerning the public/private distinction, and the tension between poetry and liberalism, we can argue that these become non-problems, because the poetic self does not require a liberal state to act as an umpire, regulating competition and preventing harm. The liberal state would not be necessary to regulate competition because every individual would be able to defend themselves. As a poet, one would be amongst equals: a poet could prevent him/ herself being redescribed. Further, as the public language game could not be appropriated, and enrichment stemmed from creating a private language, it is hard to conceptualise just why a poet would want to redescribe another poet – there would be, *literally*, nothing to gain. Therefore any attempts at regulation by the state would amount to unnecessary and illegitimate limitations upon individuals' freedom to enrich themselves.

Of course some may be less poetic. In which case we could try to defend liberalism by arguing that the less poetic, under liberal principles, are provided protection by the state. However, this argument for liberalism does not stand up. For the less poetic would be dependent upon the public language game to derive their identities, and this language game is created and recreated by the more poetic. In other words, the less poetic would fail to be human because they would fail as poets and be humiliated by relying on the creative work of another for their identity. If some form of protection were sought by a restriction on language (which is hardly a feature of liberal states, and more a feature of some Orwellian nightmare), then the more poetic would be restricted in their attempts to create an ever richer public language game, from which new private vocabularies could be created. Culture would be impoverished in order to protect the weak. Therefore liberalism would be illegitimate because it would fail to protect the less poetic and, in addition to this, it would prevent the more poetic from enriching themselves and creating a more poetic culture. What this means is that the Nietzschean emphasis on poetry is in practice wholly antithetical to liberalism, and that for a political system to be legitimate, it would have to be some form of elitist system which allowed poets to harm the less poetic.

So, to avoid metaphysics we are counselled to focus on practices which, in the case of politics, entails an ethnocentrism which eschews references to a transcendental subject or romantic conceptions of history. Such ethnocentrism would have to judge the practices of a political system by the norms of that political system, as there could be no appeal to something beyond the community, such as a transcendental self or history. This, however, would result in a strong form of normative relativism whereby every political system provided 'social justice', provided that it 'worked' according to its own norms. Such a position would be immature because, although avoiding metaphysical references to something beyond practices, it would prevent us having the courage to use own our reason to evaluate a political system. The prevailing norms would be dogma that had to be accepted, which meant that the status quo would be divinised. One would have to accept the given order.

Against such normative relativism, and ethnocentrism, Rorty argues for liberalism as a model of the good society. *In place of every community being equally just, in its own terms, Rorty, in effect, argues that liberalism provides the good society for all humanity, by being in accord with a universal human essence, which transcends its contingent socio-historical location.* (In which case liberalism may not be an historical contingency, but an inevitable outcome, given that it is in accord with the defining human essence). The subjects of an authoritarian political system have an identity forced upon them, and therefore have their humanity denied, by being humiliated and prevented from being poetic; whilst the citizens of liberal democracy have a polity which prevents harm, and which allows individuals the freedom to poetically enrich themselves.

This means that in place of reference to socio-historically contingent practices, we have metaphysical speculation about a transcendental self, with a metanarrative about this self being used to justify liberalism as a blueprint for the good society. On these terms, social justice can only be achieved in liberal states, because only liberal states prevent harm and allow the freedom for self-enrichment. The public/private divide can be used to furnish the good society for all. As we have seen though, the Nietzschean notion of the self as a poet does not actually fit in with liberalism. Liberalism could not prevent harm and if a liberal state did try to regulate the public language game then it would restrict poetic agency and limit the creativity of those who refashioned the language game. In which case, *a metanarrative about the self would require one to argue for some form of elitist society*, which allowed the poetic the freedom they needed. This freedom may include the freedom to harm others, by reworking culture in new ways, and imposing this on those who are unable, or less able, to be poetic. Again the outcome would be an immature politics, because a metanarrative about the self would provide a definitive justification for a political system which allowed poets to harm non-poets. There could, *ex hypothesi*, be no questioning of this metanarrative, and the good society would be accepted as such, when poets were free to recreate culture, even if this entailed humiliating others.

(3) Practices within liberal democracies

If we turn our attention from issues of social justice concerning the good society, to consider social justice in terms of the actual practices within liberal democratic states, then we our turning our attention from poetry and private languages to concrete – material – practices in civil society. This is because within existing liberal states, poetry will be confined to the private sphere so as to avoid harming others. Poetry in this context, though, is broader than individuals' final vocabularies. It now includes all forms of theory and any attempt to problematise the given, meaning that the *public sphere is the sphere for concrete practices, which conform to established ways of going on*, and the private sphere is the sphere for discursive practices (which would include philosophical justifications of the liberal model of the good society). Hence Rorty argues that instead of 'asking what's the problem?' we should adopt the attitude 'if it isn't broken, don't fix it', and 'save problematizing for weekends' (1996, p. 44). In the public sphere we simply 'get on with things' and in the private sphere we may think up schemes which question the given, but we should see such schemes as aspects of a private attempt at poetic self-enrichment, rather than as going beyond appearances to the underlying truth.

The conception of politics offered here is both positivist and conservative. In trying to remove theoretical problematisations from the public sphere one has to take the view that the political order is simply given, and that any changes will be reactive piecemeal changes to overcome discrete, clearly-bounded problems. The pragmatic emphasis on the given, or 'the manifest', would become the positivist view that we can have a direct access to a 'manifest truth'. Indeed, any attempt to create theoretical explanations of any sort would have to be regarded as an objectionable metaphysical attempt to go beyond the observable facts to 'something else'. Politics therefore would deal with atheoretical 'facts'. This positivism results in conservatism because by removing theory, we have to focus on already-existing ways of going on. We cannot think up new practices for the sake of innovation alone, because that would mean 'stepping back' from practices to theorise those practices. We may introduce new practices *reactively*, to overcome some specific practical problem, but we cannot instigate change for the sake of change, because that would entail using theory *qua* private poetry to explain practices, and to act as a foundation to justify or reject certain practices. After all, to instigate change in a non-reactive way would be to use theory to problematise the facts, by constructing a political problem via private poetry, instead of resolving problems after (factual) problems appear.

This emphasis on practical issues leads Rorty to argue that, as regards economics, '[t]here is nothing sacred about either the free market or about central planning; the proper balance between the two is a matter of experimental tinkering' (1987, p. 565). In a sense this is certainly true, but it overlooks how the 'balance' is not just an issue of securing economic growth, but of also dealing with issues of distributive justice, which are intrinsically normative, and therefore highly contested issues. If growth were the only concern, then an authoritarian capitalist order may be 'justified', but if our concern is broader than this, then we enter the remit of normative debate which, by its nature, problematises the given.

In his 1997 William E. Massey Sr. Lectures in the History of American Civilisation, published as *Achieving Our Country* (1998b), Rorty switches his attention from what may be described as rather a technocratic state-centred politics, with the state resolving non-normative factual problems, to focus on different groups in civil society. In this work, Rorty defines the Left as being concerned with issues of social justice regarding, for example, fairness of wealth-distribution, whereas the Right do not think any reforms are required. Rorty criticises the Left for changing from a 'reformist Left', which dealt with such material issues, to a 'cultural Left', which is 'spectatorial', because it has retreated from practical problems in civil society to theorising identities via romantic speculation about 'the other'. Hence we have 'women's history', 'black history', and 'gay studies', but no 'unemployment studies', 'trailer-park studies', or 'homeless studies' (1998b, pp. 79-80). That is, issues of inequality concerning lower class groups are ignored because they are not 'other' enough.

This should not, though, be taken to contradict my argument so far. For although Rorty laments the change in the Left, with it abnegating its social responsibility to effect changes for material social justice, he nonetheless sees social reform in terms of rectifying anomalies within a system which otherwise works. When Rorty argues that the Left ought to improve social justice by seeking reforms, he is not arguing that there are structural problems within the social status quo or that we ought to seek out problems by problematising the given. So the Left is not to regard poverty as a structural problem requiring a major reorganisation of socio-economic relations, or to start questioning the existence of inequality itself. Rather, the task of the Left is to respond reactively to problems within the status quo, after they emerge. So, if workers protest about pay and conditions in one company or economic sector, then the Left may take up their case, but not question capitalism *per se*. This has a rather paternalist flavour to it, which Rorty makes explicit when he comments that 'bottom-up' initiatives for labour reform have proved successful, although they stand more chance of success if linked to 'top-down' initiatives by the secure middle class (1998b, pp. 52-4).

This argument is linked to what amounts to a pluralist conception of the state. Groups in civil society mobilise over a specific, clearly demarcated, substantive issue, and if their case is reasonable, then the neutral state will produce a policy to resolve matters. Rorty does recognise the danger that the state will be influenced by powerful monied interests (of the 'over-class'), but he believes that there is no reason to hold that the state is intrinsically or necessarily disposed to serve powerful material interests. If presented with a clear empirical case for a specific reform, especially if backed by an active Left and a paternalist middle class, the state may well respond favourably to a case for reform.

So, when it comes to discussing issues of social justice in terms of the actual functioning of liberal democracies, the focus is on material practices, with poetry being confined to the private sphere, for private use only. Thus the evaluation of liberalism is not in terms of an abstract discussion about a poetic self *vis-à-vis* the public/private divide, but in terms of material relations in the public sphere of civil society, and the state's relationship to such relations. As theory is classed as poetry, it is confined to the private sphere along with any normative questioning of the status quo – meaning that the status quo has to be accepted as legitimate, without question. If problems arise then these are specific anomalies within a system which is held to 'work'. Such problems may be resolved reactively by the state, or by a reformist Left presenting a case for a specific reform to a neutral state. In this case what separates Left and Right is not a question of values about the legitimacy or otherwise of the status quo, but a question of activity, with the Left and the Right having the same values, but with the Left being more active than the complacent Right. Hence Rorty is able to describe Lyndon Johnson as a 'part-time Leftist', on the basis that he put reforms in place to help American children, whilst slaughtering Vietnamese children (1998, p. 44).

Such a position is 'immature', in the sense I've been using, because it divinises the status quo. There can be no normative questioning or evaluation of the status quo, or liberalism, or capitalism, and instead we have to accept the actual ongoing practices within liberal states. We cannot develop alternative practices because that would entail constructing some form of 'theoretical' explanation of the given. This would mean arguing that practices ought to be based not on the existing ways of proceeding, but on a piece of private poetry, which presumes to offer a better way of going on, because it has seen some 'truth' contrary to established practices. If a practical problem arises within such ongoing practices then either the state can rectify this to restore equilibrium, or groups in civil society can mobilise to effect a practical small-scale change to previous practices. So social justice is presumed to be embodied in existing practices, and we are precluded from trying to assess such practices in terms other than their continued utility. We cannot use our reason fundamentally to question the status quo, and at best, the Left may introduce piecemeal reforms to improve that status quo.

(4) Conclusion

If we consider issues of social justice in terms of the good society then we must necessarily engage in some form of metaphysical speculation. This is because the very purpose of conceptualising the good society is to say that certain political relations are justified, because they are in accord with what it is to be human, or because they are the inevitable outcome of some historical process. In short, defining the good society is a foundational enterprise, because something beyond practices is sought to legitimise those practices.

This does not, though, leave us with a dichotomy between metaphysical arguments for the good society and the strong normative relativism which stems from ethnocentrism. Instead, we may consider social justice by assessing practices within political systems. To do this would require making some form of truth-claim. This need not be foundational in an epistemic sense: it need not assume that we have any direct access to an underlying 'Fact' which will explain everything. In place of such direct access, our knowledge would be theoretically mediated, and fallible. Such knowledge-claims would offer different interpretations based on different empirical evidence and different interpretations of the same evidence.

Taking such an approach would be 'mature', because it would allow us to use our own understanding, rather than rely on a metaphysical metanarrative or divinising the status quo. We may then question how good (or not) liberalism is in realising its principle of equality of opportunity; to what extent (if at all) capitalism and democracy are incompatible; whether instances of ascribed status inequality, such as racism and sexism, are functional or antithetical to capitalism; and so on. In doing this we would be raising the issue of structural problems and problematising the given, in place of fetishising the putative facts of the status quo. This, of course, is the task of social science, and it is this science that Rorty's pragmatism eschews, by holding that theory and problematisations are private-sphere – or 'weekend' – activities, which is why his original assessment of liberal practices divinised the status quo.

Whether liberalism ought to be replaced, or not, is a metaphysical question about defining the good society. Nevertheless, by having a non-positivist theoretically mediated access to social reality, which will problematise the status quo, we may escape from our self-imposed immaturity, and have the courage to use our own understanding to assess just how well liberalism serves social justice.

Notes

1 A different version of this essay appeared as an article in *Res Publica*, Vol. 6, No. 1, February 2000. Whereas that article dealt with the individualism-communitarianism debate, this chapter is more concerned with arguing that Rorty is trying to maintain the Enlightenment conception of politics as emancipatory, whilst changing the philosophical terms of reference. Hence I argue that Rorty accepts Kant's definition of the Enlightenment, whilst rejecting Kant's metaphysics.

2 Rorty draws upon the work of the later Wittgenstein, to describe cultures as 'language games'. However, Rorty's Nietzschean argument about poetry is antithetical to Wittgenstein's argument that there can be no 'private languages', because the argument for self-enrichment (by reworking the public rules of a language game) is an argument to create new private rules, or private uses of language.

3 Some describe Wittgenstein as a behaviourist, but unlike behaviourists, Wittgenstein does not deny the existence of a self, on the grounds that denying the existence of a pseudo-entity was meaningless. This was pointed out in conversation with me by Professor Roger Trigg.

References

Ball, T. (1990), 'Review Symposium On Richard Rorty', *History Of The Human Sciences*, Vol. 3, No. 1 (February), pp. 101-104.

Bhaskar, R. (1991), *Philosophy And The Idea Of Freedom*, Blackwell, Oxford.

Critchley, S. (1996), 'Is Derrida A Private Ironist Or A Public Liberal?' in C. Mouffe (ed.) *Deconstruction And Pragmatism*, Routledge, London.

Dews, P. (1990), 'Review Symposium On Richard Rorty', *History Of The Human Sciences*, Vol.3, No. 1 (February), pp. 108-114.

Fraser, N. (1990), 'Solidarity Or Singularity? Richard Rorty between Romanticism and Technocracy', in A.R. Malachowski (ed.), *Reading Rorty: Critical Responses To Philosophy And The Mirror Of Nature (And Beyond)*, Blackwell, Oxford.

Fukuyama, F. (1992), *The End of History and the Last Man*, Free Press, New York.

Geras, N. (1995), *Solidarity In The Conversation of Humankind: The Ungroundable Liberalism Of Richard Rorty*, Verso, London.

Kant, I. (1992; orig. 1784), 'An Answer To The Question: What Is Enlightenment?' in H. Reiss (ed.), and H.B. Nisbet (trans.), *Kant's Political Writings*, Cambridge University Press, Cambridge.

Laclau, E. (1996), 'Deconstruction, Pragmatism, Hegemony' in C. Mouffe (ed.) *Deconstruction And Pragmatism*, Routledge, London.

Rorty, R. (1980), *Philosophy And The Mirror Of Nature*, Blackwell, London.

Rorty, R. (1987), 'Thugs And Theorists: A Reply To Bernstein', *Political Theory*, Vol. 15, No. 4 (November), pp. 564-80.

Rorty, R. (1989), *Contingency, Irony And Solidarity*, Cambridge University Press, Cambridge.

Rorty, R. (1991), *Objectivity, Relativism And Truth: Philosophical Papers volume 1*, Cambridge University Press, Cambridge.

Rorty, R. (1996), 'Response To Simon Critchley' in C. Mouffe (ed.) *Deconstruction and Pragmatism*, Routledge, London.

Rorty, R. (1998a), *Truth And Progress: Philosophical Papers Volume 3*, Cambridge University Press, Cambridge.

Rorty, R. (1998b), *Achieving Our Country: Leftist Thought In Twentieth-Century America*, Harvard University Press, London.

Warren, M.E. (1990), 'Review Symposium On Richard Rorty', *History Of The Human Sciences*, Vol. 3, No. 1 (February), pp. 118-22.

9 The Individual at the End of History

LUBICA UČNÍK

Introduction

The year 1989 signifies many things to many people.[1] The meaning of 1989 is so diverse that it is impossible to reach any consensus on the matter. Richard John Neuhaus begins his article on Havel by recounting supposed beliefs 'by some' that '[m]aybe our cultural salvation will come from the East'. Those unnamed some 'have given up on a decadent West mired in materialism and blinded by debonair nihilism' and wait, perhaps, for 'their cue from Pope John Paul II' that after 'the Revolution of 1989' we will recover the Christian soul of Europe, meaning East and West. (Neuhaus, 1990, p. 77). Francis Fukuyama heralds the events in Europe in 1989 as the final victory for liberal democracy the world over and concludes that this marks the end of history. From now on, there is only one reliable model of the state to assume and that is liberal democracy (Fukuyama, 1992). On the other hand, we might ask with Jacques Rancière (1995, pp. 2-3) why this proclaimed ending took so long, and hence call into question the purported end. Rancière muses,

> Yet, viewed from closer range, this configuration holds some surprises. Thus the same conspicuous American who noisily proclaims the end of history with our decade also tells us, more quietly, that this is the very same end proclaimed by Hegel in 1807, even if this means leaving us in doubt: Has it taken history this particularly overburdened-two-centuries-long interval to get its death over with because getting rid of the last vestiges is always slow, or because of the fateful error of the interpreter, Marx, who saw in the Hegelian promise not the end of history at all, but merely the end of prehistory?

Accordingly, we might follow Misha Glenny who speaks of the mastery of the 'rational over the irrational' (Glenny, 1993, p. 2) in the form of a victory of a free market over a planned economy, a victory that announces 1989 as the rebirth of history. Václav Havel speaks of the triumph of the citizens against the State in Central-Eastern Europe, or a victory of the powerless. Renata Salecl alleges that the subsequent development in Central and Eastern Europe did not assume the form of liberal democracy, and this to the chagrin of observers from the West[2] (Salecl, 1992; Salecl, 1994). Slavoj Žižek uses Lacanian psychoanalysis to demonstrate the victory of passionate national desires over the free market logic (Žižek, 1990; Žižek, 1992; Žižek, 1994a; Žižek, 1994b; Žižek, 1996). Finally, John Gray contends that the model which countries of Central and Eastern Europe want to emulate is 'the Anglo-American exemplar' (Gray, 1995, p. 39). Gray further argues that this 'transplantation of Western models that are themselves unstable and in varying degrees of crisis in their countries of origin' (Gray, 1995, pp. 37-8) is in the end highly problematic. His allegation amounts to a warning that this policy might lead to the destruction of an economic system in the countries of the origin of the model as well, that is in the countries of the so-called First World.

There is, however, one underlying assumption in all these claims: the presupposition that post-socialist countries should rescue the individual from the rubble of the collectivism of previous socialist experiences.[3] The concept of the individual is a contentious issue in contemporary debates about the constitution of political philosophy. Moreover, it is not only pertinent to politico-philosophical discourse but is an ethical problem as well. The question of how to live a good life with others is important to our everyday living. What exactly, then, does 'an individual' mean? The aim of this paper is to explicate how the concept of the individual is used in the discursive practices of the post-socialist countries.

The 'rebirth' of the individual in post-socialist Europe

Havelková, reflecting upon the dissolution of 'Really Existing Socialism'[4] in Czechoslovakia after 1989, points out in *A Few Prefeminist Thoughts* that,

> The totalitarian government thoroughly suspended individual subjectivity in the form of people's autonomous development as citizens, as owners, as thinking beings, as acting subjects, and as men and women shaping their own lives (Havelková, 1993, p. 66).

The claim is that the recently dismissed socialist system of administration facilitated the way of collectivist thinking, and thereby suppressed the individual. The very concept of individualism, which has been questioned in the Western philosophical milieu by writers with different ideological affiliations, became the rising 'protagonist' in the vocabulary of a new post-socialist society. The problem is, though, that the concept of the individual is appropriated without any critical examination in post-socialist countries of Central and Eastern Europe. Furthermore, this uncritical appropriation of the concept of the individual creates another dangerous coupling for women in particular. Within the discourse of Marxist ideology, women were subsumed under the all encompassing category of the proletariat; with the rebirth of liberal individualism in Central and Eastern Europe, the same problem re-emerges, albeit varying in a different discursive framework. This time woman is subsumed under the concept of the individual. Nevertheless, the result is the same – women are left out from theoretical discussions once more. Havelková, despite her insistence on 'collectivist' discursive thinking in the context of 'Really Existing Socialism', inevitably betrays the vocabulary of individualism which underpins her argument. Havelková, summarising the problems based on the constitution of 'Really Existing Socialism', writes,

> The negative improvement of the position of women as compared with that of men was accomplished through a *degradation of all individuals to objects*. ... Hence, the problems of subjectivity and identity are not perceived in this society as specifically female ones. In theoretical terms, identity based on sex is still approached as a sub-problem. There are ... two reasons for making the 'general human' superior to the 'specifically female'. First, the problem is not one concerning women more than men; and second, in its emphatic form it is an essential problem of all (Havelková, 1993, p. 66, emphasis added).

What is interesting in Havelková's exposition, for the present discussion, is the imperative – which she shares with many writers from post-socialist countries, as I have already indicated – to liberate the individual, 'the general human', from the garbage of collectivism. Yet, her exposition *is* couched in the language of individualism. In the context of her argument, Havelková inevitably points out the problem inherent in the understanding of the concept of an individual as an essentially non-gendered abstraction. Havelková outlines the ideological imperative of 'Really Existing Socialism' as a 'so-called general development of personality' which the government has 'presented as the supreme goal of social development' (Havelková, 1993, p. 67). Havelková insists that this has amounted to the dismissal of the individual as such from any political consideration. Socialist governments achieved this policy through practices which put the 'collective interest' of the whole society as a prime objective of public discourse. Havelková elaborates,

> This relates to another ideological principle that undermined the autonomy of the individual – people's separation from property. A *person*'s general development was said not to be connected with property (Havelková, 1993, p. 67, emphasis added).

One of Havelková's inferences, therefore, is that the supreme goal of the present post-1989 government is to reinstate the individual as a citizen, consumer and, above all, an owner.

Kicková and Farkašová advance a similar claim. With regard to the past and present experiences of people who lived under the 'Really Existing Socialism', they write,

> The *individual* [wa]s seen as part of the collective; the individual's development depend[ed] on the quality of the social conditions, and the final goal [wa]s not the *individual's development* but the advancement of society. ... The idea of individual independence [wa]s replaced by one of social dependence (Kicková and Farkašová, 1993, p. 90; emphasis added).

Once more, the argument is predicated on the 'individual'. Only the individual's dependence on or independence from the social order is questioned, while the individual as such remains an unquestioned presupposition – a 'given'. Furthermore, Kicková and Farkašová assert that now, in the post-socialist society, young women tend to understand their lives differently. The assertion is that,

> [l]iving for the present is more a preference of women in the younger generation. It entails the direct experience of things of value, the effort to love more for oneself, but also being more utilitarian in regard to consumption. There is less use of the future tense in their language. There is a generational change in values and goals, more directed toward individualism than to collectivism. From an orientation toward the future, it moves to an orientation toward the present, from enthusiasm to scepticism, from self-sacrifice to self-advancement (Kicková and Farkašová, 1993, p. 92).

This argument implicitly rests upon an abstraction of the individual who is oriented more towards herself, consumes wisely, rejects the past and future (or history) because she lives for the present and regards her self-advancement as the very opposite of intersubjectivity. For Kicková and Farkašová, the individual is presented as a free floating, consuming, self-seeking person while the idea of intersubjectivity is inevitably represented in negative terms as self-sacrifice.

The problematic character of this assumption could be juxtaposed to the most repeated claim about the discredited system, propounded in this instance by Salecl:

> For communist ideology to function, it was ... necessary to control what was taught in school. ... but privately (students) did not believe in (communist ideas). Although students performed communist rituals (praising the leader, engaging in communist types of parades, wearing Komsomol insignia, etc.), they retained a cynical distance towards such rituals. This cynical distance actually enabled the system to function: the Party did not believe in such rituals either, but as long as people performed them publicly, the system functioned regardless of how critical people were in private (Salecl, 1994, p. 54).

Salecl here asserts the widespread rejection of the dominant communist ideology, and by the same logic, presumably 'collectivism' as well. This claim maintains that there were critical people who privately rejected the dominant ideological discourse. The moment one asserts a critical stance of people, one has sustained the language of the Enlightenment where it is reason as such that is available to each person individually to make her judgement. This contention re-phrases the assertion by Havel in his now famous essay "The Power of the Powerless", where he writes,

> Because the regime is captive to its own lies, it must falsify everything. It falsifies the past. It falsifies the present, and it falsifies the future. ... It pretends to persecute no one. It pretends to fear nothing. It pretends to pretend nothing. Individuals need not believe all these mystifications but they must behave as though they did or they must at least tolerate them in silence ... For by this very fact individuals confirm the system, fulfil the system, make the system, are the system (Havel, 1985, p. 31).

In Havel's version of the accusation, each individual is already understood as a self-defining subject who, for the sake of peaceful living, conducts themselves as 'pretending' to believe the socialist order or putting up with the system 'in silence', thus perpetuating the system in all its strength. The idea of the subject always underpins the notion of individualism, collectivism, the nation, and so on. As Heidegger argues,

> Man [sic, passim] as a rational being of the age of the Enlightenment is no less subject than is man who grasps himself as a nation, wills himself as a people, fosters himself as a race, and, finally, empowers himself as lord of the earth. ... for man always constantly remains determined as I and thou, we and you (Heidegger, 1977, p. 152).

I want to claim that most of the arguments waged in the heated debates of pre-1989 (Battěk, 1985; Benda, 1985; Černý, 1985; Hájek, 1985; Havel, 1985; Hejdánek, 1985; Kosík, 1995; Kusý, 1985; Ruml, 1985; Šimečka, 1984; Uhl, 1985; Vohryzek, 1985; Zvěřina, 1985), and after, were, and still are, couched in the teleological understanding of the historical development of a society and the individual and not the collective. In Havel's Hegelian words,

> ... life, in its essence, moves towards plurality, diversity, independent self-constitution and self-organization, in short, towards the fulfilment of its own freedom (Havel, 1985, p. 29).

Historical interpretations did not cease after the 'Velvet revolution' in 1989. Perhaps the best exposition of this understanding is outlined in the article 'Emancipation of Women. A Concept That Failed' by Kicková and Farkašová. They write,

> Collectivism existed not only as a theoretical principle but also as a real form of social organisation in which our whole lives played themselves out from childhood to old age. This naturally left behind very specific traces in *the individual* and in the social consciousness of our people. The idea of historical progress and of an objective historical necessity is deeply embedded in this consciousness. It expressed itself in people's conviction that society was moving toward a better, more perfect and just form. The linear concept of historical progress was evident in daily consciousness. The small, even the gigantic injustices did not break the basic faith that it must some day get better, although one did not know how, when, or where. And anything that was part of that process was itself good (Kicková and Farkašová, 1993, p. 91, emphasis added).

Here, collectivism is equated with a linear conception of historical progress and then dismissed as a utopian vision of the good life, achievable somehow, somewhere, some day, for the individual. In contradistinction to previous arguments, Šimečka understands 'Really Existing Socialism' differently. He writes,

> 'Existing socialism' has turned 'a movement totally geared to the future into a self-satisfied present. It has thus stolen from socialism any future it might have had' ... (Šimečka, 1984; cited in Havel, 1985, pp. 21-2).

This implies that (presumably 'real' or 'original') socialism was a historical movement, which was, in the process, somehow deprived of its *telos* and, furthermore, Šimečka, *pace* Kicková and Farkašová, asserts that it is this 'self-satisfied present' which is characteristic of socialist systems.

How can we make sense of these different descriptions? I want to suggest that Hegel's theory of history is crucial to our understanding of certain developments (and texts) coming from Central-Eastern Europe. For the purpose of this paper, I will mostly use an account given by Gillespie to outline the 'historical' development of the concept of history as it is still understood in Central-East European countries. First and foremost, I want to consider Hegel's perception of history as a linear progression towards a universal resolution of 'society'. Secondly, I will consider Hegel's 'Euro-centric' understanding of 'progress' on a universal scale. Finally, I will briefly deal with Hegel's treatment of the dialectical resolution of human history.

Hegel's scientific project

Hegel's project of a 'scientific understanding' of history must be located in the era in which he lived. The Enlightenment had undermined Christianity's claim to be the only source of knowledge, with science claiming for itself the power of reason to explain the nature and therefore the world. This decline of religious power was coupled with technological inventions which seriously undermined Scriptural authority; well before the Enlightenment, Gutenberg's invention of print had enabled a wide reading of the Bible, and therefore, increasing possibilities of dissent. Any alternative interpretation of the Bible certainly weakened the legitimised reading of the Scriptures by the Catholic Church. Humans now filled the space vacated by God. History as a 'science' could come about only when humanity became the 'centre of the Universe' and, consequently, also the sole object of historical inquiry. Therefore, the idea of history, as we understand it today, presupposes an individual who is caught up in the historical process as a finite being.

According to Gillespie, in the eighteenth-century Enlightenment the eternal was replaced with the actual and the human as such became the focus of philosophical inquiry. With the advent of the natural sciences, which appeared to uncover laws governing nature, it was the human who was seen as master – if he could only control his natural desires, passions. To achieve this, man must conquer 'the universal law of natural causation' (Gillespie, 1984, p. 9) and procure freedom from nature. This freedom was understood as the opposite of caprice and desires, as a rational will, a will which is not contradictory but fully conscious of itself. Only when humanity becomes the master of nature, would man be free. The notion of progress has become central to the understanding of history.

Although Hegel does account for individual humans, his understanding of history is a holistic one. For Hegel freedom could be actualised or realised only in a State where the self is no longer set against the natural object world, but is recognised in the conscious whole of the State. Therefore, Hegelian history begins with the formation of the State. Hegel describes three stages of development: first – the Oriental world, where only one – the despot – was free; then the Greek and Roman world, where only some men were free, excluding slaves, women, foreigners; and lastly the Germanic world, where people, through Christianity's teaching, began to understand that all humans must be free. Hence, Hegel asserts that

> The German Spirit is the Spirit of the new World. Its aim is the radicalization of absolute Truth as the unlimited self-determination of Freedom — *that* Freedom which has its own absolute form itself as its purport (Hegel, 1991, p. 341, emphasis in the original).

Hegel, following Kant's lead, also asserts that,

> ... to *explain* history is to depict the passions of mankind, the genius, the active powers, that play their part on the great stage ... (p. 13, emphasis in the original). Passions, private aims, and the satisfaction of selfish desires are ... most effective springs of action. Their power lies in the fact that they respect none of the limitations which justice and morality would impose on them; and that these natural impulses have a more direct influence over man than the artificial and tedious discipline that tends to order and self-restraint, law and morality (Hegel, 1991, p. 20).

Hence, Hegel's claim is that movers of history are precisely those finite individuals with all their passions, hatreds, and desires. And yet, the Absolute Spirit aims precisely toward 'order, self-restraint, law, and morality' in its final stage, striving towards freedom for humanity. How can we reconcile those two opposing moments between the finite individual and the Absolute Spirit – between passions and freedom? It is here that Hegel asserts his understanding of progress as *Aufhebung*,[5] or the dialectical move where those very opposites unite at an ever expanding synthesis, and yet, at the same time, preserving those opposites within itself. Hence, the 'order' of Absolute Spirit is no longer imposed on the self from outside, but the self recognises itself to be self-legislated. The subject becomes aware of the law as a part of her own free self-constitution.

Hegel talks about an individual as being subject to history because, as he argues, 'the universal must be actualised through the particular'. Even if the goal of history is to perfect humanity so it can realise its freedom, any particular human is not important for Hegel in the big picture of history and, yet, history progresses through individuals. Essentially, what is important is the relationship between nature and humans and their subsequent re-union through freedom. According to Hegel, the decisive moment in history is the diremption of natural consciousness into the soul and the Absolute spirit. To understand this diremption of spirit, one has to look at the Enlightenment project that singled out the individual against society as the property owner and therefore the agent of its own destiny. It is this exclusive stress on the individual, particularly within the Anglo-Saxon tradition that Rousseau, Kant, and Hegel successively tried to overcome. Thus their intellectual projects have to be understood as attempts to integrate those free-floating individuals back into the context of society while, at the same time, retaining their autonomy.

Dumont reminds us that the idea of a society (or a collective of post-socialist discursive formulations) must always be understood as predicated on the idea of an individual. As he writes,

> The point to be borne in mind is that the stress on things, the mastery over things, is throughout a property of the individual, not of the society as a whole. It begins with private property in Locke … (Dumont, 1992, p. 105).

Therefore, the Enlightenment's idea of the individual, as an autonomous, rational property owner, is crucial to the understanding of history as the quest of *Geist* towards freedom. The problem, of course, is how this historical journey towards freedom is understood. As a recent example from the Czech Republic documents, it is not always freedom for all.

> A delegation of Czech Roma on 2 June (1998) handed over to the mayor of Ústí nad Labem a protest against a plan to isolate a tenement block of Romani families behind a wall. A spokesman for the Association of Roma in the Czech Republic said the plan is an 'insult' to all the Roma in the country. He added that if the plan is implemented, other towns will follow suit and 'then you will have ghettos, followed by ovens, and that will be the

> end of the Roma'. Mayor Ladislav Hruška said the wall is 'not racially motivated' but just intended to 'separate the decent people from those who are not,' (Reuters reported: Radio Free Europe/Radio Liberty, 1998).

The use of the same example after a year stresses the problematic character of social justice if freedom is predicated on the idea of the individual. The restrictive measures are not necessarily enforced by the external agencies. Perhaps, Rousseau's observation that 'Man was born free, and he is everywhere in chains', expresses this particular situation better (Rousseau, (1762) 1988, p. 49).

> Czech Roma agree to being fenced off. The Romany Rainbow organization, which represents rent defaulters in an Ústí nad Labem town district, on 15 April (1999) agreed with the local council on the construction of a fence to separate Roma from houses opposite their apartments, CTK reported. The fence will be 1.8 meters high and made out of ceramics. In 1998, the town council announced plans to build the fence, ostensibly to protect residents from the noise and the rubbish produced by the Romanies. The district's mayor hailed the decision as a breakthrough reached without 'any special mediators or human rights activists from outside Ústí nad Labem' – a hint obviously aimed at Czech Human Rights Commissioner Petr Uhl, who said he will block any attempt to build the wall, a statement he repeated after hearing of Romany Rainbow's decision. (MS, Radio Free Europe/Radio Liberty, 1999).

I want to suggest that Foucault's project might be more helpful in understanding of this 'self-disciplining' by the Romanies. As Foucault writes, 'a 'new micro-physics' of power' produces 'discipline [a]s a political anatomy of detail' (Foucault, 1991, p. 139).

Foucault's genealogy

Perhaps it is necessary to ask different questions in order to understand the discursive preoccupations with the individual in post-socialist countries. In this context, I want to consider Foucault's genealogy. Foucault rejects a certain mode of narrative history; it is not just the story he rejects but the methodology of traditional (evolutionary) history. Foucault also rejects the theory of ideology as a means to interpret events.

> Continuous history [is] the indispensable correlative of the founding function of the subject: the guarantee that everything that has eluded him [sic, passim] may be restored to him; the certainty that time will disperse

> nothing without restoring it in a reconstituted unity; the promise that one day the subject – in the form of historical consciousness – will one again be able to appropriate, to bring back under his sway, all those things that are kept at a distance by difference, and find them in what might be called his abode (Foucault, 1986, p. 12).

On the Foucaultian model, there is no underlying *meaning* which a critic, historian, analyst would be able to 'recover'. Foucault, following Nietzsche, speaks about a history of the present; history is constructed from the present point of view. That is, historical narration is constructed to disrupt and invigorate the present, so that the 'historical events' retrieved, newly discovered and re-described, explain the present state of affairs. On this model, *Zeitgeist*, ideology, *Weltanschauung*, etc. are devices to be used as explanatory tools through which we unite dispersed events. For Foucault, however, there is no unitary narration of progress and rationality inherent in the past; there are only *ad hoc* discursive events. 'Truth' is not universal but historically contingent, and determined by the power relations and knowledge produced within specific discursive practices and institutions. Power (in contrast to ideology) for Foucault is not a unitary negative force, but positive and productive and permeates the whole social body. Power relations do not come from above as a restraining force, but are everywhere.

> Small acts of cunning endowed with a great power of diffusion, subtle arrangements, apparently innocent, but profoundly suspicious, mechanisms that obeyed economies too shameful to be acknowledged, or pursued petty forms of coercion – it was nevertheless they that brought about the mutation of the punitive system, at the threshold of the contemporary period. Describing them will require great attention to detail: beneath every set of figures, we must seek not a meaning, but a precaution; we must situate them not only in the inextricability of a functioning, but in a coherence of tactic. They are the acts of cunning, not so much of the greater reason that works even in its sleep and gives meaning to the insignificant, as of the attentive 'malevolence' that turns everything to account. Discipline is a political anatomy of detail[6] (Foucault, 1991, p. 139).

Foucault's project seeks to undermine the long held Western tradition of hermeneutics, in the sense of the interpretation of events by some privileged subject or institution.[7] Foucault also shows how 'man' emerged in the philosophical discourse of the seventeenth century as an embodiment of reason, unceasingly dividing, calculating, ordering, measuring and interpreting things and events. Through different institutional practices, disciplinary power techniques produce 'docile bodies' with calculated precision; they produce self-sufficient, self-policing, self-analysing subjects. The point, then, is not to look for a hidden meaning, for the explanation of 'Really Existing Socialism' as a collectivist enterprise, but to look at different institutional practices, power relations and economies of knowledge proliferating at that particular time. The question is not 'why' but 'how' and 'what'. What were the disciplinary practices that allowed/ disallowed certain events, practices, and regimes of knowledge to become legitimate? What was 'sayable' and when? How did certain discursive events come to be juxtaposed and become legitimate while others were suppressed and became mute? However, the most important point for my argument is Foucault's insistence that any text must be seen as an active and productive component of different discursive practices, not a reflection of them; that is, a text, does not *reflect* the underlying 'consciousness' or *Zeitgeist* of a period; rather, the text participates in the production of that 'consciousness'.

Charta 77[8] should be seen in this light. It was not a case of detecting the pathological symptoms of 'Really Existing Socialism'; on the contrary, Charta 77 was a productive construction of different ways of thinking and understanding the world. By the same token, texts written after 1989 do not disinterestedly describe the evils of the preceding regime and the goodness of the current one, those texts generate the understanding of events, and they create that understanding as such.

Conclusion

In this instance, the comment by Louis Dumont on the passage from Marx's *German Ideology* seems pertinent,

> ... in a stateless group in which the division of labour prevails, ... each member must be the locus of a contradiction between his private interest and the common interest. This situation, we are told, leads to the common interest assuming the form of a State; yet this State is at the same time an illusory community. I interpret this to mean that, as a separate entity, the State cannot remain identical with the common interest as such. But a logical aspect seems to be left out; a differentiation has occurred. The citizen no longer has to care immediately for the common interest, since the State is now in charge of it; ... there is a close interdependence between the

> existence of the State and the unrestrained assertion of private interest by the citizens (Dumont, 1977, pp. 141-2).

I want to suggest that this description of the State is more appropriate for State Socialist societies where the State and the Communist party asserted power over every aspect of public life. 'Really Existing Socialism', through different discursive practices, excluded citizens from the participation in the political and public domains, encouraging them, by the provision of 'consumer goods', to concentrate on the private, personal, subjective domain of their lives. Thus, discursive configurations of 'Really Existing Socialism' inadvertently, 'produced' the formation of 'individuals' interested only in their own private affairs. So it is not surprising that this idea of negative freedom, the freedom *from* the state or from other individuals is at present firmly embedded in the consciousness of the post-socialist subject.[9]

Finally, the idea of recovering the individual from the collectivist rubble misses the point. The individual is always already present, at least discursively. Fukuyama may have a point: there may indeed be no space to think otherwise than in the terms of liberalism, a kind of hegemony of the language of the Enlightenment. Therefore, the point of any critique should be to reformulate this very abstraction of the private individual and her participation within the public sphere. Herein lies the possibility for intervention; to begin to question the 'naturalness', the 'obviousness' of always-already established identities by pointing towards different, alternative histories. The individual is not a pre-given entity, which needs to be recovered anew from collectivist debris, but a constructed discourse which we can produce anew by filling the empty space of origin with a new articulation of what it means to be a person.

Notes

1 This paper was first read at the conference 'The Liberal Order: The Future for Social Justice?' at the Palacky University, Olomouc, Czech Republic, 7-12 July 1999; I thank participants for their contribution and advice. I also thank Claire Colebrook and Horst Ruthrof for their helpful criticism of earlier versions of this work.

2 The West is so disappointed with non-democratic developments in the East because it is searching in the East for the rebirth of its own democracy, the rediscovery of its own lost origins (Salecl, 1994, p. 149/n.16).

3 Neuhaus, for instance, writes, 'From beneath the rubble have emerged human beings very much like ourselves, except, just maybe, made stronger by the long night of oppression' (Neuhaus, 1990, p. 77).

4 The term was explained by Miroslav Kusý (1985). The expression 'Real Socialism' was used in Czechoslovakia and later on, all states professing to live by Soviet Marxist Ideology. Kusý writes, 'Real Socialism is not a Czechoslovak invention. Our politicians and ideologists merely took it and applied it. Originally it defined membership in the Soviet bloc: outside the bloc is no real socialism' (1985, p. 153). Furthermore, the Communist Party (and by extension the government), instead of maintaining that our society works towards the 'bright future' of classless, and therefore stateless, society, announced that the socialism as it is practised is already hic et nunc – hence, the socialism is already real and existent. Hence, from the proposition 'The classic Marxist authors, Stalin included, treated the etatist conception of the socialist state negatively' (ibid., p. 154) to the 'fact' – 'The socialist state is the main achievement of the working class' [Bilak] declared bravely in Sofia (Pravda, 18.12.1978)' (ibid., p. 154). So, 'Real socialism is what we have now!' is how Vasil Bilak defined the present reality' (ibid., p. 157).

5 This is a Hegelian term meaning that history as the movement of Absolute spirit at the same time abolishes and preserves both a thesis and antithesis in the higher unity of synthesis. It is sometimes translated as a sublation.

6 The paragraph begins: 'There can be no question here of writing the history of the different disciplinary institutions, with all their individual differences. I simply intend to map on a series of examples some of the essential techniques that most easily spread from one to another. These were always meticulous, often minute, techniques, but they had their importance: because they defined a certain mode of detailed political investment of the body, a 'new micro-physics' of power; and because, since the seventeenth century, they had constantly reached out to ever broader domains, as if they tended to cover the entire social body' (Foucault, 1991, p. 139).

7 The Western philosophical tradition inherited the 'art' of exegesis, which began and was perfected by the Catholic Church in the Church's effort to 'interpret' the Scripture. When the 'rationality' of man was asserted in the seventeenth century, it was the thinking, rational individual who took over the function of hermeneutics.

8 The manifesto 'Charta 77', released on 3 January 1977, was inspired by the abuses of human rights in Czechoslovak Socialist Republic. Its release was prompted by the event of Czechoslovakia signing the Helsinki Agreement Treaty. The Helsinki Agreement was a UN Treaty designed to ensure that certain human rights are endorsed in the signatory states.

9 On the contrary, in countries with a capitalist mode of production, the private sphere includes those non-government organisations, such as charities, which assume the role of carer for differing aspects of common interests not catered for by the capitalist State. Therefore, citizens are, partially at least, encouraged to think about others less fortunate.

References

Battěk, R. (1985), 'Spiritual Values, Independent Initiatives and Politics',in J. Keane (ed.), *The Power of the Powerless: Citizens against the State in Central-Eastern Europe*, M.E. Sharpe, Inc., Armonk, New York.

Benda, V. (1985), 'Catholicism and Politics', in J. Keane (ed.), *The Power of the Powerless: Citizens against the State in Central-Eastern Europe*, M.E. Sharpe, Inc., Armonk, New York.

Černý, V. (1985), 'On the Question of Chartism', in J. Keane (ed.), *The Power of the Powerless: Citizens against the State in Central-Eastern Europe*, M.E. Sharpe, Inc., Armonk, New York.

Dumont, L. (1977), *From Mandeville to Marx. The Genesis and Triumph of Economic Ideology*, The University of Chicago Press, Chicago and London.

Dumont, L. (1992), *Essays on Individualism. Modern Ideology in Anthropological Perspective*, The University of Chicago Press, Chicago and London.

Foucault, M. (1986), *The Archaeology of Knowledge*, translated by S. Smith, A.M., Tavistock Publications Ltd, London.

Foucault, M. (1991), *Discipline and Punish. The Birth of the Prison*, translated by A. Sheridan, Penguin, Harmondsworth.

Fukuyama, F. (1992), *The End of History and the Last Man*, Avon Books, New York.

Gillespie, M.A. (1984), *Hegel, Heidegger and the Ground of History*, The University of Chicago Press, Chicago and London.

Glenny, M. (1993), *The Rebirth of History. Eastern Europe in the Age of Democracy* (new edition), Penguin, Harmondsworth.

Gray, J. (1995), *Enlightenment's Wake. Politics and Culture at the Close of the Modern Age*, Routledge, London and New York.

Hájek, J. (1985), 'The Human Rights Movement and Social Progress' in J. Keane (ed.), *The Power of the Powerless: Citizens against the State in Central-Eastern Europe*, M.E. Sharpe, Inc., Armonk, New York.

Havel, V. (1985), 'The Power of the Powerless. To the Memory of Jan Patočka', in J. Keane (ed.), *The Power of the Powerless: Citizens against the State in Central-Eastern Europe*, M.E. Sharpe, Inc., Armonk, New York.

Havelková, H. (1993), 'A Few Prefeminist Thoughts' in N. Funk and M. Mueller (eds) *Gender Politics and Post-Communism: Reflections from Eastern Europe and the Former Soviet Union*, Routledge, New York.

Hegel, G.W.F. (1991), *The Philosophy of History*, translated by J. Sibree, Prometheus Books, Buffalo, New York.

Heidegger, M. (1977), *The Question Concerning Technology and Other Essays*, translated by W. Lovitt, Harper & Row Publishers, New York.

Hejdánek, L. (1985), 'Prospects for Democracy and Socialism in Eastern Europe' in J. Keane (ed.), *The Power of the Powerless: Citizens against the State in Central-Eastern Europe*, M.E. Sharpe, Inc., Armonk, New York.

Kicková, Z. and Etela F. (1993), 'The Emancipation of Women: A Concept That Failed', in N. Funk and M. Mueller (eds) *Gender Politics and Post-Communism:*

Reflections from Eastern Europe and the Former Soviet Union, Routledge, New York.

Kosík, K. (1995), *The Crisis of Modernity: Essays and Observations from the 1968 Era*, J.H. Satterwhite (ed.) Rowman & Littlefield Publishers, Inc., Lanham, London.

Kusý, M. (1985), 'Chartism and 'Real Socialism'' in J. Keane (ed.), *The Power of the Powerless: Citizens against the State in Central-Eastern Europe*, J. Keane (ed.), M.E. Sharpe, Inc., Armonk, New York.

Neuhaus, R.J. (1990), 'Havel Living in Truth', *National Review*, 42 (21), pp. 77-78.

Radio Free Europe/Radio Liberty. (1998), *RFE/RL Newsline* (Vol.2. No.105. Part II) Prague, Czech Republic, 1998 [cited 3 June 1998], available from http://www.rferl.org/newsline.

Radio Free Europe/Radio Liberty. (1999), *RFE/RL Newsline* (Vol.3. No.74. Part II) Prague, Czech Republic, 1999 [cited 16 April 1999], available from http://www.rferl.org/newsline.

Rancière, J. (1995), *On the Shores of Politics*, translated by L. Heron, (*Phronesis*,) Verso, London, New York.

Rousseau, J. ((1762) 1988), *The Social Contract*, translated by M. Cranston, Penguin Books, Harmondsworth.

Ruml, J. (1985), 'Who Really is Isolated?' in J. Keane (ed.), *The Power of the Powerless: Citizens against the State in Central-Eastern Europe*, M.E. Sharpe, Inc., Armonk, New York.

Salecl, R. (1992), 'Nationalism, Anti-Semitism, and Anti-Feminism in Eastern Europe', *New German Critique (An Interdisciplinary Journal of German Studies,)* Fall, pp. 51-67.

Salecl, R. (1994), *The Spoils Of Freedom: Psychoanalysis and Feminism After The Fall of Socialism*, Routledge, London and New York.

Šimečka, M. (1984), *The Restoration of Order: The Normalization of Czechoslovakia 1969-1976*, translated by A.G. Brian, Verso, London.

Uhl, P. (1985), 'The Alternative Community as Revolutionary Avant-Garde' in J. Keane (ed.), *The Power of the Powerless: Citizens against the State in Central-Eastern Europe*, M.E. Sharpe, Inc., Armonk, New York.

Vohryzek, J. (1985), 'Thoughts Inside a Tightly-Corked Bottle' in J.Keane (ed.), *The Power of the Powerless: Citizens against the State in Central-Eastern Europe*, M.E. Sharpe, Inc., Armonk, New York.

Žižek, S. (1990), 'Eastern Europe's Republics of Gilead', *New Left Review*, September/October, pp. 50-62.

Žižek, S. (1992), 'Eastern European Liberalism and its Discontents', *New German Critique. (An Interdisciplinary Journal of German Studies,)* Fall, pp. 25-49.

Žižek, S. (1994a), 'Enjoy Your Nation as Yourself', in his *Tarrying with the Negative. Kant, Hegel, and the Critique of Ideology*, Duke University Press, Durham.

Žižek, S. (1994b), 'Introduction. The Spectre of Ideology' in S. Žižek (ed.), *Mapping Ideology*, Verso, London, New York.

Žižek, S. (1996), 'The Fetish of the Party' in W. Apollon and R. Feldstein (eds), *Lacan, Politics, Aesthetics*, State University of New York Press, Albany, New York.

Zvěřina, J. (1985), 'On not Living in Hatred. To my Friends and Enemies' in J. Keane (ed.), *The Power of the Powerless: Citizens against the State in Central-Eastern Europe*, M.E. Sharpe, Inc., Armonk, New York.

10 'Community' – An Instrument of Social Order other than the State? A Rhetorical Perspective on Contemporary American Critiques of Liberalism

PETRI KOIKKALAINEN

(1) Introduction

In Western and especially American political theory of the last few decades the issues of social justice have mainly been addressed through theoretical frameworks connected to some form of 'liberalism' – utilitarian, contractarian, libertarian, or welfarist. Hence, social justice has often meant 'distributive justice', a contract or consensus between autonomous and self-interested citizens about the proper or legitimate distribution of political power, money and other resources.[1] Furthermore, the institution responsible for safeguarding social justice has quite self-evidently been the state. When the state has been called the 'welfare state', its philosophical presuppositions have still been regarded as 'modern' and usually 'liberal' despite the possibly collectivist implication of the term.[2]

However, this state-centred and broadly speaking 'liberalist' hegemony in political theory has recently shown some signs of weakening. Liberalism as a governing ideology has acquired new 'communitarian' and 'republican' challengers, which instead of the fair distribution of power and other resources emphasise such concepts as 'virtue', 'morality', or 'community'. At the same time, the state as a supreme political authority is challenged both globally, by the international market economy and political integration, and locally, by different communities and cultures claiming their right to self-determination. As the name of arguably the most visible 'new' movement in political theory – communitarianism – suggests, the concept of 'community' has acquired an especially central position in both theoretical and practical critiques of the modern state and of its apparent dominating ideology, liberalism. Many influential strands of this critique spring from American debates, but ideas like 'the third way' or 'balancing rights with responsibilities' now enjoy popularity also in Europe, promoted both by politicians (e.g., Tony Blair, Gerhard Schröder, Martti Ahtisaari) and theorists, often more or less directly linked to the political decision-making system itself (e.g., the British professor Anthony Giddens, and Dr. Alpo Rusi, adviser to the the former President of Finland Martti Ahtisaari).

My starting point is to assume that a change of political agendas or 'paradigms' has been attempted in American and to some degree in European politics. Questions about morality, community, or identity seem to have taken priority over 'old' disputes about developing the welfare state, reducing class tension, or pursuing an ethnically or sexually emancipated society. The 'new paradigm' has allowed new possibilities for political theorists and practitioners, but it has placed new limitations on them as well.

The approach of this paper to these changes is centred on an analysis of political language and rhetoric; how different actors explain and legitimate the transition from the 'old' to the 'new'. I try to provide an interpretation of some conceptual and historical preconditions that have helped develop the 'morally conscious' new paradigm. My main academic interest concerns the writing of the 'political past', or presenting politically purposeful accounts of the social and political events of recent decades. I presume that it is typical for critical thought (be it, for example, theoretical questioning of liberalism or partisan critique of the welfare state) to rewrite the past of political thought and action, and that theoretical and political claims are often validated by invoking these practical interpretations of the past.

I wish to demonstrate a certain linkage between the 'political theory' and 'political practice' in these American debates. This means, for example, that political critique (as in electoral campaigns) is often presented as a critique against political theory or 'philosophy'.[3] Equally, many academic texts of 'political theory' or 'political philosophy' contain explicit suggestions toward the current political state of affairs and the practical organising of political or social matters.[4] This may not be surprising in itself, but if the degree of this mutual involvement is compared with the European (or at least the Nordic) situation, it is evident that this kind of 'border-crossing' between the academic world of theory (or philosophy) and the practical world of politics is, despite the aforementioned academic advisers of our heads of states, far less visible than it is in America.[5]

(2) Historical argument in a political text: progress, change and return

In European politics the emphasis on the well-being of 'communities' is perhaps most commonly associated with the politics of the 'new' centre-left, while in the United States the concept of 'community' can equally well belong to the arsenal of the political right. The mid-term Congressional elections of 1994 showed a victorious Republican Party with a remarkably conservative program, placing a heavy stress on morality, community, and religion. One of the most important reference points of the speeches and pamphlets of this campaign was the idea of an autonomous citizen who was assumed to relate critically and warily toward the federal administration and its central political bureaucracies. The moral and political judgements of the ideal citizen were said to be guided by a historically mediated 'common sense', closely linked with the American form of life developed in the local communities. This 'citizen's perspective' typically placed the remote and bureaucratic central political administration against the ordinary citizens and their communities, in which the uncorrupted American ethos was still presumed to prevail. In the book *Restoring the Dream. The Bold New Plan by House Republicans*, this argument was presented concisely and conclusively:

> The United States is predicated on the idea that Americans and their local communities are best suited to solving their own problems, their own ways (House Republicans, 1995, p. 205).

It may be worthwhile to stop at this statement for a moment. The 'Americans' of the sentence are an elaborately defined concept. We are not discussing the properties of just 'anyone' here, any individual in any group without any further specifications. If we consider replacing the word 'Americans' with plain 'individuals', or 'persons', we may notice a difference. The expression 'Americans' increases the force of the argument by giving it a clear contextual reference point. Accordingly, the 'local communities' of Americans seem to be something more accurately and richly defined than the commonly mentioned 'voluntary associations' or 'regional subgroups' of social scientific parlance. Another thing to be noticed is how the text binds the existence of 'Americans' and 'communities' together. We are discussing Americans and their local communities, dealing with problems concerning the American form of life, solvable by the historically mediated knowledge and moral guidelines possessed by the communities themselves. It is also stated that the existence of the United States as a nation is closely connected with a substantial idea, which the latter part of the sentence is attempting to define. Following this line of argumentation it is also possible to understand the 'idea' as a criterion in light of which it is possible to assess the current state of the nation. In other words, the United States is ideologically on the right track when it is publicly recognised that Americans and their local communities are entitled to solve their own problems, in their own ways. This politically strong entitlement is said to follow from the actual competence of the communities and individuals. According to the text they are best suited to solving their own problems.[6]

There are many different origins to the current American emphasis on 'morality', or 'communities', where the substantive morality is supposed to reside. The backgrounds and motives of the various strands may differ from each other significantly. It is, for instance, easy to conclude that the communitarian policies promoted by Amitai Etzioni (known for his Democratic associations) and his Communitarian Network are different and far more moderate than are the politics of the 'true conservatives'.[7] In the 'real world' of political associations and dissociations Etzioni's communitarians and hard-line Republicans probably have more things separating them than binding them together. However, if we look at things from a distance, Etzioni and the Republicans do share a common theme: they are both strongly concerned about the crisis resulting from the decline of private and public morals, and they both support the idea of *return* to some 'original' or 'traditional' values which have been prevalent in the past, but have declined in the recent decades. This return is said to be the proper remedy against the erosion of the moral standards of private and political life.

Even though the famously radical 'Republican Revolution' of 1994, headed by the now retired Speaker of the House of Representatives Newt Gingrich, ultimately ended in a political defeat, its practical influence may not be as easily dismissed. For example, in the 1996 presidential election the Democrats had to formulate much of their own rhetoric in accordance with the themes that made the Republicans victorious in 1994: strengthening family values and moral order, fighting crime, assuming responsibility of one's own life.[8] In the formulations of the Republican Party these notions were given a clear political emphasis:

> Getting Washington out of the way ... is the crucial first step in the long process of returning authority and responsibility to where they belong – to

> our families and neighborhoods, churches and charitable organizations (House Republicans, 1995, p. 205).

In this quotation 'Washington' – the central political and bureaucratic administration of the federal state – is explicitly presented as an element in conflict with 'Americans' and their communities. At the same time it is affirmed that the discussion is about power and its legitimate use. The right place of 'authority' is said to be in families and communities, not in Washington. As the argument proceeds, 'we must now reverse the direction of the mighty river of power that for thirty years has been flowing away from the people and toward Washington' (ibid.). Now it is evident that the text also contains a crystallised definition of a political program. The attempted change of the 'site of power' is described as going through a 'long process'. What is specifically important, the nature of this 'process' is *returning*, which gives the text a distinct historical meaning. We (the audience of a political program) should attempt to reinstate a legitimate state of affairs that existed in the past. Authority and responsibility should be handed back to where they rightly belong.

'Returning authority and responsibility to where they belong' represents a common type of a political argument. In this paper it is considered as a particularly interesting example of political language because of its clear reference to historical time. In other words, the argument supposes that a more legitimate state of affairs has existed some time in the past of the American nation. Different arguments of this kind seem to form a distinct 'historically conscious' mode of political rhetoric common in the current American politics. This mode of political language and rhetoric is more closely analysed in the forthcoming sections.

(3) The 'Communitarian Paradigm'

The critique against 'liberalism' and the 'welfare state' (which concepts are in day-to-day American politics often used to signify one and the same thing[9]) has resulted in a redefinition of conceptual borderlines not only in the world of daily politics, but also in the study of political ideologies and political philosophy. At least since the beginning of the 1990s, it has been possible to find in the texts of Anglo-American political theorists a rough consensus about some kind of 'paradigmatic' change in the focus of research, caused to a large extent by the communitarian or republican[10] critiques against current 'Rawlsian' or 'welfare' types of liberalism. According to the interpretation given by the American political scientist

Patrick Neal, the predominant debate of the 1970s handled the confrontation between the 'utilitarian' and 'contractarian' versions of liberalism. This debate was manifested especially in the various critical responses given to Rawls's famous (and strongly contractarian) *A Theory of Justice* (1971). Neal claims that since the early 1980s there has been a significant change in the focus of research, and that Alasdair MacIntyre's and Michael Sandel's still widely read critiques of liberalism can be seen as starting points of this 'revolution'.[11] According to Neal, these critiques led to a reorganisation of the 'ideological structure' of the discipline of Anglo-American political science, so that the 'liberals', at this time a more united group,

> began self-consciously to speak directly to the issue of 'defending liberalism' (Neal, 1993, p. 623).

This change of attitude, Neal writes, was a sign of neutralisation of the old 'rights vs. utility' debate inside the liberal camp, and a sign of a strengthened will of the liberals to find some common ground in defence of liberalism against the especially 'communitarian'[12] challenges coming from the outside. This change of orientation probably tells us both about the efficiency of the communitarian critique and about the significant differences between the critique and its target, liberalism.

In his book *The New Golden Rule* from 1996, sociologist Amitai Etzioni[13] gives a representative account of the 'historical change' of the political agendas. Etzioni draws a historical scenario, according to which a change has occurred between two significantly different ways of conceptualising the political state of affairs. The two modes of thinking are here referred to as the 'old paradigm' and the 'new paradigm', roughly following Etzioni's own use of the terms. It is a bit unclear whether Etzioni's account is meant to be a description of a thing that has already happened or a vision of a desirable future state of affairs. At least it can be said that Etzioni seems to regard the change he describes as beneficial or worth wanting. In short, Etzioni talks about change in which the 'old paradigm', operating with the concepts of liberalism, welfare state, and economic rationality, gives way to the 'new paradigm', which speaks in terms of morality, virtue, and order. The basic reference points can be picked up from the following definition by Etzioni:

> [T]he old map centers around the role of the government versus that of the private sector, and the authority of the state versus that of the individual. The current axis is the relationship between the individual and the *community*, and between freedom and order (Etzioni, 1997, p. 7; italics in

original).

Etzioni elaborates this interpretation by naming some traditionally conflicting conceptual pairs (linked to the old 'left-right' opposition), that, according to Etzioni, no longer are the proper or best possible ways to address social or political problems:

> Given this different framework, it makes sense to view libertarians, liberals, laissez-faire conservatives, neoconservatives (usually considered right-wing), and civil libertarians (often considered liberal, if not left) as belonging in various positions on one *side* (not pole) of the intellectual-political space because they all focus – albeit to varying degrees – on the need for autonomy, and pay relatively less attention to the needs for social order. When it is necessary to refer to all these lines of thinking together, I refer to them as individualist. On the other side of the space are social conservatives (often lumped with libertarians and laissez-faire conservatives), who are relatively less directly concerned with autonomy, often focusing more on the need to shore up the moral order, and if necessary have it undergirded by the state (ibid.; italics in original).

When we look at Etzioni's account of the new paradigm ('the current axis'), we can notice that the defenders of the welfare state of the 'old left' have found new and perhaps surprising allies, all of which are placed under the new group title *Individualists*: liberals, libertarians, laissez-faire conservatives, neoconservatives. The other side of the political space has changed even more. In Etzioni's scheme the proper opposition of Individualists are *Social Conservatives*, who should not be associated with the 'old right' of libertarians and laissez-faire conservatives. Social Conservatives 'are relatively less directly concerned with [individual] autonomy, often focusing more on the need to shore up the moral order, and if necessary have it undergirded by the state' (ibid.). Interestingly, none of the political streams or ideologies of the old paradigm are placed under the 'new paradigm' categorisation, Social Conservatives, but they have all been placed into the Individualist category.[14]

If the pivotal political concepts of the 'earlier time' (probably 1960s to 70s) – government, state, private sector, individuals, – were things related to the economic relations and the administrative competencies of the (federal) state, then the figures of the 'current time', community and order, refer to the ethos or substance of life in a political community. The modern conception of subjectivity and political agency (stress on the rights of individuals and [negative] freedom[15]) is 'already' present on both sides of the 'old paradigm'. The limitations of the modern conception are inherent in the 'old paradigm' as a whole, and according to Etzioni's reasoning, these limitations cannot be overcome by the means provided by the old paradigm. In the intellectual horizon provided by the 'new paradigm', the 'individualist' modes of political thought may therefore appear as *remnants of an outdated mode of political thinking.* In this way they may also appear as outdated and incompetent ways to approach the current social problems. The 'new paradigm', on the other hand, may give the political struggle a sense of touching the essence of some philosophically or morally important problems, or engaging in a meaningful criticism of the 'contemporary culture'. The 'politics of morality' is obviously different from the 'politics of distribution'. It provides means to handle topics that are wholly different from the problems dealt with the concepts commonly attached to the 'economism' or 'abstract individualism' of the liberal and distinctly modern 'old paradigm'. Whereas the old paradigm referred to the 'welfare state' and its economic and political conflicts (a 'paradigmatic' example being the competition between the interests of socio-economically defined classes), the new paradigm refers to an ethical community and the substantial definition of its basic values or its ethos.

Etzioni does not want his name (or the name of his Communitarian Network) to be associated with the social conservative or 'fundamentalist' positions emphasising the rights of community and social and moral order. However, this may be less significant than the fact that Etzioni underwrites the paradigmatic intellectual horizon in which the opposite sides are Individualists and Social Conservatives, and that the 'optimal' political solution may, according to him, be found between these extremes. 'The communitarian quest, as I see it, is to seek a way to blend elements of tradition (order based on virtues) with elements of modernity (well-protected autonomy)' (ibid., p. xviii). This is also the main novelty of Etzioni's communitarian theory, and the means he can provide to revise the old framework of political debates. Etzioni's own position is moderate, but his explicit aim is to transform the political practices that have been under corrupting influence during the last few decades. The direction of that change would be toward the position emphasising community and order, thereby strengthening the substantial ethos of the community. This is how we could 'return to a virtuous equilibrium' (ibid., p. xix), that overgrown individualism and contempt of morals has reduced the possibility of since the 1960s. In virtue of its theoretical approach, 'the communitarian thinking leapfrogs the old debate between left-wing and right-wing thinking and suggests a third social philosophy' (ibid., p. 7). In his particular opinions Etzioni differs significantly from the conservative Republicans, but if we look at their rhetoric from a distance, they appear to share a common horizon of setting political problems. That is, if they are arguing with each other, they are arguing about the same and commonly defined things.[16]

(4) From state citizenship to community membership?

A further significant or 'paradigmatic' difference between contractual liberalism and the communitarianism of Etzioni can be seen in the following formulation:

> In a communitarian society (and in quite a few others) *values are handed down from generation to generation rather than invented or negotiated* (ibid., p. 93; italics in original).

As mentioned before, the 'communitarian paradigm' is designed to be a vehicle of social restoration and moral reform. Etzioni's 'new golden rule', 'Respect and uphold society's moral order as you would have society respect and uphold your autonomy' (ibid., p. xviii), is set up as a straightforward answer to the decline of moral standards and decent behaviour that began in the 1960s. In this sense Etzioni's use of the concept 'paradigm' provides an interesting analogy with T.S. Kuhn's use of the same concept, and ultimately with Kuhn's account of a scientific revolution. For Kuhn, one of the most important sociological consequences of a scientific revolution is a *restoration of order* in a previously anomaly-ridden scientific society, i.e., a society in *crisis* (Kuhn, 1970, p. 94; cf. Etzioni, 1997, pp. xvii-xviii). Another and possibly a more familiar aspect of the Kuhnian theory of revolutionary change, the appearance of a qualitatively new horizon of problem-setting and solving, can be seen in Etzioni's theorising as well. To put it briefly, Etzioni's communitarianism is about restoring 'social order', but an order that is in some important ways different from the 'modern state' with its inherent crises, confusions, and anomalies. The content of 'a new kind of order' can be approached by studying Etzioni's treatment of the concept of positive law:

> In contrast, I introduce the principles that for a society to be communitarian, much of the social conduct must be 'regulated' by reliance on the moral voice rather than the law, and *the scope of the law itself must be limited largely to that which is supported by the moral voice* (Etzioni, 1997, p. 139; italics in original).
>
> Therefore I see a compelling reason for communitarians to stress that *law in a good society is first and foremost a continuation of morality by other means* (ibid., p. 143; italics in original).

The idea of the law as 'first and foremost a continuation of morality by other means' is in a marked contrast with much of the theorising about the normative basis of the modern constitutional state. Diverse thinkers such as Max Weber, Carl Schmitt, or Quentin Skinner have in different contexts described the modern legislative process, as well as the powers of execution and jurisdiction, as formal and settled procedures, in which any substantial or traditional morality is by definition in a secondary role.[17] Etzioni, however, distances himself from the 'modern' viewpoint which prioritises procedurally settled laws and their formal legitimacy over the shared moral convictions of the citizens as the basis of the integrity of the political community. For Etzioni, the institutionalised and conflict-oriented 'politics' is secondary to a substantial 'morality', which is practised by different groups and communities in the 'non-political' social world. As is evident from the following quotation, this also leads to a standpoint which places the modern state and its conception of political citizenship into a secondary role compared with 'society' and membership in its different 'communities'. To put it in more general terms, Etzioni prioritises 'virtue' over 'law', and the 'social' or 'moral' over the 'political':

> [T]he communitarian society is not first and foremost one of law-and-order, but one based on shared moral values that the members affirm. It is a society primarily based on virtues and on laws that embody them. For the same reasons, the main social body is not the state (or even the polity) and the main actors are not citizens, but the body is the society (as a community of communities) and the actors are members in it. Social action, such as that which occurs in and among family members, neighborhoods, voluntary associations, and communities, has priority over political action (ibid., pp. 140-141).

Writers such as Etzioni or Robert Bellah's group (in their famous interview study *Habits of the Heart: Individualism and Commitment in American Life,* 1985) give individualism and contractual relations a certain legitimate place in the American form of life. Entrepreneurship, hard work, individual innovation and fair play are rightful parts of the American ethos as well as religion or voluntary help. However, in addition to these 'individualist' values, these writers stress the importance of a publicly recognised substantial morality: a formal liberty as such is not enough to convey true meaning and content to people's lives. The possibility of social and political criticism is opened up by the claim that contemporary social practices, as well as contemporary ways of interpreting and understanding social practices, have failed to appreciate the importance of a moral framework that could support a genuine sense of communality and mutuality:

> [We] seem to be hovering on the very brink of disaster, not only from international conflict but from the internal incoherence of our own society. What has gone wrong? How can we reverse this slide toward the abyss? ... What has failed at every level from the society of nations to the national society to the local community to the family is integration: we have failed to remember 'our community as members of the same body', as John Winthrop put it (Bellah et al., 1985, pp. 284-285).

According to the analysis provided by Bellah's group, the United States is in a crisis symptomised by the lack of internal coherence, caused to a large extent by the 'modern' or 'individualist' conception of handling public affairs, i.e., *the politics of interest.*[18] As Bellah's group states, '[w]e have committed what to the republican founders of our nation was the cardinal sin: we have put our own good, as individuals, as groups, as a nation, ahead of the common good' (Bellah et al., 1985, p. 285). This situation can be compared with an earlier and more 'communal' period of American history, and in this comparison the present situation is seen as an era of moral degradation. Without the coherence and predictability provided by a commonly accepted code of morality, the current politics of promoting special interests and guarding achieved benefits has become a morally inadequate and 'only semi-legitimate' business.[19] Relying on the wide interview material collected during the preparation of the study *Habits of the Heart*, Bellah's group recommends revitalising the two morally coherent trends already present in American public culture, namely the *biblical* and *republican* traditions:

> The erosion of meaning and coherence in our lives is not something Americans desire. Indeed, the profound yearning for the idealized small town we found among most of the people we talked to is a yearning for just such meaning and coherence. But although the yearning for the small town is nostalgia for the irretrievably lost, it is worth considering whether the biblical and republican traditions that small town once embodied can be reappropriated in ways that respond to our present need (Bellah et al., 1985, pp. 282-283).

Bellah's group posits Massachusetts's first governor John Winthrop (1588-1649) as a typical or 'paradigmatic' example of the biblical tradition. For the Puritan sects led by Winthrop, the ultimate criterion of earthly success 'was not material wealth but the creation of a community in which a genuinely ethical and spiritual life could be lived' (Bellah et al., 1985, p.

29). Freedom was not a licence to do anything not explicitly forbidden, but instead a 'moral' freedom for the things good, just, and honest (ibid.). The exemplifying figure of the republican tradition, Thomas Jefferson (1743-1826), worried about the possible corruption of the leaders of the nation, and he saw the future of his country as dark and shadowed by a threat of tyranny if the content of the citizens' life was to be 'in the sole faculty of making money'. The idea of a 'pure' or 'neutral' liberty that would allow people to do whatever they think pleasant – for example, to dedicate themselves to accumulating wealth – was, according to Bellah et al., insufficient to both Jefferson and Winthrop. 'However important formal freedom was to either of them, freedom took on its real meaning in a certain kind of society with a certain form of life' (Bellah et al., 1985, pp. 30-31).

The structure of Bellah's argument[20] and his use of historical examples suggest an evaluative comparison between the traditional and the contemporary forms of life. The crux of the argument is to show that neither the modern American society of the end of the 20th century, nor the predominant modern political philosophy of the same era, can recognise a satisfactory model of social or political order, 'a certain kind of society with a certain kind of life' (Bellah et al., 1985, pp. 30-31), in which freedom could attain its real meaning. The constitutional system, built in part to safeguard individual rights, is corrupt because it has distanced itself from some of its most important original purposes. A 'neutral' or 'formal' liberalism is a part of this alienation, since it explicitly denies any teleological or substantial definition of the 'common good'. A fundamental crisis can be said to exist in various spheres of the American life: in personal relations it leads to a dissolution of families and spiritual isolation; in popular culture it leads to a fragmentation of tastes and glorification of sex and violence; in public life it leads to a predominance of special interests at the expense of the public good. 'Washington is corrupt to its core', wrote Etzioni in *New York Times* in 1982, referring to the influence of vested interests in national decision-making (Etzioni, 1984, p. xi). According to Etzioni, the institutional political decision-making system is no longer guided by the needs of the national community or the common good, but by narrow and selfish group interests (Etzioni, 1993, p. 217). In this sense also the political system is alienated from its original purposes.

The critique against the political system is typically directed against the central (federal) administration and the elites closely linked to it. Politically and economically strong interest groups are said to use the tools of political power for their own benefit at the expense of the quiet majorities in the periphery. Hence, there is a strong local dimension in the contemporary critique of modern liberalism. The people who still possess the genuine American ethos and understanding of the proper ways to handle public affairs do not live or exercise influence in the political and intellectual centres of the federal republic. A good example is the social compact model developed by Jean Bethke Elshtain, which in a strongly communitarian fashion, emphasises traditions, historically developed communities and the social constructedness of human identities. 'In the world of social compact, human beings are ends in themselves, not means', she writes (Elshtain, 1995, p. 106). When asked about the possibility of such communities in the 'real life', Elshtain answers in the following way:

> There are pieces of such communities in small-town, rural and urban America, in communities where people struggle to preserve their way of life against forces of dissolution. Often, religious communities aim explicitly to counter ultraindividualism and provide an institutional framework which nourishes alternatives. ... The social compact inspiring such movements is local, bounded, grassroots; it is a community, not a state, and its ethos is preserving, not acquiring. Instead, they are organized to defend and sustain what remains of a way of life not permeated utterly by, and defined exclusively in, individualist or contractual terms (Elshtain 1995, pp. 107-108).

Elshtain directs her expression 'the forces of dissolution' explicitly against liberal contractualism and the individualistic and even egoistic lifestyle of the big cities (ibid., pp. 103-108). This position gives the communitarian critique a further means of distinction and a strong means of political argumentation based on a cultural and geographical difference.[21] A clearly defined counterpart gives the critics a possibility to say something concrete about the existing political and social practices. According to Elshtain, getting rid of the corruption requires forces that have not been infected by the same disease (ibid., p. 108).

In his analysis of corruption Etzioni reaches a similar conclusion. According to him, successful political reformers, 'like Archimedes, *must find a point of leverage outside the political world* in order to be able to change it. ... *Thus the challenge for the politics of change is to find ways to mobilize the great underrepresented majorities*' (Etzioni, 1993, p. 227; italics in original). The ultimate aim of Etzioni's reformatory 'politics of change' is 'to replace a government by and for deep pockets with a political system that is based on the principle of "one person, one vote," one that is responsive to all the members of the community' (ibid., p. 246). Agreeing with Elshtain or Bellah's group, he says this could happen by re-appropriating or re-invigorating such moral norms and institutions that the culture of liberal individualism has eroded. The precise recipe for this renaissance may be still in the making, but at least it is clear that the modern state in its present forms is not 'such an institution'.[22]

(5) History and 'life politics': a concluding remark

Etzioni, among other writers cited above, criticises contemporary social relations as being too individualistic, too atomised, too greedy, and speaks about a 'return to equilibrium' in which the 'modern' conception of individual freedom would give some ground to traditional forms of communal life. In this confrontation between 'modernity' and 'tradition' concepts and figures like 'history', 'time', or 'our common past' play a central role.

The idea of a close relationship between 'tradition' and 'community', as present in Etzioni's or Bellah's group's writings, is closely reminiscent of, for example, Alasdair MacIntyre's conception of a meaningful human practice. For MacIntyre, a human practice (for example, a religion or a scientific discipline) can remain 'authentic' or true to its nature only through virtuous action (MacIntyre 1981, pp. 177-181, 191-192; compare with Etzioni's phrase 'order based on virtues', Etzioni 1997, p. xviii). If the strong and appealing language of 'tradition', 'moral order', or 'virtue' is compared with the 'instrumentality' of the ultimately individualist philosophical presuppositions that are said to lie behind the contemporary 'welfare state', a difference can be noted. The moral language possible to the 'individualist' or 'modernist' may in the worst case appear as an openly negligent viewpoint towards the major problems of our time, and in a slightly better case it can be seen as a well-meaning but toothless moral toolbox if the nature of 'our problems' is taken into serious account. In this situation, the argument implies, we have to turn our eyes to 'our common past' for morally sound solutions. For Etzioni, this past was by no means perfect, but alongside its admittedly negative aspects, there was a social and moral coherence worth missing:

> In the fifties we had a well-established society, but it was unfair to women and minorities and a bit authoritarian. In the sixties we undermined the established society and its values. In the eighties we were told that the unbridled pursuit of self-interest was virtuous. By the nineties we have seen the cumulative results (Etzioni 1993, p. 248).

The style of political argumentation taking shape here is not only 'historically conscious', but also openly emotional and nostalgic.[23] It may be argued that one of its purposes is to make an appeal to the middle-aged and older generations and their long life experience, especially to their possible perception of how the praised 'progress' and 'development' can also lead to negative consequences.[24] In this respect the argument is not only preparing ground for restoring some philosophical or political tradition of thought, but it is also preparing ground for a promise of an emotionally or spiritually rewarding 'journey back home', for example, to the safe childhood of the 1950s, when many things later problematised and politicised were still clear and predictable.

At the same time it seems evident that the argument contains a strong political message: we are speaking of changing society normatively in ways that can hardly be regarded as solely 'philosophical' or 'cultural'. As Etzioni writes: '*We need to return to a society in which certain actions are viewed as beyond the pale,* things that upright people would not do or even consider' (ibid., p. 24; italics in original).

The purpose of this article has been to concentrate on the distinctly political aspect embedded in popular notions concerning modern individualism, relativism, and ultimately alienation. More precisely, this article has attempted to show how it is possible to formulate 'historical' arguments that can work as politically useful counter-conceptions, against which it is possible to formulate 'new' positive programs or paradigms, which may now appear as clear improvements. These arguments have a recognisable reference to the 'social reality' as commonly perceived, and they assume their place within a certain type of understanding of contemporary history. The recent decades' era of individualism and relativism can be interpreted as a historical watershed, after which it is possible to return to a more 'balanced' practical politics, and a more 'balanced' theoretical understanding of politics as well. The possibility of this return, however, is dependent on a rethinking and reorganising of the socio-political world so that the political authority of 'the state' is diminished and the moral authority of 'communities' is increased. The same structure of argumentation seems to be applicable both 'academically', in various critiques of liberalism, individualism, and modernity, and 'practically', for example, in strategic positions and rhetorical figures suitable for use in political party programs. Whether or not these changes or developments (from 'old' to 'new', 'politics' to 'morality', 'state' to 'community') are to be seen as 'positive' or worth pursuing, remains a question of political judgement par excellence.

Notes

1 For a further explication of this terminology, see for example Rescher (1982, pp. 5-18).

2 A political analysis using this framework is provided, for example, by Robert N. Bellah's research group. In what they call 'Welfare Liberalism', '[t]he public good is defined as national harmony achieved through sharing the benefits of economic growth', while the opposing force, 'Neocapitalism', 'sees us not as a polity but as an economy, in which the population is an all-inclusive "interest group", chiefly concerned with "a healthy, vigorous, growing economy that provides equal opportunity for all Americans"'. Their conclusion: 'the Welfare Liberal vision ... shares with Neocapitalism a fundamental assumption about the relationship between public and private life. The purpose of the government is to give individuals means to pursue their private ends' (Bellah et al., 1985, pp. 263-265).

3 Political campaign texts often criticise individualism, atomism, relativism, or the academic mind-set of the 1960s, themes which would at least in Finland (the author's home country) be understood as concepts of academic research rather than of daily politics. See, for example, the following remark by the prominent Republican figure Jack Kemp: '[T]his is something different and deeper than a crisis of crime, a crisis of the economy or a crisis of welfare ... this moral relativism indicates a crisis of confidence in our own ideals ... Ending this moral ambiguity – attempting to reintroduce into our culture the ideas of right and wrong – is the first commitment of meaningful cultural renewal' (Kemp, 1994).

4 For detailed examples, see Etzioni (1993, pp. 11-12, 24); Bellah et al. (1985, pp. 282-303); MacIntyre (1981, pp. 253-255); Taylor (1991, p. 23).

5 An institutionalised form of the connection between the academic world and practical politics are the *think tanks* with their typical employee, the academically trained *policy entrepreneur* (to follow economist Paul Krugman's terminology), who is 'like the professors, a professional intellectual, but of a different sort' (Krugman, 1994, p. 11).

6 In addition to the aforementioned, I understand the statement under analysis to lead to the following possible consequences: i) The United States as a nation is something specific, because its existence is guided by a specific idea; ii) the citizens of the United States when they are seen as 'Americans' are something more specifically defined than just 'individuals', that is, abstract or even atomistically seen persons; iii) therefore the American citizens and their communities have some specific normative or moral competencies to solve the problems in their communities; iv) the social, moral or political problems of the United States in general should be seen as problems about the current moral status of the communities, or about the current well-being of the 'American idea'. The solutions to the problems should be found accordingly.

7 See, for example, *Contract with America. The Bold Plan By. Rep. Newt Gingrich, Rep. Dick Armey and the House Republicans to Change the Nation*

(Gillespie and Schellhas (eds), 1994) and *Contract With the American Family. A bold plan by Christian Coalition to strengthen the family and restore common-sense values* (Introduction by Ralph Reed, 1995).

8 In a telling example, the incumbent president Bill Clinton (who began his first presidency under a liberal flag) had to invoke the moralising language of 'family values' to ensure his re-election:

> 'Teen pregnancy is not simply foolish and costly, it is destructive to children, to families, to our society. It is *wrong*. ... Don't get pregnant or father a child until you are ready to shoulder that immense responsibility. If you do, we will help you only as long as you help yourself. And you can't walk away from that responsibility. If you do, we make you assume it' (Clinton, 1996, pp. 71-73).

9 See, e.g., House Republicans: 'Most of what is wrong with America today is a result of years of bureaucratic empire-building in Washington and a long-standing liberal mindset that whatever is wrong, government will fix it. Liberalism's fixes welfare, urban handouts, public housing, the Department of Education are now visible and widely acknowledged failure' (1995, p. 38).

10 By 'republicanism' is meant here not only a stream of daily American politics, but also a tradition of political thought, significant figures of which have been, for example, Thomas Jefferson or Hannah Arendt. Of contemporary researchers at least John Pocock, Quentin Skinner, and John S. Nelson have paid considerable attention to republican political theory.

11 MacIntyre (1981) and Sandel (1982). Sandel's book especially is an explicit and detailed critique of Rawls.

12 Neither MacIntyre nor Sandel, however, accept the label 'communitarian' as applicable to themselves.

13 Etzioni is the leading figure of the organised Communitarian Network in the United States. It would probably be unfair to equate MacIntyre's or Sandel's critiques of liberalism with the programs of Etzioni's group, but it is a virtue of Etzioni that he gives a clear operational definition of the change described in the previous paragraph. Furthermore, Etzioni's open associations with Democratic politics demonstrate the ability of the 'new' issues to jump over old political borderlines.

14 Along the same lines, the conservative American philosopher Allan Bloom sees libertarianism, 'the most popular form of the right in the 1980s', as 'the right-wing form of the left', because of its moral laxity (Bloom, 1987, p. 85). The source of the moral decline of society, according to Bloom and many others, is in the academy, especially in the academic Left of the 1960s and its intellectual inheritors. Critiques have been targeted, by Bloom and others, against relativism, multiculturalism (especially in Cultural Studies), neglect for the classical canon of the Western thought, students' and teachers' lack of interest in historical phenomena, fragmentation of the University's discipline structure, the 'Company Man' operating style of the professors, postmodernism, new French philosophy, feminism, and political correctness.

15 Critical accounts commonly refer to the 'negative' conception of freedom: freedom is absence of external hindrance to subject's action. A commonplace is the beginning of *Leviathan*'s chapter XXI, which says: 'Liberty, or Freedome,

signifieth (properly) the absence of Opposition; (by Opposition, I mean externall Impediments to motion;)' (Hobbes, 1968, p. 261; cf. Barber, 1989, p. 62ff; and Skinner, 1998, pp. 4-16).

16 This common horizon was well illustrated by Etzioni during his recent visit to Helsinki: 'The Religious Right', Etzioni said, 'raised all the right questions, but gave all the wrong answers. Communitarianism seeks to give the best, or better answer to those questions' (author's notes of Etzioni's lecture at the Department of Sociology, University of Helsinki, 24/8/1998).

17 Legislation, according to the stereotypical 'modern' view, is first and foremost a process of political decision-making, not a process of transforming any substantial morality into authoritative commands. Accordingly, the authority of a 'modern' power-holder is based on a 'morally neutral' position of superiority in the state hierarchy, the position itself being temporally and conceptually precedent of any current appointee of the office (see, e.g., Skinner, 1989, pp. 91-92; also Schmitt, 1985, pp. 43-44). The position of authority once given is (at least in principle) independent of the moral traits, family background, or religion of the office-holder. The classic and fundamental formulation of this idea is Hobbes's 'artificial person', *Leviathan,* the sovereign user of public reason and the sole giver of laws, all of whose actions are directed towards public security and well-being. The decisions of the sovereign lawgiver have their legitimacy in the fact that they are decisions of a public and authorised reason, not in that they would be based on any single substantial conception of morality, truth, or justice (cf. Hobbes's formulation: *auctoritas non veritas facit legem*). If this is applied to a representative parliamentary democracy, we may perceive the compelling status of the laws as not a consequence of their truthfulness, but as a consequence of a political authority conveyed through the representative process of legislation, which process is seen as legitimate by a majority of the people.

18 See Bellah et al. (1985, p. 200). The other, more legitimate forms of politics (according to Bellah) are *the politics of community* and *the politics of the nation* (pp. 200-203).

19 '[J]ustice and the common good can be addressed at the level of national consensus. But social movements quickly lose their moral edge if they are conceived as falling into special pleading, as when the Civil Rights movement was transformed into 'Black Power'. Then we are back in the only semilegitimate realm of the politics of interest' (Bellah et al., 1985, pp. 202-203).

20 By this I mean, for example, the structure (the well-crafted consequence of interviews and historical examples) of Bellah et al. (1985).

21 See also historian Allen J. Matusow' s account (Matusow, 1984, pp. 3-4): 'The liberal mood of 1960 was largely defined by elite intellectuals residing on the East Coast, principally in New York City and Cambridge, Massachusetts. Constituting an intense subculture at the center of nation's communication network, these intellectuals –nearly all of them liberals – shared a world view that profoundly influenced the political climate'.

22 Cf. MacIntyre (1981, pp. 253-254): 'Nothing in my argument suggests, let alone implies, any good grounds for rejecting certain forms of government as necessary and legitimate; what the argument does entail is that the modern state is not such a form of government'.

23 Cf. the following quote from Gingrich (1994, p. 166): 'The Capitol once stood as a shining example for the entire world of free people governing themselves. Republicans want to return that trust to the American people. For more than forty years, the Democrats ran the Congress with an iron fist, ruining the tradition and trust created by our Founding Fathers'.

24 The most common time-span mentioned in the critical accounts of 'the American political past' is limited to about two or three generations (while the early Puritan tradition, the struggle with the British Empire, or the founding of the nation are almost invariably presented in a favourable light). This gives some reason to believe that the political problems addressed through this kind of rhetoric are not only about 'history' and its right interpretation, but also about 'justice between generations', national heritage and the right way to treat it. In a recent example, the Republicans' attack against president Clinton's supposed immorality has been interpreted by the media as the World War II generation's last attack against the excesses of the 'flower generation' of the 60s.

References

Barber, B.R. (1989), 'Liberal Democracy and the Costs of Consent', in N.L. Rosenblum (ed.), *Liberalism and the Moral Life,* Harvard University Press, Cambridge, Mass. and London.

Bellah, R. N. et al. (1985), *Habits of the Heart. Individualism and Commitment in American Life,* University of California Press, Berkeley et al.

Bloom, A. (1987), *The Closing of the American Mind: How Higher Education Has Failed Democracy and Impoverished the Souls of Today's Students*, Simon and Schuster, New York.

Christian Coalition (1995), *Contract With the American Family. A Bold Plan by Christian Coalition to Strengthen the Family and Restore Common-sense Values* (Introduction by Ralph Reed), Moorings, Nashville, Tennessee.

Clinton, W.J. (1996), *Between Hope and History. Meeting America's Challenges for the 21st Century*, Times Books, New York.

Elshtain, J.B. (1995), 'The Communitarian Individual', in Etzioni (ed.), *New Communitarian Thinking. Persons, Virtues, Institutions, and Communities,* University Press of Virginia, Charlottesville and London.

Etzioni, A. (1984), *Capital Corruption. The New Attack on American Democracy,* Harcourt Brace Jovanovich, New York.

Etzioni, A. (1993), *The Spirit of Community. The Reinvention of American Society,* Touchstone, New York.

Etzioni, A. (1997), *The New Golden Rule. Community and Morality in a*

Democratic Society, Profile Books, London (1st American edition 1996).

Gingrich, A. and House Republicans (1994), *Contract with America. The Bold Plan By Rep. Newt Gingrich, Rep. Dick Armey and the House Republicans to Change the Nation*, E. Gillespie and B. Schellhas (eds), Random House, New York (various printings and editions).

Hobbes, T. (1968), *Leviathan*, C.B. MacPherson (ed.), Penguin Books, Harmondsworth (originally published 1651).

House Republicans (1995), *Restoring the Dream. The Bold New Plan by House Republicans. What We Pledge to Do Now to Strengthen the Family, Balance the Budget, Replace the Welfare State*, Republican National Committee, S. Moore (ed.), Times Books, New York.

Kemp, J. (1994), 'A Cultural Renaissance'. Remarks delivered 22/2/1994 at a conference entitled 'Culture Wars: The Battle Over Family Values', sponsored by the Shavano Institute for National Leadership of Hillsdale College. Transcript available(15.12.1999): http://www.empower.org/html/pubs/speeches/renaissance.htm.

Kuhn, T. S. (1970), *The Structure of Scientific Revolutions*, (2nd edition), University of Chicago Press, Chicago.

Krugman, P. (1994), *Peddling Prosperity. Economic Sense and Nonsense in the Age of Diminished Expectations*, W.W. Norton & Co., New York and London.

MacIntyre, A. (1981), *After Virtue*. University of Notre Dame Press, Notre Dame, Ind.

Matusow, A.J. (1984), *The Unraveling of America. A History of Liberalism in the 60s*, Harper & Row, New York et al.

Neal, P., (1993) 'Vulgar Liberalism', *Political Theory*, vol. 21, no. 4, November.

Rescher, N. (1982), *Distributive Justice*, University Press of America: Lanham, Maryland (originally published:, Bobbs-Merrill, Indianapolis, 1966).

Sandel, M. (1982), *Liberalism and the Limits of Justice*, Cambridge University Press, Cambridge.

Schmitt, C. (1985), *The Crisis of Parliamentary Democracy* E. Kennedy (trans.), MIT Press, Cambridge, Mass. and London (originally published 1923/1926).

Skinner, Q. (1989), 'The State', in Ball, Farr and Hanson (eds), *Political Innovation and Conceptual Change*, Cambridge University Press, Cambridge.

Skinner, Q. (1998), *Liberty before Liberalism*, Cambridge University Press, Cambridge.

Taylor, C. (1991), *The Ethics of Authenticity*, Harvard University Press, Cambridge, Mass. and London.

Unpublished:

Notes on Amitai Etzioni's lecture in the Department of Sociology, University of Helsinki, 24/8/1998.

11 Communitarianism and Immigration: Walzer on 'Members and Strangers'

PHILLIP COLE

Left political theory addresses the problems of the distribution of freedom and welfare within bounded political communities, but rarely addresses the question of how membership of these communities is to be fixed (see Canovan, 1996).[1] There seems to be an assumption that the question of membership can be set aside, but the fact remains that it can only be set aside on the added assumption that it is answerable in ways that are compatible with the central principles of left political theory – in other words, on condition that the policing of the external boundary of the community is in harmony with the moral and political principles that are applied within that boundary. However, once this issue is raised, it becomes clearer how difficult this external question of membership is: can we draw a boundary that constitutes insiders and outsiders in a way that embodies the principles of equal respect and concern for humanity as such – not only insiders – that are the central commitments of left political theory?

One exception to this failure to address the question of membership is Michael Walzer, who makes it the subject of a chapter in *Spheres of Justice* (Walzer, 1983; parenthetical references in the text will be to this work unless otherwise stated). He argues that political communities need a shared identity, and that the only way to ensure this is by choosing members; therefore political communities have the right to determine their membership with policies of admission and exclusion. These policies are constrained in two ways: first, by the community's understanding of itself; and second, by the principle of mutual aid for 'necessitous strangers'. But beyond this, the political community has the right to operate principles of admission and exclusion of its own choosing. Walzer defends his position by arguing that a political community is in important ways like a club, and to the extent that clubs have the right to constitute their membership, so too should political communities. What emerges, then, is a specifically communitarian justification of immigration controls.

There are problems with Walzer's treatment of the issue. The first concerns his use of various models of membership such as the club and the family: he derives both too much and too little from these particular models, and there are others available which give very different answers to these questions. The second is the extent to which the communitarian approach allows any 'external' criticism of communities' self conceptions and their membership practices as unreasonable. The third is the extent to which Walzer's approach is compatible with the principle of the moral equality of persons, which many would see as paramount. In the next section I will present Walzer's thesis on membership, and deal with the problems I have raised in subsequent sections of this paper.

(1) Members and strangers

Walzer describes a political community as a world of common meanings: language, history and culture produce a 'collective consciousness' (p. 28). National character is a myth, but 'the sharing of sensibilities and intuitions among the members of a historical community is a fact of life' (p. 28). While historical and political communities may not coincide, in a political community the moral settlement of issues must still appeal to common meanings that are available to all citizens. One of these common meanings must be membership itself – membership is what the members of a political community understand it to be. This means that as members of the political community we must choose criteria for membership '... in accordance with our own understanding of what membership means in our community and of what sort of community we want to have' (p. 32).

One possible principle of membership is the principle of mutual aid (p. 33): duties owed to persons generally, in the absence of any cooperative arrangements. According to this principle, positive assistance is required if 'it is needed or urgently needed by one of the parties', and 'if the risks and costs of giving it are relatively low for the other party' (p. 33). Mutual aid is a possible external principle of membership, and is independent of the view of membership taken by the community – it is owed to strangers regardless of that view. However, Walzer concludes that 'the force of the principle is uncertain' (p. 33).

The only two ways of avoiding the question of membership is either a system of global libertarianism in which all are independent economic units, a world of strangers; or a system of global socialism, where there is a single collective system, a world of members. However, '... neither of these arrangements is likely to be realized in the foreseeable future' (p. 34); and more importantly, there are good arguments against either arrangement which show that there is a need for immigration and naturalization policies. Such policies will be shaped by arguments about (1) the economic and political conditions of the host country; (2) the character and 'destiny' of the host country; and (3) the character of political communities in general. The subject of discussion for Walzer is (3), because it is our understanding of political communities as such that determines whether we think they have the right to determine their membership by their own criteria. However, as we only have 'dim perceptions' of what a political community is (p. 35), Walzer proposes to examine it by appealing to clearer perceptions of smaller units, specifically neighbourhoods, clubs, and families. These three, then, become models of membership which can, or cannot, be applied to the political community itself.

The first model that Walzer discusses is that of the neighbourhood, which he takes to be a 'random association' (p. 37): an association without an organised or legally enforcable admissions policy (p. 36). People choose neighbourhoods, and are not chosen, except to the extent that economic factors constrain such choices. Walzer agrees with Henry Sidgwick that such a model is unsuitable for the state, as there would be no 'patriotic sentiment' and therefore a lack of cohesion (Sidgwick, 1881, pp. 295-6).

While Walzer rejects the neighbourhood as a model for membership, he thinks clubs and families do provide more convincing models.To the extent to which he considers that political communities have the right to determine their membership, he takes it that the nation state is like a club, in that no one has the right of entry: 'The members decide freely on their future associates, and the decisions they make are authoritative and final' (p. 41). We may feel there are moral obligations to admit in some cases -- for example a group of 'national or ethnic "relatives"'; and in this sense states are like families: '... it is a feature of families that their members are morally connected to people they have not chosen, who live outside the household' (p. 41). This means the household can be a refuge in times of trouble, and states behave in the same way: 'They don't only preside over a piece of territory and a random collection of inhabitants; they are also the political expression of a common life and (most often) a national 'family' that is never entirely enclosed within their legal boundaries' (p. 42).

And so Walzer concludes that nation states have the right to determine their membership: they are not like neighbourhoods, but are like clubs and families in certain respects: that is, no one has a right of entry, and where we do feel a moral obligation to admit, it will be to people who belong to our national 'family'.

There are two problems Walzer acknowledges he must deal with before his account is complete: firstly, 'alien' groups already within the national boundary; and secondly, the problem of 'necessitous strangers'. On the first issue, Walzer declares that the nation state has no right to expel 'alien' groups already within its territory. Such groups have a 'territorial or locational right' (p. 43). Walzer comments (p. 43):

> Initially, at least, the sphere of membership is given: the men and women who determine what membership means, and who shape the admissions policies of the political community, are simply the men and women who are already there. New states and governments must make their peace with the old inhabitants of the land they rule.

The second problem is more complex. To what extent are nation states obliged to take in necessitous strangers under the principle of mutual aid? For Walzer, the question is how the principle of mutual aid applies to political communities. To some extent, this will depend on 'territorial extent and population density' (p. 45). Here Walzer comments on the White Australia policy, introduced in 1901 and only abolished completely in 1973. Given the amount of space, the right of white Australians to exclude 'necessitous men and women' could not be defended (p. 46).

Thomas Hobbes makes the point that where a country is not sufficiently inhabited, people have the right to move in as long as they do not harm the original inhabitants (Hobbes, 1968, p. 367). If those original inhabitants try to prevent them getting what they need to survive, for then sake of 'things superfluous', they can be read as breaking the fifth law of nature, of mutual accommodation, and so are responsible for the state of war that must follow (Hobbes, 1968, pp. 209-10). Walzer points out that Hobbes takes 'things superfluous' to be anything not needed for survival, but this is too narrow. The conception of what must be protected has to be 'shaped to the needs of particular historical communities', and so would include 'ways of life' (p. 47). In the case of white Australia, 'ways of life' in any significant sense were not at stake, and so the exclusion of necessitous strangers was not justified.

But still, to what extent do we have an obligation to let in 'immigrants from poorer countries?' (p. 47). Henry Sidgwick says that immigration of this kind must be restricted once it interferes with the local standard of living, especially that of the poor (Sidgwick, 1881, pp. 296-7) – but Walzer suggests that restrictions can be introduced before that stage, by giving aid to necessitous strangers where they happen to be: '... the community might well decide to cut off immigration even before that, if it were willing to export (some of) its superfluous wealth' (p. 48). This means, then, that a state can refuse entry to migrants whose economic position has become untenable, and can instead send some kind of economic aid or relief to where they happen to be.

Economic migrants, then, including those who are 'necessitous', can be justifiably kept out under Walzer's scheme. What of refugees? Walzer defines refugees as people who need membership itself, rather than wealth or territory (p. 48). Once more, obligations to refugees are limited, in this case to any refugees we helped to create, and to those with which we share some kind of affinity, perhaps a political one. 'Perhaps every victim of authoritarianism and bigotry is the moral comrade of a liberal citizen ...' (p. 49). Walzer thinks we do not have to make these distinctions at present because numbers are so small, but if faced with increased numbers, then we would be forced to choose between victims, and 'we will look, rightfully, for some more direct connection with our own way of life' (p. 49). If there is no affinity at all, 'there can't be a requirement to choose them over people equally in need' (p. 50). In the end (p. 50):

> communities must have boundaries; and however these are determined with regard to territory and resources, they depend with regard to population on a sense of relatedness and mutuality. Refugees must appeal to that sense. One wishes them success; but in particular cases, with reference to a particular state, they may well have no right to be successful.

And: '... political communities ... have a right to protect their members' shared sense of what they are about' (p. 50). And we can deduce that they have the right to protect this not only from strangers, but also from necessitous strangers and 'strange' refugees.

The final category is the asylum seeker, the political refugee who has succeeded in entering the territory. The question is, do we have the right to expel them? Walzer thinks not, but in a qualified sense: '... at the extreme, the claim of asylum is virtually undeniable. I assume that there are in fact limits on our collective liability, but I don't know how to specify them' (p. 51). There must be some limits, because '... actually to take in large numbers of refugees is often morally necessary; but the right to restrain the flow remains a fact of communal self-determination. The principle of mutual aid can only modify and not transform admissions policies rooted in a particular community's understanding of itself' (p. 51).

In the end, political communities have the right to shape their population, and this right frames not only the issue of general immigration, but also the issues of 'necessitous' economic and political migration. The principle of mutual aid does constrain this right, but the right also seems to limit the principle. Walzer concludes (p. 62) that:

> Admission and exclusion are at the core of communal independence. They suggest the deepest meaning of self-determination. Without them, there could not be *communities of character*, historically stable, ongoing associations of men and women with some special commitment to one another and some special sense of their common life.

(2) The models of membership

Walzer's thesis can be summarised thus: (1) political communities need a conception of themselves if they are going to be successful; (2) this self-conception needs to be protected through immigration and naturalization controls. The problem I want to investigate here is the use Walzer makes of his 'models of membership': the neighbourhood, the club and the family. Walzer reads both too much and too little into these models, and in fact none of them helps him establish either of the two claims that make up his thesis. I will discuss the family model first.

(i) The family model

It is important to remember that families are a mixture of genetic, legal and conventional connections. It is not that there are three kinds of family, depending upon whether they are genetically connected (the 'natural' family), legally connected (e.g. by adoption), or conventionally connected (e.g. a group that lives as a family in the absence of genetic or legal connection). Rather, the vast majority of families are, to an important extent, a mixture of all three. Under 'western' practices one is legally connected to one's partner through marriage, or conventionally connected where there is no legal act of marriage; genetically connected to one's children, biological parents and siblings; and conventionally connected to a wider range of members, such as one's partner's family. This means that a family is a mixture of choice and determination, in that one may choose one's partner or have them chosen for one,[2] but find oneself in a set of conventional relationships with their family which no one has chosen; and of course one lacks choice when it comes to genetic connections. Crucially, however, overlaying all of this is another layer of convention, including the family's genetic elements, which give such connections their significance. This means that even though genetic connections cannot be broken, they can lack significance in particular cases, or the conventions that normally overlay them can be broken and set aside. 'Natural' families can break up; adoptive families can be created.

When it comes to the use of the idea of the 'family' in political theory, for example in relation to the idea of the 'nation', we should therefore be cautious. The family is more often 'read' as a natural entity rather than a constructed one, and can therefore encourage an approach to identity and nationalism which modern political philosophy may find unacceptable – for example in the shape of 'ethnic' nationalisms which appeal to discredited and racist notions of shared 'blood'. Walzer, of course, would maintain a considerable distance between his own position and such notions, but he does still seem to read the family as primarily 'natural' when he refers to national and ethnic relations (p. 41), and emphasizes the connections with such people that are not chosen. Once we take into account the degree to which families are chosen and constructed, it is no longer such a useful analogy.

Of course Walzer may reply that there is still a degree to which families are 'natural' or at least unchosen, and that is the sense in which he is using them as an analogy here. But then it emerges that there is something odd with this reasoning. Walzer wishes to show that political communities can be like families, to the extent that on occasion they involve relations with 'outsiders' that are unchosen but nonetheless ethical – they involve obligations. But political communities are only like families in that respect if one believes that they involve this kind of relationship. If one rejects this kind of relationship, then political communities are not like families, in this respect, at all. The reasoning cannot be: (1) political communities are like families; (2) families involve ethical relationships with others that are not chosen; (3) therefore political communities involve ethical relationships with others that are not chosen. This would only follow if the first premise were (1) political communities are like families *in all respects*; but Walzer is not putting forward such a dubious argument. Rather, the reasoning is something like this: political communities involve ethical relations with 'outsiders' that are not chosen, and in this respect they are like families – but this is not so much an argument as an observation, and nothing more follows from it about political communities or about families. So while it may look as though Walzer is deducing something about the nature of political communities *from* the nature of families, he is not and he cannot. While Walzer makes limited use of the analogy with the family, he makes far greater use of the club model, and as we shall see the same concerns arise.

(ii) The club model

Walzer extracts most from the club model of membership, in that with a club: 'The members decide freely on their future associates, and the decisions they make are authoritative and final' (p. 41). However, to what extent is this true? A case can be made that clubs cannot have just any principles of membership – these principles can be subjected to moral and legal scrutiny and revision. One could argue that applications for membership should depend upon the goals and purposes of the club – to refuse entry to an applicant on any other grounds would look arbitrary and open to challenge. Therefore the only relevant ground for refusing membership is that the applicant will prevent the club from achieving its purposes. There are two sets of purposes here: (i) the purposes of the club as a whole; and (ii) the purposes of individual members of the club which are relevant to its constitution – the club is designed so that people can fulfil these particular purposes. It needs to be shown that the applicant will prevent the club from fulfilling its overall purpose, whatever it is, and/or that they will prevent individual members achieving their relevant purposes. It might be argued that another constraint on membership is that a club can legitimately limit its numbers. However, a limit on numbers can only be relevant if it can be shown that to admit more than that number will undermine the purposes of the club – and so the numbers criterion falls under the purposes criterion.

This model of membership can only be applied to political communities if they have purposes and their members have legitimate individual purposes. It may then be argued that a political community can refuse to admit people if they can be shown to threaten the overall purpose of the community, or if they will prevent members achieving their individual goals. For this to make sense we would have to (1) identify the overall purposes of the political community; (2) identify the individual purposes of its members that are regarded as needing protection; and (3) show how an applicant could undermine either or both of these. The question of numbers seems to be the most obvious limit – that to admit more than a certain number would threaten the community in these ways. There could, however, be more extreme examples where an individual is identified as 'undesirable' for, perhaps, political reasons – although for liberal democracies such cases would, hopefully, be very rare.

But for Walzer, there is another consideration – the political community's self-conception. The community has the right to protect its members' conception of themselves and of the community as a whole, and they therefore have the right to exclude anybody who they consider would disrupt that self-conception. This still falls under our general argument for exclusion, if we accept the claim that a self conception is essential if a political community is to achieve its purposes. But why would we accept this? We should note that the club model of membership does not help on this specific question, as it is not at all clear that a club needs the sort of shared self-conception Walzer describes in order for it and its members to achieve their goals. And so while the club model seems most useful for Walzer, it cannot help him establish his central thesis.

Walzer also assumes a single model of membership for clubs, when they may exhibit a variety of membership practices. There seem to be four possible models of membership for any unit: first, where membership is determined solely by the members; second, where membership is determined solely by the applicant; third, where membership is negotiated by members and applicants; and fourth, where membership is determined by factors beyond the control of either party. For Walzer, clubs are of the first type, neighbourhoods the second, and families the fourth; he does not seem to consider the third. As we have seen, families are not necessarily pure examples of the fourth type, and equally it seems possible that clubs could be any of the first three types, or be impure mixtures of them. Of course, it could be replied that at least *some* clubs are of the type Walzer describes in his analogy, but then why suppose that political communities are like *these* clubs in particular, unless we have already decided that political communities just *do* have the right to control membership?

This brings us to the same concern over the logic of the argument as with the use of the family model. Again the argument cannot be that (1) political communities are like clubs; (2) club members have the right to determine their membership; therefore (3) political communities have the right to determine their membership. For this to follow, the first premise would, once more, have to be (1) political communities are like clubs *in all respects*; and this is just false. Therefore Walzer cannot *deduce* the right of political communities to determine their membership from the fact that clubs (but not all of them) have this right. All he can do is offer the observation that they are similar in this respect – but this involves accepting the truth of the claim that political communities have this right. In other words, no one can be persuaded that political communities must have this right from the fact that some clubs have it, unless the question is begged. Of course, it may be that Walzer is not offering this form of deduction in his use of the club model nor the family model – but the point is then worth making that we misread him if we see the use of the models in this way; and a further point follows, that it is very unclear what work the models have left to do once this role is taken away from them.

Walzer's thesis, then, has two claims: (1) that a political community needs a shared self-conception if it is to achieve its purposes; and (2) that this self understanding has to be protected by having control over membership in the shape of immigration and naturalisation restrictions. While the club model does provide us with a reason for controlling membership, to protect the goals and purposes of the club, it does not show that a shared understanding is a ground for exclusion: firstly, because clubs do not necessarily need a shared understanding in order to achieve their purposes; and secondly, because even if they did, it has not been shown that controlled membership is necessary in order to protect that shared understanding – it may be robust enough to survive without such controls. So the club model provides us with no reason to accept either claim of Walzer's thesis. However if, for the sake of the argument, we accept that a self understanding *is* essential for a political community to achieve its purposes, we can then ask whether membership control is needed to protect that self understanding. When we look closer at the neighbourhood model, we shall see how unconvincing this second claim is.

(iii) The neighbourhood model

Although the neighbourhood is unsuitable as a model of membership, it is here that we get the most explicit statement of Walzer's arguments for immigration control:

(1) 'Neighbourhoods can be open only if countries are at least potentially closed. Only if the state makes a selection among would be members and guarantees the loyalty, security, and welfare of the individuals it selects, can local communities take shape as 'indifferent' associations, determined solely by personal preference and market capacity' (pp. 38-39).

(2) 'The distinctiveness of cultures and groups depends upon closure and, without it, cannot be conceived as a stable feature of human life. If this distinctiveness is a value, as most people ... seem to believe, then closure must be permitted somewhere' (p. 39).

(3) 'The restraint of entry serves to defend the liberty and welfare, the politics and culture of a group of people committed to one another and their common life' (p. 39). Therefore there must be a level of

> political organisation that has the right to have an admissions policy, the 'right to control immigration' (p. 39).

There are three arguments here for immigration control:

(1) The freedom of movement argument. The argument has two stages: (a) Greater freedom of movement is preferable; and (b) open borders at the state level will in fact lead to lesser freedom of movement, because localized areas will then operate with restricted borders.

(2) The distinctiveness of culture argument. Again the argument has two stages: (a) Distinctiveness of groups and cultures is valuable; and (b) such distinctiveness depends upon immigration controls.

(3) The welfare argument, which once again has two stages: (a) The provision of welfare depends upon having a fixed membership of those entitled to be taxed to provide welfare, and those entitled to receive welfare; and (b) such a membership can only be provided through having immigration controls and naturalization laws.

Now, Walzer's description of a neighbourhood as an 'indifferent association' strikes me as impoverished. As I sit and write this paper in Stamford Hill in London, the Hassidic Jewish community that makes up a significant proportion of the population in this neighbourhood is celebrating the festival of Purim, and the streets are full of noise and colour. And yet the neighbourhood, while not a random association, is open – there are no border controls or membership restrictions for the neighbourhood as such. The same story can be told within any cosmopolitan city throughout the globe, and it is a story which seems to cast doubt on Walzer's second argument, that the 'distinctive of cultures and groups depends upon closure'. Iris Marion Young points out that in the city we often find social differentiation without exclusion: 'In the ideal of city life freedom leads to group differentiation, to the formation of affinity groups, but this social and spatial differentiation of groups is without exclusion' (Young, 1990, p. 238). She says: '... groups do not stand in relations of inclusion and exclusion, but overlap and intermingle without becoming homogeneous'. And: 'In the normative ideal of city life, borders are open and undecidable' (Young, 1990, p. 239).

Now of course, Young is talking of the ideal city, and we should also note that the Hassidic community I gave as an example is not open, but has strict membership controls and methods of excluding 'outsiders' through which they maintain their identity as a group. However, the point is not so much about this particular religious group, but about the neighbourhood itself, a geographical area, which has no such controls and yet has a distinct character. One could reply that it is not so much the neighbourhood which has this character as the different groups that happen to reside there, but this would be true of any geographical space, whether it be a neighbourhood or a political state; and the point remains that this neighbourhood, by virtue of having these groups residing within it, does have a distinct character, and it does not need border controls to do it – most importantly, there is no control over who enters the neighbourhood.

Again, it might be replied that any such character a neighbourhood happens to have is fragile and passing, in that the groups that give it this character can always leave and go elsewhere – the fact that the neighbourhood has no control whatever over membership means this is always a possibility. But this is surely the same for the political state, and this reveals an important point – that if one is concerned to maintain the identity of a state, far more important than control over entry is control over exit, and Walzer, and those who follow him, do not seriously contemplate such control. Walzer says: '... this right to control immigration does not include or entail the right to control emigration' (p. 39). But: 'The fact that individuals can rightly leave their own country...doesn't generate a right to enter another (any other). Immigration and emigration are morally asymmetrical' (pp. 39-40). The source of this asymmetry seems to be that 'restraint of entry serves to defend ... liberty and welfare' (39), but restraint of exit involves 'coercion', and therefore the violation of liberty and welfare. However, the asymmetry cannot lie here, for Walzer makes it clear that the liberty that is protected by immigration constraints and violated by emigration constraints is that of members of the political community in question. If one takes into account the liberty of non-members then immigration constraints clearly involve coercion and the violation of liberty – of non-members who wish to enter. The real asymmetry here is that members have freedom of movement over the state's borders and non-members do not. What has to be explained is why members should enjoy this freedom, while non-members are deprived of it.

All three of Walzer's arguments look unconvincing when we consider another possible model of membership, which I will call the regional/provincial authority model. Most modern states have levels of local government at the provincial or regional level and below, and these local authorities have powers and responsibilities within their boundaries. Such a body can have responsibility for the provision of services such as policing, waste disposal, education, the provision of leisure facilities; and can have responsibility for taxation to raise funds to pay for these services. And yet, typically, the boundaries of such an authority operate like Walzer's neighbourhood – they are open in that the authority has no control over who enters its territory or who becomes a resident. Walzer discusses Otto Bauer's distinction between membership rights and territorial rights: an authority can have membership rights in that it has the right to tax its members, for example; and yet at the same time it can have no territorial rights in that it cannot determine who is a member (see Bottomore and Goode, 1978, pp. 102-125). Walzer considers this unsuitable for modern political communities – Bauer was writing in the time of the multi-national European empires, and now modern nations look for control over a territory: 'Nations look for countries because in some deep sense they already have countries: the link between people and land is a crucial feature of national identity' (p. 44). Also, issues of welfare, education, and so on, need to be solved within a particular geographical space.

Bauer's approach fits the regional/provincial authority model when it comes to the provision of welfare and education. Such authorities precisely have membership rights and no territorial rights, and there is no evidence that this handicaps them in fulfilling their purposes. And if we do consider Walzer's notions of 'identity' and 'place' to be important, certain examples of regional or provincial authorities do enjoy a strong sense of identity and place – people can feel strong attachments to a particular region or province or federated state, despite the fact these bodies have no territorial rights. Even neighbourhoods, which have neither membership controls nor clear territorial boundaries, can have very strong senses of identity and place, as the Jewish community in Stamford Hill demonstrates.

And so Walzer's arguments (2) and (3) are contradicted by this model of membership: closed borders are not needed in order to have a sense of distinct identity; nor are they needed for welfare provision. Of course, Walzer may reply that his argument (1) is decisive, that these regional/provincial boundaries can only be open because there is closure at the national level. But this seems to be an intuition rather than an argument, and it is difficult to see what evidence could be produced for or against it.

(3) Unreasonable identities

We have seen that Walzer's thesis consists of two claims: (1) A political community needs a self-conception if it is going to succeed in meeting its objectives; and (2) that self-conception needs to be protected by immigration and naturalization laws. In the previous section I argued that neither of these claims is obviously true, and provided some grounds for doubting them. But there is a third claim to Walzer's thesis, which is absolutely fundamental to it: (3) that it is for a political community to decide upon its own self-conception, and its decision is final. This amounts to saying that any self-conception will do. Although many on the left would find such a position unacceptable, it is central to Walzer's perspective, as the source of the self-understanding and the moral principles that govern a community can only be that community itself. His way of doing political philosophy is to 'interpret to one's fellow citizens the world of meanings that we share' (p. xiv).

David Miller characterizes Walzer's theory as 'radically pluralistic in nature'. There are no universal laws of justice. Instead, we must see justice as the creation of a particular political community at a particular time, and the account we give must be given from within such a community' (Miller and Walzer, 1995, p.2). However, to say that this means any conception will do is not quite accurate, as Walzer does qualify the claim that the authority of the members of the community is final: 'One can argue about particular admissions standards by appealing, for example, to the conditions and character of the host country and to the shared understandings of those who are already members. Such arguments have to be judged morally and politically as well as factually' (p. 40). He gives two examples of what he considers to be either an unreasonable self-conception or an unreasonable application of a self-conception (this distinction is important, and I will apply it below).

The first example picks out those in America in, for example, the 1920s, who argued for restricted immigration to defend a 'homogeneous white and Protestant country' (p. 40). Walzer argues that such a claim was both inaccurate in that it ignored the extent to which the United States was already a highly heterogeneous community, and unjust in that it set aside the original intention to create such a society – '... the moral realities of that society ought to have guided the legislators of the 1920s' (p. 40). So this is an example of an unreasonable national identity. However, we should note that this qualification of what can count as a self-conception is itself qualified, for, appealing to the club analogy, Walzer says that earlier decisions, if different, could have led to 'an Anglo-Saxon nation-state' (p. 40); and this, one assumes, would have meant that subsequent immigration controls on these grounds would have been neither inaccurate nor unjust.

The second example is of the White Australia immigration policy. As we saw in Section 1, Walzer (p. 46) criticises that policy because of the amount of space that was available:

> The right of white Australians to the great empty spaces of the subcontinent rested on nothing more than the claim they had staked, and enforced against the aboriginal population, before anyone else. That does not seem a right that one would readily defend in the face of necessitous men and women, clamoring for entry.

Although Walzer argues that what needs to be defended is not just economic prosperity and territory, but also 'ways of life' or 'life plans' (p. 47), he concludes that no significant ways of life were at stake in the case of 'white Australia'. It is important to note that Walzer's critique of the White Australia policy is set in the context of his discussion of 'necessitous strangers' and refugees: the policy cannot be defended when it comes to the exclusion of these applicants for membership. But the policy was designed to exclude strangers as such, where 'strangeness' was measured in terms of racial characteristics, whether they were necessitous or not. Walzer's critique applies to the exclusion of necessitous strangers, but he has nothing to say here about the exclusion of non-necessitous strangers on these racial grounds. This, then, is an example of unreasonable membership controls, but not necessarily of an unreasonable self-conception.

And so Walzer does provide some grounds for critically assessing self-conceptions and their application. A multi-cultural community cannot impose a mono-cultural identity and immigration controls based on that false identity; but a mono-cultural community can impose immigration restrictions to defend itself from invasions of plurality, as long as those defences are not applied too harshly to 'necessitous strangers'. These grounds may strike some as rather shallow.

If we look closer, though, we may notice that the scope for criticism is even shallower. In the case of the White Australia policy, Walzer says that while ways of life must be taken into account as well as territorial and economic considerations, there were no significant ways of life at stake in this case. 'Let us suppose,' he suggests, 'that the great majority of Australians could maintain their present way of life, subject only to marginal shifts, given a successful invasion of the sort I have imagined' (p. 47). He does concede that some individuals could come to 'need' vast empty territories for their way of life, but '... such needs cannot be given moral priority over the claims of necessitous strangers. Space on that scale is a luxury ...' (p. 47). Strangely, having argued that territorial and economic considerations are not the only ones, and that ways of life have to be taken into account too, Walzer seems to give a reading of ways of life primarily in terms of territorial considerations, assessing them only in terms of the space available to lead them. It could surely be argued that a way of life is threatened by the admittance of 'strange' refugees even though there are no territorial or economic factors at stake – one's way of life is violated by the mere presence of such strangers, however little space they take. Having introduced ways of life as an important factor when it comes to the inclusion or exclusion of necessitous strangers, Walzer seems to have left himself with few or no grounds to reject any particular way of life as unreasonable. He therefore seems to have no grounds to criticize the White Australia policy, even when it comes to the exclusion of necessitous strangers.

His critique of the 'white America' proposal is equally problematic. As we have seen, he seems to allow that if the United States in fact was, more or less, a White Anglo-Saxon Protestant nation, the community could legitimately adopt this as a national identity and defend it through its immigration policies. However, given the plural nature of the United States, such an identity could not be imposed. But why shouldn't a political community *revise* its self-conception? The United States could have decided that it would consider itself to be a White Anglo-Saxon Protestant nation for purposes of future immigration policies, and those already within the borders who did not fit that identity could be re-defined as internal 'aliens'. Note that Walzer allows for the existence of internal aliens when he considers the rights of the original inhabitants of a territory. As we saw in Section 1, such inhabitants have a locational right and cannot be expelled: 'New states and governments must make their peace with the old inhabitants of the land they rule. And countries are likely to take shape as closed territories dominated, perhaps, by particular nations (clubs and families), but always including aliens of one sort or another – whose expulsion would be unjust' (p. 43). Walzer argues that any such internal aliens must be allowed full citizenship rights, but they seem to remain alien in that they are not included in the 'dominant' national identity. The fact that the dominant (majority) group is not obliged to negotiate a *national* identity that includes *everybody* who has a legitimate right to be within the territorial boundary, seems strange.

My suggestion here is that, given the absence of such an obligation, there seems to be no good reason why a political community, which in the past had a plurality of membership and a plural identity, cannot revise its self-conception and so become more exclusive. Those re-defined as internal aliens cannot be deprived of their citizenship rights and cannot be expelled, but others like them will no longer be admitted. This would allow that the 'white America' policy could have been imposed in the 1920s without any inaccuracy or injustice. After all, if we appeal to the analogy of the club, it is always open for the current membership of the club to revise the membership rules – there seems to be no reason why they should be bound by the rules decided upon by past members. They could not expel present members who do not fit the new self-conception, but no new 'strange' members will be admitted. Of course, such a decision has to be open to democratic review, but if a particular 'nation' dominates in terms of numbers, then it would seem unreasonable to frustrate its democratic will for the sake of a small minority.

This is to take into account the extent to which 'strangeness' is a construction imposed upon others, rather than something naturally given. Who counts as 'strange' can therefore be reviewed and revised. Kitty Calavita describes the case of Spain, where people from the former colonies such as Peru were regarded as unproblematic until Spain became embodied in the European Union: once Spain became part of the EU's overall immigration policy, those people from Spain's colonial past became subject to severe immigration control, as privileged entry was granted to members of EU states (Calavita, 1998). Within Walzer's framework, there seems to be no grounds for objecting to such a revision, as long as those *already within* the territory are not expelled or deprived of their citizenship rights. But even if this is the case, it seems likely those already on the inside will be subjected to increased social *and* legal harassment because of their close connection to those now defined as outsiders.[3] And so once more, Walzer seems to have no grounds to criticize even the 'white America' proposal which he considers to be unjust. We have to wonder whether his approach has *any* scope to criticize unreasonable self-conceptions, or unreasonable applications of a self-conception.

(4) Moral equality

One basis for criticizing unreasonable self-conceptions or unreasonably restrictive membership rules is that they violate a fundamental principle of modern political philosophy – that of the moral equality of persons. Amy Gutmann identifies an assumption of human equality as the 'unifying theme of liberalism' (Gutmann, 1980, p. 18); and Will Kymlicka goes further to see the 'duty to treat people with equal consideration' as the basic principle upon which any modern political theory can be assessed (Kymlicka, 1990, p. 34), endorsing Ronald Dworkin's view that every plausible political theory is based upon equality as the ultimate political value (Kymlicka, 1990, p. 4).[4] Michael

Walzer shares this assumption, when he says that he does not know what characteristics make us equal, but (p. xii):

> The answer has to do with our recognition of one another as human beings, members of the same species, and what we recognize are bodies and minds and feelings and hopes and maybe even souls. For the purposes of this book, I assume the recognition. We are very different, and we are also manifestly alike.

This principle of moral equality causes difficulties for liberal political philosophy when it comes to any form of immigration control -- for membership practices, in the end, make a distinction between 'insiders' and 'outsiders' which excludes those defined as 'outsiders' from any share in the goods that are shared amongst 'insiders'; and it is difficult to find any criteria to make this distinction which is not arbitrary from a liberal point of view. The principle of moral equality precisely gives arise to this concern to eliminate arbitrariness from social and political practices, and leads John Rawls to condemn as unfair any distribution of resources which rests upon what he sees as the arbitrary properties of 'social starting positions, natural advantages and historical contingencies' (Rawls, 1978, p. 56); these, for Rawls, are the 'fundamental inequalities'. The arbitrary nature of resource distributions under capitalism therefore becomes the central problem for liberal theories of social justice (see Kymlicka, 1990, pp. 85-6). If we see the membership problem as a question of distribution – which is precisely how Walzer characterizes it (p. 29) – then the same worries about arbitrariness arise, especially if we are concerned with natural and historical contingencies.

Of course, this concern over arbitrariness has its place in a liberal viewpoint which holds the principle of moral equality as universally valid, and Walzer does not occupy this position. But this does not mean he can evade the difficulties the principle raises for immigration practices, because it may well be that 'our' political community holds a political philosophy which is itself liberal and democratic, and therefore has the principle at its core. Whether we are 'universalist' or 'local' liberals we hold the same principle – the only difference is that in the former case the principle can be critically applied globally, while in the latter case the principle can only be critically applied to our own community and any others that also claim to be liberal democracies. Joseph H. Carens (1995, p. 346) makes the point that liberals must be guided by the principles of their own tradition even if they do not seek to impose those principles globally, only locally; and one such fundamental principle is that of moral equality:

> No moral argument will seem acceptable to *us*, if it directly challenges the assumption of the equal moral worth of all individuals. If restrictions on immigration are to be justified, they have to be based on arguments that respect that principle.

In the end, Carens does not believe that any such argument is possible, and therefore open borders with complete freedom of movement is the only consistently liberal position. Immigration and naturalization practices, as such, therefore present a deeply serious problem for liberal political theory, whether we interpret liberal principles globally or locally.

This, of course, is to shift the level of argument from Walzer's level 3, the character of political communities as such, to level 2, the character of a particular community, which in this case happens to be liberal democratic. Walzer may reply that if 'our' self-conception is of a liberal democratic state, then his approach shows, perfectly consistently, that we have to put in place immigration and naturalization policies that reflect this particular self-conception. However, this tells us nothing about how to solve 'our' problem – of how immigration and naturalization controls *can* be made compatible with liberal democratic principles. And so on this extremely complex but crucial political question, Walzer's approach to membership seems to shed no light whatsoever.

Conclusion

Walzer's thesis on membership consists of three basic claims: (1) That political communities need a shared self-understanding – that states need a national identity; (2) that they have the right to protect that identity through immigration controls; and (3), that within some limits, a state's national identity cannot be subjected to external criticism. In this essay, I have argued that Walzer has not shown that states *need* a national identity; and even if they do, he has not shown that this identity *needs* to be protected through immigration controls. I have also questioned the coherence of the third claim, in that it seems a state's self-defined identity, within Walzer's scheme, cannot be subjected to *any* external criticism at all. Finally, Walzer does not make it clear how membership controls can be made compatible with what seems to be a central commitment of a modern political philosophy, whether taken globally or locally – to the moral equality of persons.

This final problem raises fundamental issues for political philosophy that go beyond Walzer's approach. There seems to be a fatal tension at the border of the liberal democratic state – it may be that practices of exclusion cannot be coherently justified within the terms of a recognisable liberal democratic theory.[5] If we do take seriously the claim that the commitment to the moral equality of humanity is the defining centre of liberal democratic politics, then we are entitled to expect to find that commitment at the heart of the central practices and institutions of states that describe themselves as liberal democracies. That it is not present in some of the most important practices – immigration and naturalization – must lead us to question the extent to which the states that most jealously claim the title 'liberal democracy' have any right to it. If T. H. Green was correct in his argument that the degree of recognition that the principle of moral equality applies to others beyond our 'tribe', ultimately to all peoples, is a measure of the historical progress of humanity (Green, 1883, pp. 217-231), then, contrary to some suggestions, history has clearly not come to an end in western capitalist states.

Notes

1 This essay was researched and written while on research leave funded by the Arts and Humanities Research Board and the School of Humanities and Cultural Studies at Middlesex. I would also like to thank my colleagues in the Philosophy, Religious Studies and Cultural and Intellectual History Academic Group for their support. Thanks are also due to Bob Brecher, Doris Schroeder and Paul Gilbert for their comments, and to the participants at the 'The Liberal Order: The Future for Social Justice?', Palacky University, Olomouc, Czech Republic, July 7th-12th, 1999, for their lively and challenging consideration of the original paper. Dr Roshi Naidoo's support and belief was, as always, foundational.
2 Having one's partner chosen for one has always been an important part of the 'western' convention of marriage, often overlooked by essentialist characterizations of 'eastern' conventions.
3 See my 'The Limits of Inclusion: Western Political Theory and Immigration' (Cole, 1998), where I expand on why this would happen.
4 See Dworkin, 1977, pp. 179-83; Dworkin, 1986, pp. 296-301; Dworkin, 1987, pp. 7-8.
5 See my *Philosophies of Exclusion* (Cole, forthcoming), for a more detailed treatment of this issue, and my 'The Limits of Inclusion" (Cole, 1998).

References

Bottomore, T. and Goode, P. (eds) (1978), *Austro-Marxism*, Clarendon Press, Oxford.

Calavita, K. (1998), 'Immigration, Law, and Marginalization in a Global Economy: Notes from Spain', *Law and Society Review*, vol. 32, no. 3, pp. 529-566.

Canovan, M. (1996), *Nationhood and Political Theory*, Edward Elgar, Cheltenham.

Carens, J.H. (1995), ' Aliens and Citizens: The Case for Open Borders', in W. Kymlicka (ed.), *The Rights of Minority Cultures*, Oxford University Press, Oxford.

Cole, P. (1998), 'The Limits of Inclusion: Western Political Theory and Immigration', in *Soundings*, Issue 10, Autumn 1998, pp. 134-44.

Cole, P. (forthcoming), *Philosophies of Exclusion: Liberal Political Philosophy and Immigration*, Edinburgh University Press, Edinburgh.

Dworkin, R. (1977), *Taking Rights Seriously*, Duckworth, London.

Dworkin, R. (1986), *Law's Empire*, Harvard University Press, Cambridge, Mass..

Dworkin, R. (1987), 'What is Equality? Part III: The Place of Liberty', *Iowa Law Review*, vol. 73, no. 1, pp. 1-54.

Green, T.H. (1883), *Prolegomena to Ethics*, ed. A.C. Bradley Clarendon Press, Oxford.

Gutmann, A. (1980), *Liberal Equality*, Cambridge University Press, Cambridge.

Hobbes, T. (1968; orig. 1651), *Leviathan*, Penguin, Harmondsworth.

Kymlicka, W. (1990), *Contemporary Political Philosophy: An Introduction*, Clarendon Press, Oxford.

Miller, D. and Walzer, M. (eds) (1995), *Pluralism, Justice, and Equality*, Oxford University Press, Oxford.

Rawls, J. (1978), 'The Basic Structure as Subject', in A. Goldman and J. Kim (eds), *Values and Morals*, Reidel, Dordrecht.

Sidgwick, H. (1881), *Elements of Politics*, Macmillan, London.

Walzer, M. (1983), *Spheres of Justice: A Defence of Pluralism and Equality*, Martin Robertson, Oxford.

Young, I.M. (1990), *Justice and the Politics of Difference*, Princeton University Press, Princeton.

12 Liberal State and Polity in the Era of Globalisation: Social Injustice, Governance and Resistance in the Global-Local Nexus

MAJID YAR

Introduction

Over the past decade the concept of 'globalisation' has become common currency, figuring in debates both in academia and in the wider public arena. 'Global speak' is increasingly becoming a part of the phenomenological and discursive reality of Western societies. In this paper I wish to explore one strand of the complex and multifaceted character of globalisation, namely its role in the generation of patterns of social inequality and injustice, and the possible and emergent forms of political mobilisation and resistance against such global processes. Substantively, I will propose two arguments. Firstly, that the specifically global genesis of patterns of inequality/injustices presents a challenge to liberal-democratic politics which has traditionally focused on the nation state as a form and avenue of political action. I argue that the globalised character of such economic, environmental and cultural processes exceeds the interventionary capacity of the nation state as a level of political organisation. Secondly, I challenge the formulation that the most appropriate response to globally generated inequalities, and the attendant 'crisis' of national politics, is simply a 'scaling-up' of political discussion, organisation and mobilisation to a global level via transnational political actors and agencies, a 'solution' associated with recent advocacy of 'global civil society'. I argue that coterminous with the emergence of global forms of political association and mobilisation we can simultaneously see the revivification of *localist* and contextually embedded forms of social and political movement, as the negative and inegalitarian effects of global processes impact upon specific locales and meet with resistance. In conclusion, I argue that patterns of inequality and injustice generated by global processes appear to be inciting forms of political resistance at *both* global and local levels, and these must be seen as deeply interconnected and equally significant for the furtherance of emancipatory struggles for social justice.

Globalisation and injustice: economic, environmental and cultural dimensions of inequality

Like many concepts which come quickly into academic fashion and become associated with the *Zeitgeist*, globalisation is a contested concept with multiple and many-hued definitions and usages, often of very variable sophistication, clarity and plausibility. Like 'postmodernism' in the 1980s, globalisation has become a 'buzz word' for the 1990s, and enjoys an equal indeterminacy in its widespread deployments. My own understanding and use of the concept can be very briefly characterised, at the most general level of analytical abstraction, as denoting *the maximal spatial extension of social relations, interactions and exchanges*. In other words, it denotes the phenomena in which relations and interactions, both individual and collective, occur between human beings who are increasingly widely dispersed in spatial terms. Viewed in these terms, what is today termed globalisation can be seen as the fullest extension of a process of 'time-space compression' (Harvey, 1990) whose emergence can be seen as a characteristic of the development of modern social formations as a whole.[1] What 'compression' describes is the process by which close temporal and spatial restrictions on social relations/interactions/exchanges (which typified life in pre-modern societies) have come to be lifted. The dynamic of industrial capitalism, coupled with the development of communication systems, mass media, transport infrastructure and technology, has served to extend cumulatively the spatial range of social interactions. Actors thus come to be 'disembedded' from narrowly confining space-time envelopes, and come to interact habitually with, and thereby affect, others heretofore inaccessible because of their distantiation in space (and so time). Hence the discussion of globalisation is basically an exploration of the processes by which social relations of all kinds are being increasingly *de-territorialised*. The extension of everyday interactions to the greatest possible spatial range (the *world-wide* flows of people, machinery, money, images, information) is what in current discussions is referred to as 'globalisation' (Featherstone, 1990, pp. 1-7). Here I wish to spotlight three dimensions or aspects of global processes (the economic, environmental and cultural) which can be seen to have problematic repercussions, generating as they do their own patterns of inequality, deprivation, exploitation and injustice.

Economic globalisation

It can be said fairly incontrovertibly that economic imperatives and logics have been a central driving force behind the emergence of globalisation. Indeed, the global processes which are of such interest today can be seen to have emerged coterminously and integrally with the development of modern industrial capitalism (Wallerstein, 1974; Sklair, 1991). Historically, we can note the obvious examples of the importation of raw materials and human resources, and the exportation of goods for sale to foreign markets as integral moments in the development of modern capitalism. The economic process, from production through consumption, can thus be seen as a spatially extended chain of flows, interactions and exchanges, which serves to interconnect suppliers, manufacturers, traders and consumers across national and continental territories. However, we can note a range of qualitative and quantitative transformations during the second half of the 20th century which have accentuated the globalised character of the capitalist economy, bringing with them the entrenchment of older patterns of inequality and the instantiation of new ones.

Firstly, we can note the extension from the resource-based and market-seeking global relations noted above, to a spatial optimisation of production in which production processes are increasingly spread across the globe (Dunning, 1993; Dicken, 1998). The development of industrial capitalism has long instantiated an international division of labour (IDL) in which production is split between developed market economies (DMEs) and less developed countries (LDCs). The former monopolise the capital-, knowledge- and skill-intensive aspects of production which entail high value-addition, while the latter are confined to labour-intensive, low skill and low knowledge-based parts of the production process which entail low value-addition. This division of labour establishes and reproduces relations of domination between DMEs and LDCs, generating ever-increasing disparities between rich and poor (Waters, 1995, pp. 70-1). This sort of economic relation has expanded massively in the course of the last twenty or so years, led by multi-national enterprises (MNEs) and trans-national corporations (TNCs), as well as various forms of subcontracting, production licensing, joint ventures, partial mergers and interfirm agreements (ibid., p.72). The fragmentation of production and its flexible dispersal/allocation to wherever labour costs are cheapest and so profit potential is greatest, has the effect of further disadvantaging the LDCs with respect to DMEs, especially as the LDCs are effectively forced to compete with each other to attract production investment by offering the lowest possible wage costs and taxation regimes, and the minimisation of labour-protection and environmental regulations which also contribute decisively to production costs.

Secondly, this spatial flexibilisation/dispersal of the production process is increasingly affecting the economies of the developed world, inciting restructuring processes which bring with them greater economic and social insecurity and disadvantage, broadening the cleavages between rich and poor in the industrialised North and West. The global mobility of capital, its capacity to locate and relocate production wherever labour and related costs, taxation regimes, etc., are most favourable, is driving a competitive process in which labour flexibilisation (casualisation, reduction of employment protection, withdrawal of trade union recognition and collective bargaining, etc.,)[2] and the minimisation of welfare provisions are instituted as means to capture inward investment. The globalisation of production and corporate reach is thus central to a process of industrial restructuring often associated with the transition of a 'post-Fordist' regime of production (Amin and Dietrich, 1991), and typically championed by neo-liberal ideologues in the name of 'free markets'. Presently, there is great pressure in DMEs toward the kind of restructuring processes associated with neo-liberal projects of Reaganism-Thatcherism (even in those countries which have heretofore retained in significant degree collectivist patterns of industrial relations and welfare corporatism). What these restructurings under pressure from economic globalisation in effect mean is the increase of job insecurity, restriction of workers' rights and entitlements, downward pressure on wages for many working people (be they located in commodity manufacture or service provision), the advent of structural (chronic) unemployment, withdrawal of welfare 'safety nets' for those unable to secure or perform paid work, and increasing polarisations in the living conditions of the poorest and richest. Globalising forces are in effect becoming both an engine and apologia for deepening socio-economic inequality, exploitation and neglect, in the advanced industrial as well as the developing world.

Thirdly, we can see the neo-colonialist exploitative international social division of labour constitutive of the globalised economy (point 1, above) being reproduced 'internally' within the advanced industrial economies, as migrant labour and minority ethnic groups are concentrated within the most marginal, casualised, poorest paid and least protected sectors of the newly 'flexibilised' Western labour force (point 2, above). The socio-economic marginalisation of migrant groups and 'racial' or 'ethnic' minorities descended from the migrant populations has been an established feature of Western societies. What can be seen at present is the refiguration of these relations of inequality in terms of the new labour patterns ushered in by globalising processes in the DMEs. Established patterns of inequality are reproduced within the frame of labour flexibilisation, as migrant and minority ethnic groups are over-represented in those sectors most profoundly impacted by the restructuring processes already discussed. Thus, for example, Saskia Sassen's (1996a, 1996b) work dealing with so-called 'global cities' shows the way in which the socio-economic structure of major Western metropoles are being constituted around an increasingly polarised division between those employed in the advanced economic sectors (corporate professional, informational and culture industries, etc.,) and those restricted to marginal, informal, manual, repetitive, insecure, poorly remunerated and devalorised labour. The latter group often comprises those from immigrant communities and minority ethnic groups. Similarly, Scott Lash and John Urry (1994) point up the ways in global economic restructuring processes are implicated in the generation of 'impacted ghettos' and a new urban underclass composed in significant part by ethnic minorities and migrants (Lash and Urry, 1994, chapters 6 and 7, pp. 145-192). These 'racialised' or 'ethnicised' relations of inequality are further accentuated and reproduced through the denial of citizenship and citizenship rights to migrants, contributing to their socio-economic marginalisation and restricting access to channels of social mobility.

Fourthly, we must note the importance of globalised financial flows, interactions, and exchanges in the refiguration of patterns of economic inequality, insecurity and hardship. It is certainly clear that in the uneven emergence of global process, financial markets constitute the most fully globalised domain of social-economic relations. As Harvey writes:

> The formation of a global stock market, of global commodity (even debt) futures markets, of currency and interest rate swaps, together with an accelerated geographical mobility of funds, meant ... the formation of a single world market for money and credit supply ... Computerisation and electronic communication have pressed home the significance of instantaneous international co-ordination of financial flows (Harvey, 1990, p. 161).

Integral to this process has been the formation of international banking groups and the establishment of international branch networks, the erosion of boundaries between different forms of financial practice and institution (banking, brokerage, financial services, consumer credit, etc.,) as mergers and takeovers have created new international financial conglomerates (ibid.; Urry, 1990, p. 14). Thus the combination of developments in the electronic means of communication and the emergence of multination and transnational financial enterprises has made possible the globalisation of finance. The exchanges associated with global financial markets now dwarf in monetary value terms the trade in material and non-material commodities, goods and services. For example, every day more than $600 billion in foreign exchange is traded, an amount equivalent to **one year's** total world trade (Lash and Urry, 1994, p. 289). In terms of speed and volume of exchanges, the density of financial transactions has overwhelmed the manufacturing economy, producing a 'paper entrepreneurialism' (Harvey, 1990) in which speculation in a global 'financial casino' (Strange, 1986) (trading in stocks and shares, commodity and debt futures, currencies, etc.,) displaces the production of actual goods and services as the focus for profit making.

What have been the socio-economic consequences of this global 'financialisation' of the economy? Firstly, the development of a globally dispersed, almost incomprehensibly complex and polycentric network of economic interrelations, transmitting its effects with near instanteneity, has rendered local, regional or national economic conditions increasingly unstable and vulnerable to shifts elsewhere in the world. Whether it's the global stock market crash of 'Black Monday' in October 1987, or the recent 'meltdown' and economic 'readjustments' triggered by the 'crisis' of South-East Asia's so-called 'tiger economies', we can see the vulnerabilities produced by unanticipated effects in the global financial arena. Secondly, the trade in finance has separated money from any connection to value created through material process and production, and has taken on a life of its own, with 'value' being 'created' and 'destroyed' by the $billions within hours according to the moods, whims, rushes, panics and rumours sweeping global financial markets. The values of companies and currencies are increasingly decided by the free-floating and self-referential 'hyper-reality' of the financial field, making it ever more difficult to create stable conditions for production and planning. Similarly, the uneven balance of power between finance and industry renders the latter vulnerable to finance-led takeovers, leveraged buy-outs, hostile take-overs, and so on, and makes industrial enterprises the potential objects of destructive asset-stripping, liquidation and 'rationalisation' motivated by an interest in maximising gains in the short term (Bud and Whimster, 1991, p. 5; Harvey, 1990, p. 162). The 'casino' economy, that of fly-by-night investors oriented to instant profit, begins to dictate the employment and investment decisions of industrial enterprises, and short-term gains override the long-term well-being of companies and their employees. For individuals employed by such concerns the combination of these developments means increased uncertainty and vulnerability to job-losses, increasing vulnerability to tightly-bound and amplified chains of cause-and-effect circulating through the global economy, and further pressures toward casualisation, wage-restraint and a general deterioration of working conditions as the short-term profit-maximisation impelled by financial speculators and institutional investors (such as pension funds) takes ascendancy. If the global financialisation of the economy has made 'winners' out of the professionalised financial sectors (market traders and brokers, fund analysts, bankers, accountants, information and communication specialists, etc.,) and made millionaires and billionaires out of 'paper entrepreneurs' (such as George Soros), then it is equally helping to make 'losers' out of large sections the industrial and post-industrial working classes.

Environmental globalisation: the risk society

In recent years, perhaps the aspect of global processes which has been most closely attended to, inspiring a new consciousness of the world as a 'single place', has been industrial modernity's deterritorialisation of environmental problems. Scientific, political and popular discourses of global environmental interconnectedness now constitute an integral part of our understandings of ourselves and the world we inhabit. In this section, I wish to outline an account of the emergence of global environmental problems by drawing upon Ulrich Beck's (1992) theory of late modernity as a 'risk society', and to highlight the ways in which this dimension of globalisation affects different groups and individuals in different ways, thereby reinforcing established patterns of inequality and generating new ones.

The basis for Beck's account is the claim that today's global environmental hazards are the unintended consequences or side-effects of industrial modernising processes. The development of modern industrial societies (both market capitalist and state socialist) have been oriented around economic growth, the on-going expansion of the production of goods. Yet what modernising projects have remained blind to (at least until very recently) is the production of environmental 'bads' that has accompanied industrialism. The industrial process, from the extraction of raw materials, the creation of technological and transport infrastructure, the deployment of production processes in manufacturing and agriculture, to the consumption of goods by end-users, has produced a constant stream of side-effects in terms of pollutants, toxins, destruction of natural habitats and plant and animal species, desertification, rising water levels, soil erosion, climate change, biological and genetic mutations, and so on. As the side-effects have accreted and amplified over time and with industrial expansion, they have begun to make manifest their damage and endangerment not only to human health in terms of illness and disease, but to the viability of the planetary ecosystem as whole. In the advanced economies of the Western world, the relative decline in urgency over questions of material well-being (the drive to produce more goods) is giving rise to a parallel concern with the management and avoidance of the unwanted 'bads' that industrialism has brought in its wake (Beck, 1992, pp. 19-25).

Now the overall expansion in the scale of industrial processes (as Western economies have grown) and their worldwide dispersal (as previously non-industrial regions have played 'catch-up' to the West by pursuing modernising programmes), have generated a globalisation of environmental hazards. The side-effects of industrial process are no longer socio-spatially confined to the workforce of a particular enterprise or to the populations located in the immediate vicinity of such enterprises. Rather, they are geographically dispersed to an extended spatial scale, affecting 'distant others', and contributing cumulatively to global environmental degradation. Acid rain, oil spills and discharges of industrial wastes, radioactive and chemical leakages and catastrophes, CFC-induced ozone depletion, genetic modifications of plants and animals, and the 'greenhouse' effect are just some of the instances of global dispersal.

In terms of who is threatened, who is disadvantaged, and who suffers from the environmental hazards unleashed by industrial modernity, there is an ambiguity. On the one hand, people occupy different 'social risk positions', and these often follow the established inequalities of class position (ibid., p. 23). Thus, for example, the owners and managers of industry can afford to move to the suburbs, thereby 'buying out' from the immediate environmental threats to their health and well-being produced by the industrial processes from which they profit; meanwhile, industrial workers on the 'factory floor' are exposed daily, and the poor lack the resources to escape the degraded urban industrial environment in which they and their asthmatic children choke on car fumes and are poisoned by lead emissions and other toxins. Similarly, we see the exportation of hazardous manufacturing processes and industrial waste to the developing world (made possible by the economic globalisation already discussed), thereby passing the risks of industrialism onto distant others while continuing to enjoy the economic benefits (for example, the poisoning of the Ogone people and their lands by Shell in Nigeria, or the death, maiming and blinding suffered by thousands of Indians from the failure of Union Carbide's plant at Bhopal). Yet, on the other hand, ecological disasters are sublimely indifferent to class and geography, to social distinctions and national boundaries. Who gets poisoned can depend on which way the wind is blowing, and when the entire planetary ecosystem is under threat, there's nowhere to hide even for the rich and privileged. New lines of social injustice and inequality appear as the consequence of globalised environmental risks, which pass under, over and around political borders, rendering us all, at different times and in different ways, profoundly vulnerable.

Cultural globalisation; information and inequality

Finally, I wish to address the globalisation of culture and its implications in terms of the constitution of patterns of social injustice and inequality. The debate around the international and global dispersion of culture is relatively long established, and has typically been concerned with the supposed homogenisation and standardisation of culture brought about by the mobility of persons, the establishment of transnational collectivities and organisations (so-called 'third cultures' (Hannerz, 1990)), the advent of means of mass communication (print, radio, television, film, satellite, internet) and corresponding forms of mass, popular culture which achieve global distribution via the 'culture industries'. These trends have been received and interpreted in a number of distinctive ways, viewing homogenisation as either a universalising and uniting force, as cultural imperialism ('Americanisation'), or as the triumph of the 'lowest common denominator' of the mass cultural.

However, the global cultural homogenisation thesis is not particularly persuasive in that it partakes of a 'hermeneutic naiveté', assuming that all culture and communication will be received by different people in different contexts in identical ways, or that audiences and interpreters are passive 'sponges' who simply absorb cultural flows without resistance or creativity. What interests me more here is the way in which the intensification of communication and cultural exchanges (in terms of distance, density and velocity) brings with it forms of social exclusion and marginalisation for certain sectors of society. In other words, like economic globalisation and environmental globalisation, cultural globalisation can be seen to entail its own patterns of inequality. In a world in which the symbolic and cultural is becoming increasingly central to the production of social relations, social positions, access to social and political influence, economic rewards, and so on, one's positioning in terms of access to the 'means of communication' and cultural flows becomes critical in establishing inclusion, exclusion, and life chances. As Manuel Castells (1996) argues, the synergetic integration of microelectronics, computing and transmission technology from the 1970s onwards has in effect started to create a global 'network society', a 'space of flows' in which a highly interdependent social universe emerges constituted around information and culture. Yet access to these networks is uneven, and so their centrality brings with it power asymmetries and exclusions. As Mike Davis (1992) argues, certain regions (be they in the developing world or in the advanced industrial countries) are becoming 'information ghettos', data and media 'black holes' which are unintegrated into the emerging global cultural networks, and whose residents are 'information poor' and deprived of the technological means and practical competencies to position themselves successfully within the new cultural hierarchies. In the 'informationalisation' of the social world, a new global underclass is emerging to parallel the new information elites.

Social injustice and the nation state

As David Held (1991) notes, there exists a deep historical and theoretical interconnection between liberal democracy and the territorially constituted sovereign nation state as a form of political organisation. The fundamental principles and practices associated with liberal democracy (the nature of the *demos*, democratic citizenship, popular sovereignty, self-determination, consent, representation, and so on) are almost inextricably entwined with the notion of a territorially-bounded, differentiated and autonomous national political unit (McGrew, 1997, p. 5). Liberal democratic theory and practice has long assumed a 'symmetrical' or 'congruent' relation between political decision-makers and the recipients of political decisions, a relation of determination and accountability between political decisions, decision-makers, and the populace, all of which are spatialised within a particular territory. Thus the people within a spatially delimited region have the power to select and hold accountable those who make decisions, and the decision-makers enjoy both the legitimacy and practical power and instruments at their disposal in order to effectuate their decisions as policies (Held, 1991, p. 139). A clear demarcation is drawn between the national and extra-national domain, with the latter either being neglected as a concern for liberal-democratic theory, or treated in terms of the relation *between* sovereign and self-determining national political entities, thus assuming the integrity and coherence of such spatially bounded polities (typified, for example, by the 'realist' school of international relations theory).

In this conception of liberal democracy, the question of social justice is framed in terms of establishing a greater congruence between the outcomes of political decision-making and the interests of 'the people' as a whole, rather than having the former represent merely the sectional interests of dominant classes, ruling elites, and so on. This can be figured in a variety of ways, from the refinement of mechanisms of democratic representation and accountability (such as electoral reform, freedom of information) to the decentralisation of political power via mechanisms of devolved and/or direct decision-making by citizens. In other words, it claims that the generation of social injustices, and the endeavour to correct them, is basically a matter of the 'internal' circuit of power, representation, access, 'voice', decision-making, and accountability within the territorially-bounded political unit. It assumes that social injustices are generated by relations, processes and exchanges which are spatially located within the national territory, and thus that they are amenable to political correction via the mechanisms and channels of the democratic process operative within that territory.

However, as already discussed, the process of globalisation presents a fundamental challenge to such 'territorialist' assumptions about both the spatial location of the engines of social injustice, and the effectiveness of political intervention located at the level of the nation-state in challenging such processes. In an increasingly globalising world, an ever greater proportion of social relations, practices and processes take place on a spatial scale which extends well beyond the boundaries of the national territory. The boundary between the 'internal' and 'external', 'domestic' and 'foreign', are being eroded as the kinds of economic, environmental and cultural interconnectedness already discussed take hold.

In a global economic system, decisions taken by transnational economic elites (for example in the financial markets or in multi/trans-national enterprises) will have profound impacts upon the citizens of a particular national territory. The power of global economic processes can be such that they exceed the interventionary capacity of national political actors. Thus, for example, in the case of Britain's forced withdrawal from the European Exchange Rate Mechanism (ERM) in 1992, we see how the decisions of foreign exchange dealers in New York and Tokyo overwhelmed the capacities of national economic decision-makers to set the level of the national currency and so effectively manage the key economic conditions within its territory. Moreover, we see national economic decision-making becoming increasingly responsive to market imperatives, shaping economic and other related policies according to the demands and requirements of transnational capital.[3] As already noted, the increasing pressures of international competitiveness, the need to capture globally mobile capital, pushes national policy decisions toward the abolition of extensive labour rights and social protection, the minimisation of taxation regimes and environmental safeguards, all in the name of satisfying transnational capital's demand for the lowest possible overhead costs as the price for locating production within a national territory.[4] Thus we see how national policy decisions, under pressure from globalising economic imperatives, become active in *accentuating* rather than ameliorating patterns of socio-economic inequality and disadvantage.

The permeability of national territorial boundaries is, if anything, even more pronounced in the case of the globalisation of environmental problems. Pollutants and toxins move freely via air, water and land, indifferent to political borders. Hence the citizenry and environment of one nation-state are endangered by the actions of individuals and organisations located elsewhere on the planet. The democratic process is pushed into impotence. On the one hand, national political decision-makers have no capacity to regulate industrial processes (burning of fossil fuels, emissions of by-products, dumping of wastes) or consumer practices (use of CFC gases, leaded petrol, car engines without catalytic converters) which happen outside the national territory (hence, for example, the Norwegian government protests in vain to the British, when the marine life in its Fjords is irradiated by emissions carried by tidal currents from the Sellafield nuclear reprocessing plant on England's Cumbrian coast). Sovereignty is undermined as the processes and practices which can have far-reaching and deleterious consequences for a national population become ungovernable owing to their extra-national origin. On the other hand, the citizenry is equally disenfranchised, having no ability to hold accountable those who undertake, or permit to be undertaken, the processes and practices which endanger their health and well-being. Both governors and governed are sidelined as the national territory becomes 'point zero' for environmental hazards arriving from elsewhere.

The picture with respect to the globalisation of cultural and communication flows is more ambiguous, but just as profound in its consequences for the liberal-democratic national system. The emergence of a globalised 'information society' has, as already discussed, generative effects in constituting new patterns of social exclusion around the variable access to means of communication and the associated opportunities for accruing cultural capital and symbolic resources. Nation states do have some scope for intervening so as to manage the effects of such processes within their own territorial domain by, for example, making/encouraging investment in technological and communications infrastructure, providing access to citizens via national media, broadcasting, and telecommunications enterprises, making education and training provisions for the acquisition of the practical competencies necessary for utilising new information technologies, and so on. However, the scope for such interventions is limited both by prohibitions of cost and the speed of the cycle of technological innovation/obsolescence. The question of access to technology and acquisition of competencies becomes largely a private matter, and thus reinforces and reproduces existing patterns of social and economic inequality, with the poorest having least access to informational networks and thereby reproducing their marginality. Moreover, the scenario facing those in the developing world is even more stark, with the lack of existing infrastructural requirements (such as reliable electricity supply and telecommunications grids) and resources for investment in high-tech, high-cost equipment (computers, satellites) resulting in the effective exclusion of those outside the advanced economies from the new global system of informational and cultural flows. This exclusion from the means of communication in turn becomes a key moment in the consolidation of the exploitative international division of labour within the global economic system (p. 189, above), as the 'information poor' are restricted to the least lucrative aspects of the production process, while those in the 'information rich' areas reap the economic benefits of their capacity to engage in 'high end' aspects of the production of goods and services.

There are a further set of issues relating to the globalisation of cultural flows which bear even more directly on the questions of the sovereignty of the nation state and the system of democratic self-governance. It is widely acknowledged that the new means of global communication (satellites, faxes, computers, and so on) are profoundly undermining the state's capacity to license and control information flows and communication processes. Many liberals and radicals have rightly welcomed this in that it undermines the state's capacity for ideological dictatorship and cultural homogenisation, thereby encouraging both freedom of expression, information and communication, and inter-cultural communication and cosmopolitanism (Hirst and Thompson, 1995, p. 419). However, there is also a profoundly counter-democratic aspect to this process, as the transnational flows of signs, symbols, words, and images evade regulation by democratic decision-making. Much has been made recently of the unregulated flows of cultural 'bads' across national boundaries ('hate speech' such as the racist, anti-Semitic and homophobic discourses of the far-right, paedophilic materials and violent pornography, and so on). The question here is not so much one of the proper limits to 'free speech' *per se*, but rather the right to democratically determine and set limits upon what kinds of speech and representation a society deems permissible. The globalisation of cultural flows undermines such democratic decision making as, for example, in a state in which inflammatory racist speech has been prohibited under anti-discrimination laws, but where such communications appear unhindered via electronic communications, such as the Internet. It is not a question of whether such speech should or should not be allowed, but rather that of the abrogation of a people's right to democratically determine their position on the matter, and make that decision effective in policy and practice.

The above overview should begin to convey some of the ways in which the economic, environmental and cultural dimensions of globalisation are undermining the liberal democratic nation state's capacity for governance within it own territory, and concomitantly its capacity to ameliorate the social injustices and inequalities that such global processes are generating. This process has been described variously in terms of the 'hollowing out', (Jessop, 1994), the 'disétatisation' (Crook et al., 1992) and the 'desovereignisation' (Held, 1991) of the nation state. What this means for liberal-democracy is the undermining of the symmetrical or congruent 'circuit' which comprises the sovereign exercise of power by political decision-makers and their corresponding accountability to a *demos* who have enfranchised them. The mechanisms of state can no longer effectively govern or regulate the spatially extended flows, interactions, exchanges and processes which constantly exceed is territorial limits; meanwhile, the people lose the capacity for self-governance over the socio-economic, cultural and environmental conditions of their own existence, as they are effected by the actions of individuals and institutions who cannot be regulated or held accountable via the democratic mechanisms of the national political system. From the standpoint of the struggle for social justice, this process constitutes a 'double negative': on the one hand, globalisation processes generate new patterns of injustice and inequality and reproduce or entrench old ones; on the other, the very *global* nature of such processes undermines the effectiveness of those channels which were once availed for challenging these patterns of injustice, namely participation in the system of national democratic politics. The upshot is that both theorists of liberal democracy and advocates of democratic emancipatory struggles against social injustice must rethink political participation and process beyond the spatial scale of the nation state.

Responses (1): global governance, global protest

One way in which the globalising challenge to liberal democracy is being addressed is by redirecting attention to the proliferation of multinational/supranational governmental and quasi-governmental institutions, organisations, agreements and regulatory mechanisms. It is argued that the disempowerment of nation states by globalising forces has incited a process of political coordination and integration on a supranational level as political actors struggle to subject deterritorialised socio-economic, environmental, cultural and other processes to effective management and regulation. This is what is now being discussed under the rubric of 'global governance' (Held, 1991; Rosenau, 1992; Hirst & Thompson, 1995). Since 1945 we have seen a proliferation of inter-governmental organisations (IGOs) and multilateral agreements and compacts oriented to ordering and regulating activities on a supranational scale.[5] These include international organisations such as the UN, WTO, (formerly GATT), IMF, World Bank, OECD, regional groupings of states such as APEC, ASEAN, NAFTA, EEC/EU, multilateral treaties such as NATO, SEATO, and OPEC, various inter-governmental protocols and accords such as nuclear test ban and non-proliferation treaties, the conventions on the 'law of the sea' (1967-1982), the Vienna Convention (1985), the Montreal Protocol (1987), the Rio Accord (1992), and so on. It has been claimed by some commentators (especially those sceptical about the 'extreme globaliser's' claims of emergent 'global disorder') that such mechanisms indicate that global processes are far from ungovernable, and that economic, environmental and other processes are amenable to regulation, given the emergence of institutions and coordination at the proper geo-political scale.

However, the emergence of such mechanisms of global governance are deeply problematic for a number of reasons:

Firstly, there is the question of democracy (or more accurately, the distinct lack of it). The kinds of institutions noted above are almost exclusively insulated from popular sovereignty and accountability, with only a tenuous and displaced connection to democratic oversight (in that the decision-makers in such organisations are selected or appointed by their respective democratically-elected national leaderships). Perhaps the exception here is the EU, which can be seen as a partially democratised form of regional proto-government, having as it does a democratically elected legislature (albeit with limited powers), as well as the judicial and executive branches associated with the 'separation of powers' in the ideal-typical liberal democratic state. This is, however, an exception to the rule, and we can note that there is a very substantial 'democratic deficit' where such mechanisms of global governance are concerned.

Secondly, there is the deep-seated interconnection of such mechanisms of global governance with the interests and agendas of transnational capitalism and the economic and political elites of dominant states (Cox, 1996). Institutions such as the IMF, World Bank, WTO, OECD, can be seen as fulfilling an all-important function as 'disciplinary institutions' for global market capitalism, creating the most favourable conditions for the movement of capital and production of goods, dismantling national barriers and protections which might hamper the profit potentials for MNEs, and so on. The economic and political power concentrated with such institutions functions as a 'crowbar' for forcing recalcitrant nation states to open up for capitalist exploitation of their natural and human resources, and almost invariably embeds developing countries in a structure of dependency and debt which works to the advantage of the advanced industrialised world. Under the aegis of such institutions, the staggering disparities of income and resource use between rich and poor has continued to widen, as they become the facilitating agents for an economic globalisation process which is an engine of injustice and disadvantage. Similarly, the institutions of global governance can be active in engendering rather than diminishing global environmental problems, as with the USA's insistence at the recent (1998) Rio Summit on global climate change that the advanced industrial countries be permitted to buy 'pollution rights' from the developing nations, thereby ensuring that the production of harmful carbon dioxide emissions by the world's worst polluter nation continues unabated. In short, the developing institutions and mechanisms of global governance do not necessarily represent either an extension of democratic politics or a corrective for the social injustices generated as part of globalisation processes; indeed, they can and have heretofore tended to push in the opposite direction.

Given the aforementioned difficulties, it is important to recognise the centrality of other kinds of associations, solidarities, identities, communities and organisations in furthering the agendas of democratic accountability and social justice in the face of globalisation. I refer specifically here to the emergence of what has been called 'global civil society' (Falk, 1994; Wapner, 1995; Walzer et al., 1998). 'Civil society' very loosely refers to that sphere of manifold and diverse public or quasi-public associations, identities and social relations which stand outside the formal institutional spheres of state and economy, out of which alternatives and challenges to those institutional configurations emerge in the forms of social movements and popular protests and mobilisations (cf. Cohen and Arato, 1992). While civil society has traditionally been conceived within the framework of national societies, one of the positive consequences of globalisation processes has been the establishment of the conditions of possibility for extending civil associations across national boundaries (for example, via electronically mediated communication, transport infrastructure, and the many other socio-technological structures which have made possible time-space compression processes). Recent years have seen a proliferation of international non-governmental organisations (INGOs), as well as many more informal networks and associations, many of which represent transnational mobilisations and resistance movements against global socio-economic inequalities, exploitation, environmental destruction, and so on (Ekins, 1992; Maiguascha, 1994; Runyan, 1996; Dickenson, 1997). Well known examples include Greenpeace, Friends of the Earth, The World Council of Churches, The World Council of Indigenous Peoples, The World Women's Conference, the Third World Network. Such 'subaltern counter-publics' and 'counter-hegemonic projects' represent the emergence of a global political figuration of democratising pressures and emancipatory struggles against prevalent patterns of inequity. In recent years such transnational social movements have had a number of notable successes, giving some cause for cautious optimism. These have included Greenpeace's mobilisation of popular protest against Shell's plans for the ocean dumping of its Brent Spar oil rig (Beck, 1996) and the recent Global Alliance which successfully campaigned to undermine the OECD's plans for a Multilateral Agreement on Investments (MAI), aimed at further 'liberalisation' of global markets and the relaxation of international environmental laws (FOE, 1998/1999).

Responses (2): global agendas, local action

The foregoing discussion of a 'global shift' in the figuration of governance and political protest, while attending to some very important trends, is incomplete insofar as it fails to recognise the 'localising' tendencies which accompany globalisation processes.

In recent discussion there has emerged an increasing awareness that the process of 'globalisation' is somewhat more complicated in its dynamic and ambiguous in its effects than at first proposed. This is especially true with respect to the assumption that time-space compression on a global scale inevitably leads to the dissolution of 'locality', of local social and political relations, local identity and distinctiveness. Indeed, it is becoming increasingly apparent that globalisation processes can at the same time *reinforce* the locale. This has given rise to the neologism 'glocalisation', indicating the dualistic character of global-local process (Robertson, 1992). The supposed revivification of the local under conditions of globalisation turns around a number of poles, each of which has implications for questions of governance, political protest, and struggles for social justice.

Firstly, as already noted, the processes of globalisation partially undermine or bypass the autonomous nation-state; its form is 'hollowed out', transforming it into a 'quasi' or 'weak' form. As part of this process, local and regional levels of social organisation acquire greater importance as they interact more directly in global contexts without the control or mediation of institutions and structures at the state level. Regions and locales are constituted and reinforced as coherent economic and political actors, as they are integrated into structure of local-global relations in which they are increasingly direct participants rather than simply passive subsidiaries of an umbrella nation-state. The weakening of the nation-state can thus be said to 'liberate' or 'free' locality as a significant spatial scale of social, economic and political organisation and action. Thus we can see that recent years, which have seen an acceleration and deepening of globalisation, have equally seen the rise of a new discourse about the importance of local social relations, often appearing in the political arena under the appeal to 'community' (Bellah et al., 1977). In a very significant sense, 'localisation' must be seen not as the countertendency, but as an *effect*, and indeed as an integral moment, in the dynamic of globalisation.

Secondly, as part of such processes, more localised forms of identity which tended to be occluded or undermined by the nation-state system find themselves reinvigorated. Local particularism and distinctiveness have tended to be marginalised by the push toward the formation of national cultures and identities, essential moments in the symbolic-ideological constitution of nations as coherent 'imagined communities' (Anderson, 1991). States have tended to suppress local difference and distinctiveness in order to establish their sovereignty over a spatially delimited territory which might be claimed to have some socio-cultural unity or commonality. The weakening of the national territoriality constitutive of the Westphalian order[6] has simultaneously seen a resurgence of localisms. Indeed, Zygmunt Bauman (1996) claims that these two processes have an intimate causal connection. Following the assumption that social beings abhor a cultural vacuum, Bauman suggests that the loss of older certainties and stabilities underpinned by national identities is being compensated for by a turn to localism. Globalisation's threat to the national order incites a search for new forms of belonging and community on the more intimate scale of the locale (Bauman, 1996, pp. 653-658). This in turn can engender movements for greater local autonomy, for the wresting of political decision-making away from national political institutions and toward devolved and 'grassroots' scales.

Thirdly, I have already discussed the ways in which globalising processes in the economic, environmental and cultural domains impact unevenly upon different social groups. Globalisation, as a new distribution of wealth and poverty, privilege and marginalisation, power and powerlessness, is itself *spatialised.* In other words, these patterns of inequality are spatially distributed, with certain locales emerging as 'winners' while others become 'losers' in the new distribution of economic, cultural and environmental advantages and disadvantages. These spatial distributions of shared realities contribute to the construction of local social orders, cultural identities and solidarities. For the 'losers', the negative and destabilising consequences of global processes can provoke defensive reactions in the name of local autonomy and the interests of the community. Thus globalisation processes can engender positive local potentials for resistance against the new patterns of inequality and injustice. Such local forms of resistance (which can become coherent social movements) often place the value of human needs for a clean, safe, and stable economic, social or natural environment before the logic of maximising capital accumulation. In short, the localising logic of global processes can be seen to create the conditions in which political mobilisations against those selfsame processes can emerge: globalising injustice and local resistance go hand-in-hand.

This notion of local resistance to new patterns of globally-generated social injustice can be illustrated with reference to a number of examples. For instance, recent years have seen the proliferation of environmental and other forms of social movement oriented toward local, community and 'grassroots' responses to global processes. Acting under slogans such as 'think global, act local', such movements have oriented themselves toward local initiatives aimed at contesting the inegalitarian impact of globalising processes (Lash and Urry, 1994, pp. 292-305). These have included initiatives against the domination of local economies by transnational agri-business and retail chains; resistance to the privatisation and dismantling of public and civic spaces as they are sold off to corporate developers as lucrative real-estate; protests against road-building schemes which attract and benefit inward foreign direct investment at the expense of the health and welfare of local residents; challenges to the global trade in nuclear and toxic waste reprocessing and dumping; establishment of local 'barter' schemes and 'fair trade' initiatives as alternatives to TNCs whose global trading practices entail both damage to the environment via the worldwide transportation of materials and goods, and the exploitation of the economically disadvantaged. In Britain, we have seen in recent years the emergence of an array of so-called 'LAGA' groups ('Local Action, Global Agenda') oriented to a broad-based strategy of local challenges and alternatives to globally damaging and exploitative processes. Moreover, these movements are often explicitly oriented to democratising projects, demanding effective 'grassroots' participation in decision-making processes which affect localities, thereby attempting to wrest political self-determination from the anonymous and unaccountable elites in transnational corporate and financial organisations and the almost equally unaccountable actors in the institutions of global governance.

Conclusions

In this paper I have argued that liberal political theorists' and analysts' address to the question of social justice must take cognisance of the processes of economic, environmental and cultural globalisation. I have argued that globalisation has profound import for both for the refiguration and extension of democracy beyond the model of the nation-state, and for the project of effectively challenging emergent patterns of social injustice, exploitation and inequality associated with global process. I have argued that positive (if as yet largely nascent) possibilities for radical democratic movements can be seen both at the global level in the contours of a new 'global civil society', and equally at the local level in the form of 'grassroots' resistance movements. In conclusion I would, however, like to sound some notes of caution. Firstly, it must be noted that globalisation processes, while qualitatively and quantitatively unprecedented, are very uneven. Global movements of people and material artefacts remain constrained by physical and political barriers and economic costs; meanwhile, flows of finance capital and cultural goods (by virtue of their symbolic character) are extremely advanced. Secondly, it is by no means certain that globalising forces simply spell the end (or the beginning of the end) of the state system. Rather, it has been argued that the nation state is undergoing a transformation to a new historically specific form (Jessop, 1994); it is not so much being dissolved as reconfigured into a 'post-Westphalian' form. Yet others have argued that the nation state should not be seen as a passive victim of globalising processes but as an active instigator and enabling institutional configuration, a role which ensures its continued salience in the global era (Hirst & Thompson, 1995). Thirdly, the political dynamics in reaction to global processes are not uniform or clear. While we can see the emergence of outward-looking 'cosmopolitan localisms' which seek to further democratic and universalist struggles for emancipation and justice, we can equally see reactionary 'tribalisms' which retreat into xenophobia and ethnic or cultural localism. Hence there is no guarantee that the political and cultural reactions incited by globalising forces will serve the interests of egalitarian and democratic projects. However, despite these qualifications, it seems clear that it is in the emerging spaces of the 'global-local nexus' that struggles for democratic enfranchisement and social justice must be increasingly taken up.

Notes

1 See also the similar, and highly influential, conception of 'space-time' distantiation developed by Antony Giddens (1990).
2 See, for example, the discussion of the various dimensions of 'flexibilisation' in Polliert (ed.) (1991).
3 See, for example, the British government's recent decision to appoint 200 extra diplomats to act explicitly as economic 'envoys' to be sent to key countries in order to fight for Britain's advantage in global markets (Black, 1998).
4 See, for example, the case put forward by Reich (1992).
5 By 1992 IGOs numbered in excess of 3000, compared to some 30 or so existing in the pre-WWII era (Waters, 1995, p.112).
6 The term 'Westphalian order' is used to denote the political settlement after the Treaty of Westphalia (1648) which consolidated territoriality as the dominant principle of political organisation, upon the basis of which an international order was established.

References

Amin, A. & Dietrich, M. (1991), 'From hierarchy to 'hierarchy': the dynamics of contemporary corporate restructuring in Europe', in *Towards a New Europe*, Amin & Dietrich (eds), Edward Elgar, Aldershot.

Anderson, B. (1991), *Imagined Communities: Reflections on the Origin and Spread of Nationalism*, Verso, London.

Bauman, Z. (1996), 'Glokalisierung, oder Was für einen Globalisierung, ist für die anderen Lokalisierung', in *Das Argument: Zeitschrift für Philosophie und Sozialwissenschaften*, 217, pp. 653-664.

Beck, U. (1992), *Risk Society: Toward a New Modernity*, Sage/TCS, London.

Beck, U. (1996), 'World Risk Society as Cosmopolitan Society? Questions in a Framework of Manufactured Uncertainties', *Theory, Culture & Society*, Vol 13 No. 4, pp. 1-32

Beck, U. (1997), 'Die Neue Macht der multinationalen Unternehmen', in *Frankfurter Rundschau*, 9/1/1997.

Black, I. (1998), 'Cook to recruit 200 envoys in fight for global markets', in *The Guardian*, 28/11/1998.

Bud, L. & Whimster, S. (1991), *Global Finance and Urban Living: The Case of London*, Routledge, London

Castells, M. (1996), *The Rise of the Network Society*, Blackwell, Cambridge MA/Oxford.

Cohen, J. & Arato, A. (1992), *Civil Society and Political Theory*, MIT Press, Cambridge Mass.

Cox, R. (1996): 'Globalization, multilateralism, and democracy', in *Approaches to World Order*, R. Cox (ed.), Cambridge U.P., Cambridge.

Crook, S., Pakulski, J., and Waters, M., (1992), *Postmodernization*, Sage, London.

Davis, M. (1992), 'Beyond Blade Runner: Urban Control and the Ecology of Fear', *Mediamatic* (http://mediamatic.nl/home.html).

Dicken, P. (1998), *Global Shift: Transforming the World Economy*, Paul Chapman, London.

Dickenson, D. (1997), 'Counting women in: globalization, democratization and the women's Movement', A.McGrew (ed.), below.

Ekins, P. (1992), *A New World Order: Grassroots Movements for Global Change*, Routledge, London.

Emmot, B. (1993), 'Everybody's Favourite Monsters', in *The Economist*, vol. 27, no. 3.

Falk, R. (1994), *On Humane Governance*, Polity, Cambridge.

Featherstone, M. (1990), Introduction in, *Global Culture: Nationalism, Globalisation and Modernity*, Featherstone (ed.), TCS/Sage, London.

FOE (1998/1999), *Change Your World*, 14, Dec. 1998 / Jan. 1999.

Giddens, A. (1990), *The Consequences of Modernity*, Polity, Cambridge.

Hannerz, U. (1990), 'Cosmopolitans and Locals in World Culture', in Featherstone (ed.) (1990), above.

Harvey, D. (1990), *The Condition of Postmodernity*, Blackwell, Oxford.

Held, D. (1991), 'Democracy, the nation-state and the global system', *Economy and Society*, 20, 2, May 1991, pp. 139-172.

Hirst, P. and Thompson, G (1995), 'Globalization and the future of the nation state', *Economy and Society*, 24,3, August 1995, pp. 408-442.

Jessop, B. (1994), 'Post-Fordism and the State', in Amin (ed.) (1994), above.

Maiguashca, B. (1994), 'The transnational indigenous movement in a changing world order', in *Global Transformation: Challenges to the State System*, Y. Sakamoto (ed.), United Nations U.P., Tokyo.

McGrew, A. (1997): 'Globalization and territorial democracy: an introduction', in *The Transformation of Democracy: Globalization and Territorial Democracy*, McGrew (ed.), Polity/Open University, Cambridge/Milton Keynes.

OECD (1992), *Globalisation of Industrial Activities*, OECD, Paris.

Polliert, A. (ed.) (1991), *Farewell to Flexibility?*, Blackwell, Oxford.

Reich, R (1992), *The Work of Nations*, Vintage Books, New York.

Robertson, R. (1992), *Globalization: Social Theory and Global Culture*, Sage, London.

Rosenau, J. (1992), 'Governance, order and change in world politics', in *Governance without Government: Order and Change in World Poltics*, J. Rosenau & E.O. Czempiel (eds), Cambridge U.P., Cambridge.

Runyan, A.S. (1996), 'The Places of Women in Trading Places: Gendered Global/Regional Regimes and Inter-nationalized Feminist Resistance', in *Globalization: Theory and Practice*, E. Kofman & G. Youngs (eds), Pinter, London/New York.

Sassen, S. (1996a), 'Rebuilding the Global City: Economy, Ethnicity and Space', in *Re-Presenting the City: Ethnicity, Capital and Culture in the 21st Century Metropolis*, A.D. King (ed.), Macmillan, Basingstoke/London.

Sassen, S. (1996b), 'Analytic Borderlands: Race, Gender and Representation in the New City', in King (ed.), above

Sklair, L. (1991), *Sociology of the Global System*, Harvester Wheatsheaf, Hemel Hempstead.

Strange, S. (1986), *Casino Capitalism*, Blackwell, Oxford.

Urry, J. (1990), 'Globalisation, Localisation and the Nation State', Lancaster Regionalism Group, Working Paper 40.

Wallerstein, I. (1974), *The Modern World-System*, Academic Press, New York.

Walzer, M. (ed.) (1995), *Toward a Global Civil Society*, Berghahn, Providence/Oxford.

Wapner, P. (1995), 'Politics beyond the state', *World Politics*, 47, April 1995, pp. 311-340

Waters, M. (1995), *Globalization*, Routledge, London.

13 Territorial States: What Are They Good For? Who Needs Them?

DANIEL KOFMAN

> [A] restaurant menu is organized into a group of similar or equivalent items constituting the appetizer, another group of items constituting the main course, and so on. We choose one item from the group of equivalent items (pardigmatic class) called appetizers, say the soup, and we concatenate it with an item from the equivalence class of main courses, which is then concatenated with an item from the class of desserts, so that our order to the waiter constitutes a sort of sentence.... A national form of life is determined by the equivalence classes (paradigms) and concatenations the nationalist society offers its members in every area of life ...
> (Margalit, 1997, pp. 82-3).

> As the idea of the nation-state achieved its hegemony as a territorial, all-purpose political organization, it affected aspects of citizens' identity. Out of the myriad ways in which each person can be characterized, one's territorial location in a nation has come to assume overwhelming importance ... The territorial nation has been the bundle or basket into which other facets of our lives are fit ... In a restaurant, one can order '*a la carte*'; but as far as our identities are concerned, we must take what nations have bundled together, which amounts to '*table d'hote*' ... [I] will develop a vision in which our choices will partially redress the balance between *a la carte* and *table d'hote*. Government *a la carte* will seem natural to citizens in the twenty-first century.'
> (Elkins, 1995, p. 29).

It has been noticed that liberal philosophy, though much concerned from the start with justifying the authority of states, has had little if anything to say in the way of justifying the territorial nature of states.[1] Although a world divided into territorial states was a still emerging phenomenon at the dawn of liberalism, that sovereignty should be organised territorially seems not to have been for early liberal thinkers an issue meriting much attention,[2] let alone a system in need of justification. Similar inattention characterises modern classics of philosophy, from Hart's *Concept of Law* to Rawls' *A Theory of Justice.*[3]

Of course, contemporary philosophers have wielded contractarian devices for purposes far beyond those of liberalism's founders. But although distributive justice has moved to the centre of their concerns, it is still the same territorial state, albeit grown considerably stouter with age, to which they have looked for the agency of distribution. And while some echoes of 'cosmopolitan justice' have resonated since Grotius and Kant, those have tended to be confined to aspirations for peaceful relations between states, not global social or economic justice, let alone a global justice that would put in question territorial statehood.

Recently, in particular with the end of the Cold War, an assortment of challenges to the presumption of territorial sovereignty has issued forth from many disciplines, including from a handful of philosophers questioning the normative justification of this presumption. The challenges posed are as diverse as their sources, but appear to be commonly inspired by the conviction that '[t]he human future suddenly seems open' (Pogge, 1992, p. 48). I want briefly to survey some of these sources, and to separate a few of the sorts of questions being asked. I shall then concentrate on one particular challenge, attempt to defend a notion of territorial sovereignty against it, and finally suggest some issues about territorial rights emerging from that defense, exploration of which cannot be pursued here. But it is useful to begin with some preliminary conceptual clarifications.

Territoriality has been defined as 'the attempt by an individual or group to affect, influence, or control people, phenomena, and relationships, by delimiting and asserting control over a geographic area' (Sack, 1986, p. 19). Territorial strategies, in this sense, can range from the posting of non-smoking signs in a room or building, to the disallowing of small children into a part of the house with breakable or dangerous objects or a room to be kept clean for guests (or into the deep end of the swimming pool), the defense by criminal or youth gangs of their 'turf', zoning laws within a city or country, the erection of borders between two countries, or the declaration of supra-state zones, whether of free trade, military alliance, or environmental treaty. All these exhibit territoriality as defined above.

Three aspects of territoriality generally related to state sovereignty are exclusivity, contiguity, and durability.[4] Exclusivity generally involves controlling access to the territory and things within in it (Sack, 1986, p. 22), though it can also involve attempts to block access to the outside by restraining those within (as, say, various dictatorships do by restricting emigration or foreign travel of their subjects). With regard to states, it includes what is often called external sovereignty: that no other state's laws can apply or be enforced within its boundaries.

Contiguity has in practice admitted of exceptions, from Alaska to the Spanish enclave of Llivia within France and the Italian Campione d'Italia within Switzerland,[5] but these have tended to be rather rule-proving in the centuries since Westphalia.

Another aspect of the territoriality of states is the durability of sovereignty over a territory. Introduction of this essentially temporal concept[6] is not intended to deny that borders are sometimes modified, nor even radically expanded and contracted, as, say, the borders of the British Empire. Nor, of course, does it preclude the possibility of states coming into and passing out of existence. But at the heart of normative debates about sovereignty are claims to enduring control over some home base – claims which figure prominently in both nationalist and some cosmopolitan-liberal justifications.[7] It seems to be a necessary feature of territorial sovereignty that it have temporal duration; if boundaries could be altered at any time according to whim, or to the principle that society (including its boundaries) should be 'as voluntary a scheme as possible' (Rawls, 1971) the distinction between territorial and non-territorial authority would collapse. Durable territoriality thus expresses an intersection between space and time. It is useful to have this concept, therefore, in discussing territorial sovereignty.

Finally, it is important to mention an aspect of state sovereignty not inherently territorial, but which in the case of existing states presumes or builds upon the territorial aspects just enumerated. I call this feature clustering. Sovereign states are complements or clusters of identically-bounded administrative jurisdictions.[8] Thus, defense, health and welfare, unemployment insurance, national income policy, and so forth, are functions or jurisdictions usually clustered together by a single sovereign state; because the state is territorial, the jurisdictions are identically bounded.

With these distinctions at hand, we can begin to sort out some possible theoretical alternatives to sovereign territorial states, which actual critics sometimes fail to distinguish. First, political authority, at least conceptually, need not have any of the aspects of territoriality outlined above. It could be organised such that 'citizens' were identified and governed exclusively by who they were, not where they lived. In a given territory, rather than one set of laws applying to everyone within it, different sets of laws would apply to the respective citizens governed by them. Thus, Saudi citizens in the British Isles could have their hands amputated for stealing, while British citizens in the Arabian peninsula would be immune to such punishments, but subject to laws, say, prohibiting sexual harassment.[9] Here, neither exclusivity, contiguity nor durability obtain, and the 'state', such as it is, moves wherever its citizens move. Who would administer and enforce the laws in such a regime? Who would pay for roads and bridges in a given territory, and who would be eligible to use them? These and other questions could be answered in a variety of ways; rather than speculate about them here, however, my immediate purpose is simply to present this *extreme non-territoriality* (as I will call it) as a conceptual possibility.[10]

Another possibility is to retain exclusivity, but to relax the other two territorial conditions, so that new states could be formed or dissolved at ease, whether as enclaves or otherwise. Alternatively, one could retain durability in the sense of a permanent base, but relax exclusivity by allowing relatively free immigration and enabling non-citizens to be governed to some extent by their own laws. Exclusivity, of course, admits of degrees, as is the case even with current practice (think of foreign embassies or autonomous areas, for instance).

Yet another possibility, which I will discuss at some length, does not explicitly challenge the *territoriality*, as I have defined it, of individual government functions, but declusters the single sovereign state into different functions with different administrative boundaries.[11] Indirect implications of this arrangement for the exclusivity aspect will be examined later. Here we may simply note that challenges to the clustered sovereign state can be made without denying the desirability of administering discrete functions territorially (and for reasons independent of territoriality *per se*), but such that the territoriality of the state is not unaffected. This explains why it is necessary to address questions about the meaning and justification of sovereignty when attempting to analyse rights to territory.

These possibilities are of course not exhaustive of the alternatives to a sovereign territorial state, but are helpful reference points for the discussion below. I turn now to the brief general survey. As stated above, sources, motivations, and concerns have been diverse, though interrelated. First, the end of the Cold War, coupled with various trends that go under the catch phrase 'globalisation', have created a unique sense of possibility. The trends identified with globalisation are primarily developments in communications, unprecedented movement of people and capital across borders, the latter facilitated by the removal of trade barriers, and the concomitant development of global commodities markets. The actual changes as well as possibilities opened up have encouraged philosophers and others to think more concretely in terms of institutional as opposed to mere ethical cosmopolitanism. Against this background, sovereign states are increasingly viewed as impediments to the development of international institutions suited to the global scope of such concerns as world peace, human rights monitoring and enforcement, environmental protection, global development and for some, distributive justice.

Some writers, consequently, call for a single global state (e.g., among philosophers, Nielsen, 1988). Others, though concerned to articulate a version of institutional cosmopolitanism, reject that view (Beitz, 1979; Pogge, 1992; O'Neill, 1994) on the grounds that the proposed concentration of power would, if anything, reproduce the evils of a sovereign state on a grand scale. I shall not discuss this question here.

A similarly motivated view regards nation-state sovereignty as an obstacle to cosmopolitan justice (Luban, 1985a, 1985b); institutionally, it regards the sovereign state system as inimical to the desirable development of a robust international legal system with effective powers of enforcement, and broad jurisdiction in the areas of human rights protection and prevention of war. The chief concern of this debate revolves around the rights and duties of intervention. This issue is also largely beyond the concern of this paper, but a conceptual clarification is in order. The view that sovereignty is incompatible with international mechanisms of enforcement is most closely associated in international relations with realist and neorealist conceptual coupling of state sovereignty with international 'anarchy',[12] and in jurisprudence with the Austinian view that international law was strictly speaking not law at all as it was not backed up by effective sanctions. Both points were challenged by Hart. The Austinian claim is unconnected with present concerns, but regarding the former point, Hart commented that, when speaking of sovereign states,

> the word 'sovereign' means here no more than 'independent'; and, like the latter, is negative in force: a sovereign state is one not subject to certain types of control, and its sovereignty is that area of conduct in which it is autonomous....For if in fact we find that there exists among states a given form of international authority, the sovereignty of states is to that extent limited, and it has just that extent which the rules allow. (Hart, 1994, p. 223).[13]

As a citizen can be free yet constrained by laws, a state can be sovereign within a legal system (Hart, 1994, p. 223).[14]

Another debate concerns whether the European Union (and possibly other trading blocks) has already effected the demise of sovereignty (as argued, for instance, by Neil MacCormick, 1993).[15] While the conceptual question is not of particular interest for this essay, some normative aspects are tangentially related. (For instance, the question might be seen as turning on whether member states have retained a monopoly of force on their respective territories, or whether the supra-state power concentrated in Brussels already challenges that, along with the costs which would be incurred by a member state withdrawing from the Union. The issues of whether there is a monopoly of force and who has it are related, though not addressed explicitly, in the discussion below of Pogge's proposal to shift the power of immigration control downward to the local level).

A further controversy centres on identity. Some writers loosely labelled 'postmodernist', others advocating cultural cosmopolitanism (e.g. Waldron, Griffin), have claimed that identity is no longer nation-centred, but constituted from diverse sources removed from their historical and geographical contexts. This claim is often accompanied by a skepticism regarding the normative significance of national borders, given the presumption of ever diminishing cultural differences across them (a process accelerated by the new communications technologies and global mass consumption of uniformly standardized commodities, including overtly cultural ones like film and music).

A different view, which shall be the focus of the remainder of this essay, does not share the presumption of prevailing cultural cosmopolitanism. It holds that sovereign states, as nodes of concentrated power, can be overwhelming foci of their members' allegiances, sentiments, loyalties and identities. But it laments this fact, and calls for a dispersal or diffusion of sovereignty for reasons of peace and security, cosmopolitan justice, and ecological well-being (Pogge, 1992, pp. 61-4; O'Neill 1994, pp. 72-3; Beitz, 1979; Elkins, 1995). In this group, various proposals have been tabled about how to disperse sovereignty. All agree, however, that different governmental functions might have different optimal territorial shapes, while others need not be administered territorially at all (Pogge, 1992; O'Neill, 1994; Elkins, 1995). Moreover, if the 'unbundling' of functions leads to a deconstruction of national identity, or a drastic reduction in its significance, all the better for peace and human rights the world over. And the sooner one departs from the presumption that sovereign states have exclusive rights over territories and everything within them, the clearer one will perceive the possibility of institutional realignment according to the requirements of ethical cosmopolitanism.[16]

After reviewing the claims and arguments of this general view in some more detail, I will attempt to show some of its weaknesses and limitations. Rather than declaim reactionary paeans to the nation-state *per se*, I shall seek to show that proponents of declustering overlook certain issues and problems, confrontation with which indicates formidable constraints on the degree of desirable declustering. I shall conclude by mentioning, without pursuing it, one more set of related issues, namely those revolving around questions of territorial rights.

Declustering

Advocates of declustering take the high moral ground, seeking to rid us of outmoded ways of thinking that impede progress in human rights, global justice, environmental protection, prevention or elimination of war, and narrowing the gap between rich and poor countries. It is necessary 'to corrode the presumptiveness of unconscious assumptions – whether about territoriality, the state, or personal identities' (Elkins, 1995, p. 261). The most deeply embedded prevailing assumptions are that states should be massive concentrations of power exercising exclusive control over their own territories. '[W]ithin their own territories, national governments are free to do virtually anything they like. Such governments therefore have very powerful incentives and very broad opportunities to develop their military might. This is bound to lead to the further proliferation of nuclear, biological, chemical, and conventional weapons of mass destruction. And in a world in which dozens of competing national governments control such weapons, the outbreak of devastating wars is only a matter of time' (Pogge, 1992, p. 62). War will be made less likely by the declustering of sovereignty. This will be because there will be less at stake when power is diffuse (Pogge, 1992, p. 62) or because it will be more difficult to mobilise people with multiple and conflicting identities, loyalties, and memberships (Elkins, 1995, p. 262).

Another problem is oppression: 'Under the current global regime, national governments are effectively free to control 'their' populations in whatever way they see fit. Many make extensive use of this freedom by torturing and murdering their domestic opponents, censoring information, suppressing and subverting democratic procedures, prohibiting emigration, and so forth. This problem could be reduced through a vertical dispersal of sovereignty over various layers of political units that would check and balance one another as well as publicize one another's abuses' (Pogge, 1992). Again, '[e]xcess concentration of power within states is dangerous; so is excess independence of states from one another' (O'Neill, 1994, p.72).

The root of most evil, it seems, is the concentrated power of the sovereign territorial state. What is needed is to break apart the powerful link of government functions, nations, and territories. 'If state functions are to a significant degree decoupled from the nation, then perhaps one can imagine that the nation itself could be decoupled from territory' (Elkins, 1995, p.261). Just because some particular functions are better administered territorially, that is no reason to presume a division of the world into sovereign territorial states. 'Would it not make more sense to start with functional rather than territorial divisions of the tasks of government? And if we did so, would not the optimal territorial arrangements probably differ for different types of governmental function?' (O'Neill, 1994, p.72).

These passages do not exhaust the arguments presented by these authors; rather, they are presented in order to convey converging lines of argumentation. There are also divergences. O'Neill is most interested in disengaging different functions from each other and from a common territorial base. Pogge favours 'nested' units vertically dispersed, which is to say, some functions performed by overarching global administration, within which are nested regional and state level units, within which local units – some as small as neighbourhoods – assume new functions. Effectively, this means pushing some functions presently held by states upwards, and others downwards to deconcentrate the state.

Elkins, by contrast, is keen on non-territorial solutions as far as possible, is uninhibited by the prospect that government functions might increasingly resemble private services (or indeed be replaced by them), and is not averse to engaging in futuristic speculation about the harnessing of new technologies to make government services more 'customized'.

Reclustering

I want to turn now to consider some reasons both for administering functions territorially, and for clustering them in identically bounded jurisdictions. If these reasons hold good, they will cast at least some doubt on the desirability of the various proposals outlined above, notwithstanding their differences. I will begin with an argument about public goods, moving from there to considerations about efficiency, community, and the requisites of democratic participation.

Some goods, I take it as uncontroversial among the authors discussed,[17] are public goods. That is to say, they cannot be enjoyed by anyone without everyone being able to enjoy them. There is a fairly wide consensus that coercive taxation would be justified to finance production of these goods to the extent that would-be freeriders would choose to pay their share of the production if they couldn't freeride (Rawls, 1971, p. 267).[18] Infrastructures for water and electricity supply, roads and railways, public transport, military defense (assuming there are still some threats in the world if we start from the here and now), are some of the more obvious candidates for the sort of public goods likely to be considered essential by nearly everyone in modern societies.

Public goods are commonly said to be indivisible, but this feature conceals another one, namely that they are inherently territorial. That is to say, indivisibility implies that they are goods which all those residing in the territory where they were enjoyed would benefit from as well. (Notice that it is proximal residence, not common citizenship, which for most such goods makes the enjoyment of their benefit collective). The territorial feature is mentioned only in passing, if at all, in classical discussions of public goods (Rawls, 1971; Buchanan, 1968), but that seems to me to be because it is so obvious as to be taken for granted.

Restating the argument, then, the production of public goods requires coercively enforced taxation because everyone would want to be assured that as few as possible in the territory would freeride. Coercive taxation within the territory, however, implies a sovereign over it, as Rawls states:

> Each person's willingness to contribute is contingent upon the contribution of the others. Therefore to maintain public confidence in the scheme that is superior from everyone's point of view, or better anyway than the situation that would obtain in its absence, some device for administering fines and penalties must be established. It is here that the mere existence of an effective sovereign, or even the general belief in his efficacy, has a crucial role (Rawls, 1971, p.270).

If we grant, then, that there are some public goods, and that they are to be produced fairly, we have already presupposed an elaborate legal system, including courts, enforcement agencies, and public administration (an Internal Revenue Service); if we are furthermore democrats, we require in addition an elected legislature ultimately responsible for decisions about which goods to produce and how much. Importantly, however, it also follows that all of these will necessarily have identically bounded jurisdictions. This complex of agencies and administrations would follow even from a single essential public good, as each of the institutions mentioned is responsible for the same territory where the public goods will be enjoyed. Since there is a multiplicity of public goods, the question might arise whether each good should have its own parliamentary jurisdiction, and proper public and legal administration. But even to suggest this is enough to demonstrate its absurdity; the sheer inefficiency would be such as to make the very clustering of functions itself a public good. But there are more aspects to consider.

One of the most essential public goods is an enforced criminal code. Indeed this is also an inherently public or collective good (Raz, 1986, pp. 198-9) in that no futurist technology will ever be able to 'customise' the supply of its benefits. For a criminal code to work in a democracy, we require not only an elaborate legal system, lawyers and judges, and law schools, but also a broad range of institutions and practices which undergird these, from media to universities. In short, we require a community. But to be a well-functioning community, its elements have to work together according to shared norms and interlocking or coordinated functions. The taxation system supporting other public goods has to be integrated into the same legal code and enforced by the same agencies as those enforcing the criminal code, and it in turn has to finance many of the institutions required for the legal system to function.

The financing alone of public goods needs to be centralised in a modern society. It is necessary to have a centralised investment fund which can be shifted to specific functions according to changing need. That is, one needs a state budget, not merely function budgets. That would require an overarching body that can move investments across functions, deciding in a given year, say, to increase the health budget while cutting back in, say, road construction. In a simplified world in which the only public services were health and public highways, if the health and road jurisdictions did not coincide, and were not brought under some central authority, someone who lived in the health jurisdiction at a time when it had been hit with unforeseen costs could expect no succour from the other public fund, whatever the consequences. A common budget is thus itself a public good. It in turn would require taxation to be centralised, and again, a centralised legal framework regulating taxation.

This brings us to a central shortcoming shared by all the declustering/dispersal theories of sovereignty: They can all be convicted of what one might call the function-atomist fallacy. O'Neill looks at each function individually and asks, What is the optimal territorial arrangement for *it*? Pogge asks: 'when one thinks about it more carefully, it turns out to be surprisingly difficult to come up with examples of indivisible governmental functions. Eminent domain, economic policy, foreign policy, judicial review; the control of raw materials, security forces, education, health care, and income support; the regulation and taxation of resource extraction and pollution, of work and consumption can all be handled at various levels ... So what are the governmental functions that supposedly are vertically indivisible? Second, is their indivisibility supposed to be derived from a conceptual insight, from empirical exigencies, or from moral desiderata? And which ones?' (Pogge, 1992, p. 60).

The answer is that while none may be indivisible, there are reasons, both empirical and moral, pulling against division. The empirical ones have to do with efficient functioning; it is an empirical fact about our world that it has risks, which good governments seek to ensure against, and that our resources (including time) are scarce, so that all things equal we desire to avoid duplication. Chief among the moral reasons are equal treatment and democratic control. In a modern society, democratic participation varies, among other variables, according to the importance of the level of government: the more concentrated the power of the level, the higher the participation.[19] Typically, participation, as measured by voter turn out, media attention, and party membership, is highest for state-level elections. It seems a safe surmise that all else equal, the more diffuse sovereignty were, the less popular participation there would be. Oscar Wilde once remarked that socialism wouldn't work, because there was not enough time in the day for all the meetings that would be required. Here the point is not about socialism, nor whether all necessary meetings could be held. Rather, if sovereignty were diffuse yet all necessary meetings somehow held, who would attend them? And if elections were held, who would vote in them?

It is possible, then, that clustering political authority facilitates democracy as well as tyranny. In the bustle and complexity of modern life, few have time or inclination to follow the politics of the sewage administration, the road construction authority, the agricultural board, and so forth. But when all these are ordered in a structure reaching an apex, interest, commitment, and allegiance tend to increase (if at the cost of each individual having far less actual control). Pogge and Elkins implicitly acknowledge this in allowing that national identity will be far less important when sovereignty is diffuse. The problem is that the political community that sustained identity will be less important as well.

If government functions become diffuse and disconnected, and if interest, participation, and allegiance similarly decline, these functions will increasingly resemble private services. This eventuality might leave market enthusiasts (Elkins, 1995, pp. 79ff.) unperturbed. But consumer demand as a mechanism of ensuring accountability is not always a satisfactory substitute for public deliberation about desirable policy. The different forms of declustering, including vertical diffusion, would seem to come at the cost of abandoning an integrated community sharing a range of fundamental values, against the background of which it deliberates on public policy. An example provided by Pogge may illustrate this.

Pogge takes issue with Walzer, who wrote: 'At some level of political organization something like the sovereign state must take shape and claim the authority to make its own admissions policy, to control and sometimes to restrain the flow of immigrants' (Walzer, 1981, p. 10). The alternative, as Sidgwick had said, was 'not ... to create a world without walls, but rather to create a thousand petty fortresses' (Walzer, 1981, p. 9). Therefore, 'Only if the state makes a selection among would-be members and guarantees the loyalty, security, and welfare of the individuals it selects, can local communities take shape as 'indifferent' associations, determined only by personal preference and market capacity' (Walzer, 1981, p. 9). Somewhat intrepidly,[20] Pogge defends the neighbourhood restriction policy against the state; immigration control is a function 'much better served still' if pushed down from the state to the neighbourhood level. Pogge and Walzer agree that territorial exclusivity is justified to protect cultures; presumably they might also agree that there is a trade-off here between the value of freedom (for outsiders), which must be restricted, and the value of preserving the culture.

So what is at stake between them? If Pogge were accused of sanctioning intolerance and ghettoes, he would have available the reply that Walzer's state is a ghetto writ large, practising intolerance on a grand scale. But there are two points that weigh heavily, in my view, in favour of the ghetto writ large. First, there is an issue in need of clarification. Pogge does not state whether the policy of giving neighbourhoods control over immigration should be accompanied by giving them the force to back up this jurisdiction. In other words, he does not say whether he advocates breaking up the monopoly of legitimate force on a given territory that states, as Weber famously defined them, enjoy. The tenor of the discussion on immigration does not appear to recommend a redistribution of force, wisely, it would seem, given the horrific consequences that might result from each neighbourhood having its own militia. On the other hand, the general remarks cited earlier critical of the state monopoly of power would seem vitiated were they not accompanied by a call to break up this monopoly. But however one views the monopoly, it would surely be a worse situation if every clan, neighbourhood, and block could take up arms against its neighbour. Rather than going beyond the state, we would be back in a Hobbesian state of nature; indeed, while critics of classical contractarians raised doubts about whether a state of nature ever existed, we would now be in the business of creating it. But if, on a more charitable reading, Pogge means merely to derogate powers over immigration to neighbourhoods while the state maintains overall responsibility of enforcement, the question would then be whether the state would retain the duty and right to enforce hard won principles of desegregation, freedom of movement and access.

This brings us to the second point, namely that however much liberal national states are discriminatory in their immigration policy – and it remains a moot question how much discrimination is permissible on grounds of maintaining a national identity and favouring those with whom one has a special relationship – most such states are diverse enough that, to be liberal, they must safeguard against any internal discrimination. The difference in scale, then, between the ghettoes writ large and small, arguably translates into a difference in quality. Even the sort of selectiveness in immigration of the large ghetto and the small are bound to be different, as in the former case the policy ultimately must be defended to a large and already diverse public, against the background of non-discriminatory principles accepted by liberal courts. This does not guarantee a generous immigration policy, but it does ensure that a range of voices will at least be heard, that views will be debated in public, and that there will be some pressure to make external policy consistent with the internal. In such circumstances, chances are much greater that there will be at least a fair degree of internal tolerance, and possibly a more rational immigration policy. If neighbourhoods, on the other hand, have authority to exercise territorial exclusivity, they need consider no more than the narrowest interests of their respective members. Intolerance would breed as barriers were erected; pedestrians and prospective homebuyers would have to steer clear of xenophobic vicinities.[21]

Freedom of mobility, and a culture and legal practice of toleration, are again public goods that are threatened by function atomism. If we could separate the function of immigration control from the sort of community that could sustain toleration, we might come up with various answers to the question of which level is the optimal one to control this jurisdiction. If we take a broader view, however, or if we regard optimality itself in terms of the wide range of values that it is desirable to promote, then we are again moved in the direction of integrating this jurisdiction into the cluster of jurisdictions maintaining the community as a whole, that is, the community of the (re)clustered state.

To summarise briefly, then, critics of sovereign clustering neglect features of it, some of which contribute to, and some which even seem indispensable for, democratic community, the administration of justice, fair and efficient governance, and civic virtue. That there could be gains or losses from the realignment of this or that particular function is not in dispute. But that the declustering of sovereignty into myriad shapes or levels would be a clear benefit, let alone hold out the promise of remedy for the primary evils of the age, seems an unsubstantiated claim at best.

Finally, there is space merely to gesture toward some possible implications of the questions discussed here for the debates over territorial rights, on the one hand, and national identity on the other. These debates have been reinvigorated by increasing concerns about global justice, realignments of national borders with the end of European communism, and accompanying philosophical interest in the intersection between liberal and nationalist principles. If it is indeed the case, as I have tried to argue here, that there are limitations to desirable declustering of states, then certain implications will no doubt follow about territorial rights and national identity. First, if a territorial state remains the best way of attaining various public goods, then the primary value of territories will remain the instrumental value of enabling self-government. This value of territory is not usually acknowledged in the debate about territorial rights. Writers concerned with distributive justice and often influenced by economics regard territories primarily as repositories of economically valuable resources, including simple real estate (e.g. Steiner, 1994). Those concerned with self-determination, especially if they have read widely in the sociology of nationalism, tend to construe the value of territories in terms of their meaningfulness to nations, both as loci of significant historical events in the collective memory, and as diachronically continuous topographies informing folklore and the cultural imagination. To these one could no doubt add the military and 'geo-political' value of territories, which are the focus of the discipline of international relations. However, if it is necessary to cluster identically-bounded functions in order to meet fundamental requirements of efficiency and justice, and to ensure sufficient democratic participation (as has been argued herein), then the value of territory has to be reconceived. If there are any groups having strong claims to the right of self-government, then it will now follow that they derivatively have strong claims to the territory on which that self-government is to be established. Notice that the justification of this claim is very different from that given by Rawls (1993b). Rawls argues that states have rights to territories deriving from the advantages of giving them the responsibility for maintaining and developing exclusive parcels of land. This justification is the same as that for the institution of property: 'Unless a definite agent is given responsibility for maintaining an asset and bears the loss for not doing so, that asset tends to deteriorate. In this case the asset is the people's territory and its capacity to sustain them in perpetuity; the agent is the people themselves as politically organized' (Rawls, 1993b, p. 57).

Here the right is a general utilitarian one, albeit with an ecological flavour, analogous to Aristotle's argument for private property in *The*

Politics, that 'Men pay most attention to what is their own' (1262). On its face, it seems to allow that if some other agent (say a colonial power) could develop that same land more, it would be all to the good. It also fails to clarify (again, as it stands) who are the relevant reapers of the advantages of asset maintenance. Is it all of humanity, or the agents themselves? Also, what is entailed in this case by 'maintaining an asset'; that is, who maintained their assets better, indigenous hunter-gatherers or modern industrial states? I don't wish to imply that Rawls cannot answer these questions satisfactorily (for instance, he prohibits conquest on other grounds). But I wish to distinguish between this form of justification of the general value (to whom?) of sovereign rights to territory and the specific value, on the self-government argument suggested above, of a group's territory to it.

I have discussed self-determination elsewhere (Kofman, 1998; Kofman, 2000), and unfortunately cannot pursue it further here. It may be worth just mentioning, though, that if the considerations against declustering have merit, then it will be undesirable, and perhaps not possible, to deconstruct identity in the way proposed by advocates of declustering, and that groups with historical-cultural identities will retain fundamental interests in the instrumental value of territories for self-determination. The argument here will be very different from some standard ones in favour of maintaining national identity. The one quoted by Margalit as the epigraph to this chapter, for instance, holds that national identities provide their bearers with an arrangement of options, and that presumably it is good for them to have such an arrangement. But there are an infinite variety of arrangements of options, both within states and in a world of deconstructed or declustered former states. Why should a cultural cosmopolitan not take full advantage of the vast gamut of possibilities in a world of declustered, separately administered functions?

To argue, that is, simply that one needs an identity and that a national state provides one is too short a way with the arguments for declustering. But if declustering turns out to be undesirable on wholly independent grounds (as suggested here), then deconstructing identity – at any rate to the point where citizens cease to feel allegiance to one another, and therefore allegiance to their common institutions – will arguably be undesirable as well. Here a certain parallel suggests itself between the arguments presented here, and those, as Miller puts it, in favour of national self-determination from the state-to-nation direction of reasoning. Those arguments take statehood largely for granted (or see the only alternative to it as anarchy) and then run as follows: for states efficaciously and with a minimum of coercion to carry out various of their essential functions, mutual trust between the citizens in a state is required; this trust is most strongly engendered when the citizenry also shares a national identity. Thus, in order for public goods to be provided voluntary co-operation and therefore trust is necessary. Even a minimal night-watchman state requires a degree of trust necessary 'to support the ground rules of a market: individuals must have confidence in one another to deal fairly, to keep contracts, and to refrain from using their industrial or financial muscle to oblige the state to intervene in the market on their behalf' (Miller, 1995, pp. 92-93). Moreover, for redistributive social policies to be effective a shared identity among citizenry is again required; otherwise, mutual antagonism and competition will impede the willingness to make the necessary sacrifices for the sake of justice. Furthermore, the notion of deliberative democracy, whereby citizens debate and negotiate in good faith according to publicly defensible reasons, and compromise in order to reach consensus, also requires a degree of trust among the negotiators (Miller, 1995, pp. 93-97).

While there is an obvious parallel between these arguments and those presented above against declustering, they are also importantly distinct. The declustering argument holds that it is necessary to keep a degree of concentrated statehood intact in order to provide public goods and ensure a satisfactory level of democratic participation in governance. The state-to-nation self-determination argument, on the other hand, holds that states must have a shared nationality in order to achieve the same ends. The first is an argument for states (against declustering), the second an argument for making states into nation-states. But the similarity or difference between them turns on the degree to which the patriotic or communal allegiance need be, or be regarded, as 'national' (and what that entails). As against the arguments of Miller above, it might be the case that strategic and ethical reasoning together with the fostering of social norms and sanctions would create a sufficient degree of trust to enable the provision of public goods, the implementation of redistributive schemes, and the realisation of some participatory and deliberative democratic ideals. Indeed, it is arguably preferable to rely on these communal buttresses rather than on a shared national/cultural identity, for even the most culturally homogeneous state will have minorities, if only from immigration, and Miller's arguments seems to render problematic how such minorities will be able to benefit from redistributive schemes and to be included in democratic deliberation, if the requisite 'mutual trust' is based primarily on a national/cultural identity. The argument of this chapter, however, is first of all in favour of the continuation of states against advocates of declustering, and secondarily can lend support to notions of shared identity, but only to the extent that these are necessary to sustain states and make their production of public goods viable. Nothing in this argument *requires* that such identities be more than patriotic as opposed to culturally homogeneous. Elsewhere I have argued that a stronger argument for national self-determination is in the nation-to-state direction; that is, given that states exist, national groups ought to have rights to form their own independent states when they deem this advantageous to the flourishing of their distinct identities. Again, we can only gesture towards these arguments here; the focus has been on whether we require states in the fist place, and the suggestion has been the perhaps surprising one that normatively speaking, of all possible points of view, recent philosophical invitations to dance on the graves of the modern state may have been issued prematurely.

Notes

1 '[T]he notion of territorial dominion as a major ingredient in the concept of statehood ... is a feature given only passing notice by philosophers. The focus of orthodox political philosophy has been the connections between citizen and government, a relationship which would appear to have no geographical component whatever' (Fain, 1972, p. 18). Thomas Baldwin, after surveying the common acknowledgement by political and legal theorists that territoriality is an essential component of states, observes: 'What none of this justifies, however, is the assumption that the territorial conception of the state has legitimate application.' (Baldwin, 1992). The point is also implicit in Onora O'Neill's observation: 'Boundaries creep into political philosophy without us noticing. For example, within the liberal tradition of political discourse a theory of justice is typically employed to give some account of universal rights and of the limits of legitimate state powers, yet before we know it we are talking about the powers not of the state but of *states*.' (Though one alternative to a plurality of states is a global state, O'Neill considers primarily the possibility of breaking up sovereignty into jurisdictions of varying territory, as discussed below – (O'Neill, 1994)).

2 John Locke might seem an exception, as he appears absorbed with the role of landed estates in the constitution of state authority. But (what might be called) the standard 'jigsaw' interpretation of Locke's doctrine of territoriality, whereby the state's territory is assembled jigsaw-like from the estates of consenting citizens, fails to explain two anomalies: (1) that Locke considers the laws of the state to apply to the Commons, and (2) that he denies that an emigrant may take his landed property with him, so to speak; that is, he has no right of secession. Though there is no room to argue it here, I think a better interpretation, in that it accommodates the anomalies without ascribing to him the jigsaw view that he nowhere states, is that Locke naturally assumed without justification that political authority must be continuously territorial and stable

over time. These assumptions were becoming standard in the century in which the Peace of Westphalia (1648) formalised the emerging doctrine of territorial sovereignty.

3 Although Rawls' recent essay 'The Law of Peoples' has begun to address it.

4 The first two are discussed by Elkins (1995, p. 13), who also adds continuity: the non-embeddedness of enclaves within other nations. Continuity is usually implied by contiguity, since if one nation had an enclave within it (rendering it discontinuous), the other nation whose enclave it was would be non-contiguous. The exception is an enclave constituting an entire state.

5 The enclaves are cited by Gauthier (1994, p. 362).

6 I do not use 'continuity', meaning the temporal sense, so as not to be confused with the spatial sense (see note 4 above).

7 For instance, Rawls can be said to invoke it in his recent justification of the enduring control by peoples of the territories in which they reside (Rawls, 1993b).

It is also arguably the case that international law builds durability into its definition of statehood. The Montevideo Convention on Rights and Duties of States (1933) stipulates that a 'state as a person of international law should possess the following qualifications: (a) a permanent population; (b) a defined territory; (c) a government; and (d) a capacity to enter into relations with other states' (quoted in Dixon, 1996, p. 100). The first two features combine with the third (giving rise to the fourth) to incorporate the durability or relative permanence of governance over a given territory.

8 Some writers (e.g. Elkins, 1995) use the terms 'bundling' and 'unbundling', but as I have used 'clustering' elsewhere, I continue with it here and its antonym 'declustering'. I use the bulkier term 'identically-bounded', rather than 'congruent' employed by other writers because, strictly speaking, congruent territories need not have identical boundaries at all. A land-locked province within India can be congruent with Britain thousands of miles away; that means simply that if it were cut out of a map it would fit nicely onto the northern European island.

9 Compare this with a recent judgement of a French court convicting an African woman residing in France to eight years imprisonment for the practice of female circumcision or 'female genital mutilation', as the courts described it.

10 Although I know of no explicit proposal to organise political authority in this way, one might take the thrust of various criticisms of territoriality as pointing in this direction. (I owe this point to David Miller). A more widely discussed notion of extreme non-territoriality with parallels to political non-territoriality, is non-territorial identity. This is a major theme of postmodernism, which I will mention herein only in passing.

11 This is suggested, for example, by O'Neill (1994, pp. 72-3) and in another way by Pogge (1992).

12 Summarising the theory of the leading neo-realist, Kenneth Waltz, John Ruggie states that 'the international system is formed much like a market: it is individualistic in origin, and more or less spontaneously generated as a

byproduct of the actions of its constitutive units ... collaboration occurs 'only in ways strongly conditioned by' the structure of anarchy' (Ruggie, 1986).

13 For similar comments, see Akehurst, (1970, pp. 15-6); Brownlie, (1990); and Dixon, (1996).

14 Perhaps a point could be reached in the hypothetical reinforcement *and centralisation* of international law, concomitant with an attenuation of sovereignty, such that it would become less meaningful to speak of the sovereignty of states. Such a suggestion was in fact made by Hans Morgenthau, dean of mid-century realists. He held that sovereignty was compatible with international law such as it was, but could be undermined by a more robust legal system. However, since states would be unwilling to give up any of their sovereignty, international law would likely remain decentralized, weak and ineffective (Morgenthau, 1967, p. 300).

15 There are already some dozen books, articles, and chapters in print bearing titles like `Beyond Sovereignty', and many more that could do so. Most of their authors see sovereignty already in decline; nearly all rejoice in that recognition. To mention a few: Neil MacCormick, 'Beyond the Sovereign State' (1993); David Elkins, *Beyond Sovereignty: Territory and Political Economy in the Twenty-First Century*, (1995); Marvin Soroos, *Beyond Sovereignty: The Challenge of Global Policy* (1986); Thom Kuehls, *Beyond Sovereign Territory: The Space of Ecopolitics* (1996); Harold Hagemann, *Beyond the Nation-State* (1997); John Hoffman, *Beyond the State: An Introductory Critique* (1995); 'The End of the Affair?', Chapter 5 of Ross Poole, *Nation and Identity* (1999). But see also Anthony D. Smith, 'Beyond National Identity?' in *National Identity* (1991), who answers the question largely in the negative.

16 Ethical cosmopolitanism generally refers to the doctrine that all humans are of equal moral concern, and for each human moral agent. Doctrines otherwise as diverse as Kant's moral theory and Bentham's utilitarianism are examples of ethical cosmopolitanism. For Kant, each moral agent was obliged to test maxims of action according to their universalizability, while Bentham held *both* that a nation must neither 'do more evil to foreign nations taken together ... than it ... do good to itself', *nor* 'refuse to render positive services to a foreign nation, when the rendering of them would produce more good to the last mentioned nation, that it would produce evil to itself' (Bentham, 1843, p. 538). Ethical cosmopolitanism does not necessarily imply institutional cosmopolitanism (that there should be global institutions) or preclude special duties to co-nationals, compatriots, or family members.

17 This is explicitly discussed by Elkins (1995, p.79ff). Despite my disagreement with most of his conclusions, I am indebted to his discussion in Chapter 3, 'Economics and Territory', (Elkins, 1995).

18 Note that even Nozick's objections to the principles of fairness (Nozick, 1974, pp. 90-95) do not hold against the formulation here. His example of a public PA system set up without some person's consent (Nozick, 1974, pp. 93-4) relies on the assumption that the person might *not* have preferred the system, along with its obligations, had the entire proposition been put to him.

19 Note that we cannot say: 'the higher the level of government, the greater the participation'. Democratic participation in elections for the European Union, for instance, is so far extremely low despite it being a higher level of government in the sense of which we have been speaking. This merely illustrates the point that the critical determinant of participation levels is degree of concentration of power, not level of government per se.

20 Given that the history of the civil rights movement in the US has been in no small part a struggle against restricted neighbourhoods.

21 That this might sound familiar to visitors to some American cities is no objection to the claim; rather, it underscores how much worse the situation would be if xenophobes and racists could erect barriers by right.

References

Akehurst, M. (1970), *A Modern Introduction to International Law*, Routledge, London and New York.

Anton, J., Kustas, G.L. and Preus, A. (eds) (1990), *Essays in Ancient Greek Philosophy*, Albany.

Aristotle (1996), *The Politics* in Aristotle, *The Politics and The Constitution of Athens* (1996), S. Everson (ed.), Cambridge University Press, Cambridge

Baldwin, T. (1992), 'The Territorial State' in H. Gross, and R. Harrison (eds), *Jurisprudence: Cambridge Essays*, Clarendon Press, Oxford.

Beitz, C., Cohen, M., Scanlon, T., Simmons, A.J. (eds) (1985), *International Ethics*, Princeton University Press, Princeton.

Bentham, J. (1843), *Principles of International Law*, in *The Collected Works of Jeremy Bentham*, Vol. 2, J. Bowring (ed.), William Tait, Edinburgh.

Brilmayer, L. (1989), 'Consent, Contract, and Territory', *Minnesota Law Review*, Vol. 74, 1989.

Brilmayer, L. (1991), 'Secession and Self-Determination: A Territorialist Reinterpretation', *Yale Journal of International Law*, Vol. 16, No. 1, January 1991.

Brown, C. (ed.) (1994a), *Political Restructuring In Europe: Ethical Perspectives*, Routledge: London and New York.

Brown, C. (1994b), in Brown (ed.) 1994a.

Brownlie, I. (1966, 1990), *Principles of Public International Law*, Fourth Edition, Clarendon Press, Oxford.

Buchanan, A. (1993), *Secession*, Westview Press, Boulder, Colorado.

Buchanan, J. (1968), *The Demand and Suppply of Public Goods*, Rand McNally, Chicago.

Dahl, R. (1967), 'The City in the Future of Democracy', *American Science Review* 61 (Dec. 1967), pp. 953-70.

Dahl, R. and Tufte, E. (1973), *Size and Democracy*, Stanford University Press, Stanford.

Dixon, M. (1990, 1996), *Textbook on International Law*. 3rd edition, Blackstone, London.

Doyle, M. (1983), 'Kant, Liberal Legacies, and Foreign Affairs', *Philosophy and Public Affairs* vol. 12.

Elkins, D.J. (1995), *Beyond Sovereignty: Territory and Political Economy in the Twenty-First Century*, University of Toronto Press, Toronto.

Fain, H. (1972), 'The Idea of the State', *Nous* 6, pp. 15-26.

Gauthier, D. (1994), 'Breaking Up: An Essay on Secession', *Canadian Journal of Philosophy*, Vol. 24, No. 3, September 1994, pp. 357-372.

Gilbert, P. (1998), *The Philosophy of Nationalism*, Westview Press, Boulder, Colorado and Oxford.

Gross, H., and Harrison, R. (eds) (1992), *Jurisprudence: Cambridge Essays*, Clarendon Press, Oxford.

Hagemann, H. (1996), *Beyond the Nation-State*, North Holland, Amsterdam, Oxford.

Hart, H.L.A. (1961, 1994), *The Concept of Law*, 2nd edition, Clarendon Press, Oxford.

Hoffman, J. (1995), *Beyond the State: An Introductory Critique*, Polity Press, Cambridge

Hoffman, S. (1987), *Janus and Minerva*, Westview Press, Boulder, Colorado and London.

Irwin, T.H. (1991), 'Aristotle's Defense of Private Property', in Keyt and Miller (eds).

Keohane, R.O. (1986), *Neorealism and Its Critics*, Columbia University Press, New York.

Keyt, D. and. Miller, F.D. (eds) (1991), *A Companion to Aristotle's Politics*, Oxford University Press, Oxford.

Kofman, D. (1998), 'Rights of Secession', *Society*, July-August, 1998.

Kofman, D. (2000), 'Secession, Law, and Rights', *Human Rights Review*, 1:2,

Kuehls, T. (1996), *Beyond Sovereign Territory: The Space of Ecopolitics*, University of Minnesota Press, Minneapolis.

Locke, J. (1960, 1988), *Two Treatises of Government* (1698), P. Laslett (ed.), Cambridge University Press, Cambridge.

Luban, D. (1985a), 'Just War and Human Rights' in C. Beitz et al. (eds), *International Ethics*, Princeton University Press, Princeton.

Luban, D. (1985b), 'The Romance of the Nation-State', in C. Beitz, et al. (eds), *International Ethics*, Princeton University Press, Princeton.

Luper-Foy, S. (ed.) (1988), *Problems of International Justice*, Westview Press, Boulder, Colorado.

MacCormick, N. (1993), 'Beyond the Sovereign State', *The Modern Law Review*, Volume 56, No. 1, January 1993.

Margalit, A. (1997), 'The Moral Psychology of Nationalism' in R. McKim, and J. McMahan (eds), *The Morality of Nationalism*, Oxford University Press, Oxford.

Martin, R. (1993), *A System of Rights*, Clarendon Press, Oxford.

McKim, R. and McMahan, J. (eds.), *The Morality of Nationalism*, Oxford University Press:, Oxford.

Miller, D. (1994), 'The Nation-State: A Modest Defence' in C. Brown (ed.) (1994).

Miller, D. (1995). *On Nationality*, Clarendon Press, Oxford.

Miller, F.D. (1991), 'Aristotle on Property Rights', in J. Anton, , G.L. Kustas, and A. Preus (eds), *Essays in Ancient Greek Philosophy*, Albany.

Morgenthau, H. (1967), *Politics Among Nations*, Alfred A. Knopf, New York.

Nielsen, K. (1988), 'World Government, Security, and Global Justice', in S. Luper-Foy, (ed.), *Problems of International Justice*, Westview Press, Boulder, Colorado.

Nozick, R. (1974), *Anarchy, State, and Utopia*, Blackwell, Oxford.

O'Neill, O. (1994), 'Justice and Boundaries' in Brown (ed.).

Pogge, Thomas (1992), 'Cosmopolitanism and Sovereignty', *Ethics* 103 (October 1992): pp. 48-75.

Poole, R. (1999), *Nation and Identity*, Routledge, New York.

Rawls, J. (1971), *A Theory of Justice*, Oxford University Press, Oxford.

Rawls, J. (1993a, 1996), *Political Liberalism*, Columbia University Press, New York.

Rawls, J. (1993b), 'The Law of Peoples', in Shute and Hurley (eds).

Raz, J. (1986), *The Morality of Freedom*, Clarendon Press, Oxford.

Ruggie, J.G. (1972), 'Collective Goods and Future International Cooperation', *American Political Science Review*, Vol. 66, pp. 874-93.

Ruggie, J.G. (1986), 'Continuity and Transformation in the World Polity: Toward a Neorealist Synthesis', in R.O. Keohane, *Neorealism and Its Critics*, Columbia University Press, New York.

Sack, R.D. (1986), *Human Territoriality: Its Theory and History*, Cambridge University Press, Cambridge.

Shue, Henry (1997), 'Eroding Sovereignty', in R. McKim, and J. McMahan (eds), *The Morality of Nationalism*, Oxford University Press, Oxford.

Shute, S. and Hurley, S. (eds) (1993), *On Human Rights: The Oxford Amnesty Lectures 1993*, Basic Books, New York.

Smith, A.D. (1991), *National Identity*, Penguin, Harmondsworth.

Sooros, M. (1986), *Beyond Sovereignty: The Challenge of Global Policy*, University of South Carolina Press, Columbia, South Carolina.

Steiner, H. (1994), *An Essay on Rights*, Blackwell, Oxford UK and Cambridge, Mass.

Walzer, M. (1981), 'The Distribution of Membership' in P. Brown and H. Shue (eds), *Boundaries*, Rowman and Littlefield, Totowa, N.J.

14 Sentiment or Duty? Liberalism and International Justice

BYRON KALDIS

'Nowadays, there are no more French, Germans, Spanish or even English to speak of; there are only the Europeans.' (Rousseau, *Considérations sur le gouvernement de Pologne*, ch. III).

(1) At a time when contemporary national sensibilities are tried, and once widely accepted political ideas are burdened, by the demands of a unified Europe, while moral voices are calling for an expansion of the range of ethical standing and consideration (e.g. to animals, the environment, or the distant others), certain tensions are felt within Liberalism. This is predominately because taken as a doctrine that has purportedly invented the most viable conception of social justice, the strains Liberalism experiences as a result of the requirement to remain true to its distinctive modern identity seem to enjoin a reconsideration of its self-imposed character as an exclusively 'freestanding' political theory unrelated to either ethical or metaphysical presuppositions. Such a departmentalisation of spheres into political, ethical, or metaphysical is simply no more a datum. Neither does it appear any longer true to claim that contemporary versions of Liberalism which bypass theories of morals-by-agreement or entitlement-historical theses are better suited to ensure the continuation of the reason-based tradition or to cope better with the problems of pluralism, multiculturalism or that of justice beyond national-state borders.

This question of the possibility of expansiveness as a problem of ethical and political import is to a certain extent not entirely new, though certainly modern given its form. What Rousseau wished to castigate in the eyes of his Polish audience was the loss of a kind of patriotism that relates an individual to his or her nation not simply to a state (as older forms of patriotism had it) (cf. Cobban, 1934, ch. VI.) But the ambivalence between a eulogy to patriotic temperament and the enthusiasm for cosmopolitan ideals that Rousseau so often exhibits, is underpinned by his unique and less self-contradictory 'theory' of the central place of sentiments in morality. And it is there that we find his views on the expansiveness of the self most developed. It is such an acceptance of the need for a kind of extension that, I believe, Liberalism must face, and it is one kind of such an extension that I propose here. It is an attempt to show how Liberalism may be extended to encompass the international dimension from the point of view of the demands of modern pluralistic societies as well as from the point of view of the stark reality of hunger.

Should aid be the result of sentiment or duty? Can Liberalism deal with this question? Can the values of *political* particularism co-exist with those of *moral* universalism?

This paper is situated within the framework of the recent debate between universalist justice and particularist virtues (see section 7 below).[1] Further, it has at its background the controversy as to whether aid is an issue of right and duties, or of imperfect duties. If the general points made here are plausible, there may be room for some adjustments to Liberalism such that would enable it to deal with the problem of priorities in justice (personal, national or international), and in addition give alternative answers to the idea of obligation to help distant others avoiding solutions that employ utilitarian arguments for humanitarian objectives.[2]

The overall thesis of this paper is that the Liberal Order does not appear to be the future of social justice. Such a future would require, rather, the extension of Liberalism along the two lines suggested here: the idea of sentiment and the idea of global good (see section 4).

(2) First, some brief points about what the issues are in this area. There is on the one hand the problem of defining international 'justice' or 'order', coupled to the disagreements among historical traditions (either ignoring it or not): e.g. different traditions emphasise different civic duties or virtues depending on whether the domestic sphere is prior to a country's relations to others, or vice versa. Then, given the above, there is a second type of problems about how international justice is described in terms, not so much of its content or structure, but in view of its *scope*: are the agents in this area nations, national states, corporations, other non-governmental organisations, or only individuals as proper subjects of virtues, duties or sentiments? (E.g. Rousseau was quite clear that feelings couldn't be ascribed to states). A third type of problems has to do with the ethical overlapping of conflicting claims linking, but with a resultant fissure, the individual with his/her nation, or state, as well as relations between the collective entities alone: e.g. should states or other collective entities initiate moral activities based on principles of impartiality towards strangers in need without paying due respect to an otherwise inimical cultural climate or imposing stringent demands on person's feelings of national attachment, and the like? (More of states at section 7 below.)

Consider the problem of the opposition between, on the one hand, the universalist claims of cosmopolitan-type moral theories which require that we look at human beings by abstracting from national borders or religious dichotomies, and on the other, the demand (both theoretical and practical) to grant moral status to such collective entities or 'forms of culture' or 'forms of ethnic identity'. The conflict is obviously important for Liberalism for it throws into relief two prima facie contrasting ideals: the respect for autonomous individuals, the only justifiable claimants of interests and needs on which rights are based (this is linked to liberal reductive individualism), and other holistic entities which may claim a right to bar any 'cosmopolitan' humanitarian aid from crossing its borders on the basis that it violates a more important or higher (in a sense to be defined, of course) interest and need, namely that of a nation or other group, way of life, and so forth.[3] Impersonal standards of morality and universalizable values of ethical conduct that are supposed to be applicable in the private sphere (and severely criticised by non-universalist contemporary writers) may be said to elide criticism of the usual sort when 'exported', as it were, to deal with international issues. The point is not so much whether individual people are not, as a matter of fact, terribly 'cosmopolitan' in their ethical outlook, nor whether they ought to be so (for various well known reasons against the 'depersonalising' effects of deontology and consequentialism, alike);[4] the point is, rather, whether there exists an upper limit to what may justifiably be demanded of us as sacrifice imposed by a state or any supra-individual collective entity and fixed by sentiment on the one hand (or by-passed in a anti-universalist, particularistic manner), and by the teachings on universally binding rules of reason inherited by the Natural Law tradition, on the other (an example may be trades union conduct in relation to so-called 'guest workers').

(3) Should Liberalism (inescapably within the globalized contemporary reality) worry about international justice as theory and practice? Should Liberalism abstain from such an engagement and deny that it is possible (nor desirable, perhaps) to give a coherent theoretical answer thus leaving it up to individual persons to decide whether espousing Liberalism must also be in tune with their ethical or other stance *vis-à-vis* humanitarian issues? In this latter case the theoretical requirement of Liberalism's non-interference with ethical possibilities is met, and the individual is left to solve the problem by placing one's self in an ethical – non-political – 'privacy'.

But why should there be a problem for Liberalism? Two possible answers: (1) Consistency: this has to do with the scope of a theory, and may also take two forms, internal or external consistency. Now, Liberalism must be consistent, partly at least because if we discover that its foundations or justifications are the same as those used to govern the morality of international relations, then consistency demands that this be taken into account; (2) Compatibility: why should Liberalism trouble itself with notions such as 'sentiment', 'duty' or 'common good', as they do not strictly speaking belong to the (core of the) same philosophical tradition of social justice from which it originated? (e.g. individualism, psychological egoism, negative vs. positive freedom, etc.). Though the latter may appear suspect as a historically accurate claim, the main point at issue is rather this: to the extent that a Liberal theory recognises some of its substantive claims or formal aims as also present in the international world, there is no reason to deny them an equal status and compatibility within its domain. Consider the following: being entitled to a just (or non-contestable) claim to some kind of internationally applicable action is a theoretical and practical issue that Liberalism cannot ignore if the claimant puts forward the case as the result of a violation of the framework of social justice (perhaps, in its distributive or some other aspect) on which precisely Liberalism rests.[5] Whether the claimant is a state, nation, ethnic community or individual is a further problem that Liberalism or any other theory must solve.

(4) How can extending Liberalism allow it to encompass these other traditions? First, from the Rousseauan side it may enrich itself with the issues of (i) nationalism vs. cosmopolitanism; (ii) republicanism and the identification of political community with moral worth; (iii) the notions of sentiment and compassion. From the Natural Law side it can profit by discussions of the 'natural common good' as an element of the Thomistic definition of 'legal justice', on the one hand, while on the other it may look at the latter's discussion of generality vs. particularism in natural law and its application as well as at its notions of prudence, equity, and the like. The sentiment-aspect is more appropriate to Liberalism as far as individual responsibility is concerned and the individual person or citizen is taken as the locus of rights and duties to the extent that there are no *legal* rights connecting distant strangers but there may be *moral* rights to demand, and obligations, to do so – which is the contested point, of course.[6] Further, we may take the concept of 'duty' in two ways: either in relation to rights theories as usually, or as following from general, universalist, principles.

(5) Which kind of Liberalism may move us towards issues of international justice? Could it be any contemporary variety or should it be enriched by some of the Rousseauan insights embedded in civic republicanism? How can we legitimise *moral* (and yet ahistorical) arguments towards cross-national ethical action or extending moral status beyond borders, if that violates popular sovereignty as an entrenched democratic ideal?

To see what I mean by this, let us first turn to two contemporary varieties of Liberalism. What unites them is the general idea that Liberalism is a purely political theory and practice not any other type of doctrine. The first variety (explicitly contrasted to the second's *modus-vivendi* view by its author) is the familiar new version of justice as fairness by Rawls, now with the important addition of the idea of overlapping consensus. In this we find an explicit avowal of this position being 'itself a moral conception' and also affirmed on 'moral grounds'(Rawls, 1996, pp. 147-8). What is crucial here is that such a conception of social justice is contrasted to the merely *modus vivendi* one according to which it is not the business of liberalism as a purely political doctrine to adjudicate between any values.[7] In fact this latter version claims to be the only political theory that can do justice to the conflict of values for it can both give the best explanation of disagreement, plurality and conflicting, unranked, conceptions of the good and at the same time provide a merely 'political', non-moral, resolution of such conflicts. But despite the rather anaemic disagreement, I think it is safe to categorize both varieties as non-moral, explicitly political, theories of politics (as opposed, let's say, to moral theories of politics as in Plato, or religious theories of politics as in Augustine).

There is a second issue, much more important which not only shows the validity of such a unified classification (and its attendant problems) but it also serves the purposes of the present discussion more particularly. In their exchange, Habermas and Rawls made some rather interesting points (cf. section 2 above).[8] Habermas claimed that both liberal and civic republican theories 'have failed to understand the internal relation between public and private autonomy'. There is thus an 'unresolved competition' between Liberalism's high regard for private autonomy (encrusted in the well-known modern rights for fear of the tyranny of the majority), and its understanding the public autonomy of persons as citizens as 'derived from the principle of popular sovereignty and expressed in democratic law'. Between these two claims or entitlements Liberalism accorded priority to the former (due to its incipient individualism, one may add), while civic republicanism to the latter. The two errors have been, therefore, either to think of the so-called modern personal rights as somehow grounded on a certain moral basis, while republicanism, equally mistaken, grounds its own non-modern values or virtues on the ethics of community. Habermas wants to say that the mistake committed by both is to fail to regard the two, private and public autonomy, as internally connected and mutually presupposing one another.

Liberalism faces a 'dilemma' fuelling the 'unresolved competition': on the one hand, in a democratic regime human (personal) rights cannot, surely, be imposed from the outside by an agency that is external to the democratic process, even if they are exactly what the people would have decided upon if allowed to discuss, vote, etc.: this would have violated their public autonomy; on the other hand, that autonomy (or self-legislation in Rousseau's and Kant's modernist terms) 'cannot legitimately violate those rights by its laws': i.e. it is self-limited (recall that this is precisely one of the basic self-limitations, and hence problems, of the Sovereign Rousseau recognises quite early on in the *Social Contract*, I, 7: more below in section 6).

Though he denies that Liberalism leaves the two types of autonomy in unresolved competition, Rawls admits that the dilemma is as real as it is irresolvable. It is in fact this dilemma that brings us via this alternative route we have just traced to the same question concerning the limits to cosmopolitan ideals or sacrifices that can be demanded of individual persons. A sovereign democratic people cannot be forced to accept moral laws by external imposition, however admirable such a law. Neither can a sovereign people enact laws that violate or annul those rights without thereby trampling on justice (though acting entirely within its power and hence legitimately: sovereignty). If this predicament be accepted then it seems that a fruitful path may be open by looking at the primacy of sentiment as the (only) way to promote moral laws or principles of quasi-universalistic import that do not at the same time violate the principles of justice themselves, the core of universalistic, non-particularist, foundations. Let's see how the sentiment-side may deal with this.

(6) Rousseau's apparent ambivalence between his ridicule of the '*philosophe* who loves or prefers the Tartars in order to be disposed to love his neighbours' (as in *Émile*, I: cosmopolitans boasting their love of humanity in order to be free to hate their neighbours!) and his admiration of the 'great cosmopolitan souls' is not without explanation. Since the underlying basis of Rousseau's views is his notion of sentiment, he believes that these admirable souls can overstep the limits of borders that separate peoples simply by means of the power of the natural sentiment of compassion not by the exercise of reason as in other philosophical traditions (see Hassner, 1987, pp. 200-219). Now here lies the first

intimation of 'a theory of two cosmopolitanisms' that I would like to propose.

The first kind adumbrates a universalism founded on general, rational, principles; here the central ideas revolve around the notion of duty familiar in rationalist ethics. In the other kind, the central idea is that of sentiment and particularism founded on natural compassion that overcomes national barriers, as in Rousseau. So the extension or expansiveness that we are trying to ensure for Liberalism may start by acknowledging these two sources of cosmopolitanism. Furthermore, Rousseau's thesis of the primacy of sentiment may provide the missing link between 'justice' as a universalistic all-inclusive ethical principle embodied in institutions and 'virtue' as its particularist contrary.[9] The recent debate between these two schools is all too familiar. If such a rapprochement between the two ideas may be proven plausible then it may also be especially relevant for expanding Liberalism's views on social justice along the international avenue. Natural Law theory may be regarded as another missing link furnishing the parts mentioned above at section 4 (and see also below 8).

Here we should be reminded that even for Rousseau (what I have said in note 12 apart) it was clear that, even if compassion allows us to overcome borders, it is not by itself alone adequate (it needs to be guided by reason and forward-looking imagination).[10] But more importantly it was quite clear to him that it is impossible to achieve impartiality through pity and sympathy; the danger of proximity, though necessary or inevitable, contradicts the characteristic of generality or universalizability stressed later by Kant. Yet an important insight we may get from Rousseau (noticed by Orwin too) is that too much proximity or dependence may lead us to lose sight of the common good as this is memorably defined in the relevant passages of the *Social Contract*; one such remark, however, is especially valuable as it points forward towards the Kantian stricture against the empirical self's inclinations and other such contingencies of the world claiming the status of directors of moral action (the foundation of morality being from then on entrusted to a priori practical reason alone): 'by giving each citizen to his country, [it] secures him against all personal dependence' (*Social Contract*, I, 7).

Thus this tension within Rousseau's thought between the naturalness and particularism of compassion (which cannot provide the grounds of obligation) and republican reason and deliberation over the common good is instructive. We must employ the language of sentiment only with caution, if we are to extend Liberalism.

(7) Let us now turn to problems arising when attempts to provide a synthesis of universalism and particularism are carried over to the international area. In discussing the content of principles of justice, O'Neill (1996, pp. 161 ff.) follows the Kantian logical criterion of universalizability of moral maxims in laying down her preferred principle of *rejecting* injury. She explains that a principle is non-universalizable if its adoption would 'disable some from adopting' it (166, n. 14 & cf. 59, 163, 164, n. 11), i.e. not *all*. Assuming that this is so (though doubtful, logically), the point of interest is this: if *states* are the agents involved the situation changes considerably: should we demand that all states must, by following universal, cosmopolitan, principles of rejecting injury, act so as to help and so forth? Not all states can do so, of course, since some must be the recipients of aid. Let's take then as our domain of universalizability the Western industrial states; should they *all* provide aid? Or abstain from injuring each other? How does a commitment to *rejecting* injury, as opposed to actually abstaining from injury, differ in the case of state action? Moreover we have to solve additional problems: (a) define 'injury'; (b) if (a) allows for a negative definition only, what about 'positive aid'?; and (c) if particularist *virtues* can have a role to play in social justice within states (as O'Neill's theory endeavours), could states be said to have or exhibit virtues? In the case of (a), e.g. 'injury' may be physical or moral, direct or indirect, or even replaced by 'non-violation' of other states' rights (this being more general since it leaves the content of 'injury' undefined; but are we really helped by such formulations?). The *sui generis* character of virtue is that its criticised indeterminacy and fuzzy edges may not after all be a disaster because virtue has the ability to be *self-correcting* in a kind of way that is not so mysterious. A virtuous disposition is supposed to *know* how to allocate its virtuosity; the *double modality* of virtue is precisely this: that it has a dual area of application as it applies both to its object and to itself.

(8) If we turn briefly to the Natural Law tradition the first thing to note is that it offers one of the richest definitions of the 'common good' as not an aggregate or merely instrumental good but as a whole to which we all participate entirely without it thereby being possessed by anyone in particular or diminished by distribution; it rests essentially on co-operative action and includes in its content moral goods such as justice and other virtues. But is there such a substantive equivalent as a 'global common good', something over and above a mere set of conditions within which individual communities are protected in pursuing the widely divergent ends? The realist empirical objections to all ethical talk in international

relations (stemming from Hobbes' refusal to accept the enforcement of morals in the absence of a sword) have been proven wrong in small communities at least.[11] But the 'ethical' question as to whether there is any moral obligation still operative in a highly competitive environment in which the common good (e.g. the environment) may be a one-off affair is still sometimes answered in terms of what the 'rational' thing to do is. But if there is a stalemate here we may look elsewhere to the role of sentiment suitably combined with another idea that comes from the Natural Law tradition: the idea of the relation between contingency and contextualized decisions on the one hand and universalism and necessity (i.e. positive obligations to others beyond national ties or contractual agreements) on the other being mediated by the notion of 'prudence'. The latter may be seen as a 'a feel for the concrete *emotional* appeal of the particulars of action'.[12] Hence back to sentiment.

(9) The difficulties we have encountered are directly connected with a further problem within Liberalism: this has to do with a misguided attempt to distinguish conceptually purely historical from purely moral arguments for principles of positive obligations beyond national borders. Whereas the former rest on prior historical conditions or contractual agreements which generate obligations the latter are free of such assumptions. The fact that Liberalism seems to be unable to accommodate the latter within its own framework is indicative (despite empty rhetoric to the contrary). But efforts to analyse historical arguments as autonomous inevitably end up incorporating them under moral ones by revealing the higher order ethical principles under which they are subsumed. It is moreover irrelevant for a moral argument to try to ascertain empirically whether, e.g. states are as a matter of fact economically interdependent: why must we demonstrate that such an interdependence constitutes grounds for a 'moral community' which must not be ethically ignored?[13]

Going back to the questions at the end of section 1 above (can political particularism co-exist with moral universalism?), we may be inclined to accept that membership into a specified political community may be a 'crucial good' (as, e.g., Walzer may claim) but it is morally imperative to be able to define adequately what we want to mean by 'crucial': does it have the sense of 'primary' or that of 'ultimately determining'? Is this a descriptive or an evaluative statement? I have tried to show how certain alternative moves that may enrich Liberalism in this area may be fruitful but are not, of course, without some problems. It is not inexplicable that modern Liberalism is threatened by what it chose to ignore (in the concrete) for so long, namely questions of international ethics, aid and cosmopolitanism. That membership into a political community is not a moral issue nor a force that shapes moral persons (i.e. the reverse of ancient humanism and civic republicanism) may be drastically reconsidered. At the same time, the sirens of cosmopolitanism suitably cared for if we try to expand Liberalism along the two directions I have indicated. Whether, after such an operation, Liberalism will look very much the same is a question not so much of bowing to doctrinal purity but, rather, a question of whether we wish to live with such an unaltered political doctrine.

Notes

1 One recent 'constructivist' attempt to combine both refusing to see them as antithetical is O'Neill (1996) and cf. Miller (1995, esp. ch. 3).

2 See the powerful treatment of Unger's (1996). This is an example of utilising psychology in the pursuit of philosophical objectives. But it is also an attempt to prove that if his thesis is correct, then the principles of aid that follow are universalistic ones and not a matter of virtue or sentiment.

3 This point is different from that usually made in this connection as to the relative strength and hence respect that must be accorded to personal life plans, etc. relative to impersonal demands (see, e.g. Baxter, 1986).

4 See criticisms in Narveson (1993, pp. 138-150).

5 That the *legal*-or-*moral* right to equal treatment may be extended to equal access to resources is a problem, especially when immediate group-entities are involved: i.e. such that lie between individuals and states or governments, e.g.multinationals. On the status of collective entities see Van Dyke (1982).

6 See Sen (1988, pp. 57-68) on the need to supplement the discourse in terms of rights with robust empirical investigations.

7 Here I take as the best representative of this position Larmore's work: (1987and 1996). I have tried to refute one central claim of this position in another paper. Here I only posit the problem since I am interested in showing why Liberalism had better look elsewhere for enrichment.

8 The relevant passages are in Rawls (*idem*. pp. 409 ff). Rawls is there summarising and debating with Habermas.

9 However, we must not fail to notice that Rousseau has a rather realistic view of sentiments: for instance he reminds us in the *Discourse on Political Economy* that the sentiment of humanity becomes weaker when it encompasses the whole world; it is much better to rely on the immediate contact with citizens or to national sentiment. The ambivalence certainly reappears here. But I believe, though can hardly prove here, that Rousseau must be seen from two points of view in almost everything he professed, or as having more than one target. If one reads his *Lettre à M. d'Alembert* with this dual perspective in mind one

comes across a wealth of indications of how to resolve similar ambiguities and inconsistencies in the whole of his work.

10 See Orwin (1997, pp. 296-320; esp. on p. 315) - the dilemma 'sentiment or duty?' reappears: '[his compassionate] concern with others ... [is] unproductive of obligations of any kind. Man is not by nature social, and compassionate, being natural, affords no basis for lasting society.'

11 See Ridley (1996, esp. pp. 140-1) for a version of the ultimate bargaining game which I would argue is applicable for our case.

12 Boyle (1992), pp. 112-135. Cf. Goerner (1983, pp. 393-418): this is an iconoclastic interpretation of Aquinas' ethics and politics as not a species of law-or-rule-following kind but as one primarily of 'right' and intellectual and ethical 'virtue' in conditions of changing particularity; he points out himself that Rousseau's thought falls under the same heading: politics is ultimately beyond rules.

13 Such an implicit confusion vitiates the argument of Lichtenberg (1981, pp. 79-100) and remarks by Walzer, (pp. 103-5; also cf. Walzer, 1987, ch. 2).

Bibliography

Baxter, B. (1986), 'The Self, Morality and the Nation-State', in A Ellis. (ed.), *Ethics and International Relations*, Manchester University Press, Manchester.

Boyle, J. (1992), 'Natural Right and International Ethics' in T. Nardin and D. Mapel (eds), *Traditions of International Ethics*, Cambridge University Press, Cambridge.

Cobban, A. (1934), *Rousseau and the Modern State*, George Allen & Unwin, London.

Goerner, E. A. (1983), 'Thomistic Natural Right', *Political Theory*, Vol. 11, No. 3.

Hassner, P. (1997), 'Rousseau and the Theory and Practice of International Relations', in C. Larmore (1987), *Patterns of Moral Complexity*, Cambridge University Press, Cambridge.

Larmore, C. (1996), *The Morals of Modernity*, Cambridge University Press, Cambridge.

Lichtenberg, J. (1981), 'National Boundaries and Moral Boundaries: A Cosmopolitan View' in P.G. Brown and H. Shue (eds), *Boundaries: National Autonomy and its Limits*, Rowman & Littlefield, New York.

Miller, D. (1995), *On Nationality*, Clarendon Press, Oxford.

Narveson, J. (1993), *Moral Matters*, Broadview Press, Lewiston, NY.

O'Neill, O. (1996), *Towards Justice and Virtue*, Cambridge University Press, Cambridge.

Orwin, C. and Tarcov, N (eds), *The Legacy of Rousseau*, The University of Chicago Press, Chicago.

Orwin, C. (1997), 'Rousseau and the Discovery of Political Compassion' in C. Orwin and N. Tarcov (eds), *The Legacy of Rousseau*, The University of Chicago Press, Chicago.
Rawls, J. (1996), *Political Liberalism*, Columbia University Press, New York.
Ridley, M. (1996), *The Origins of Virtue*, Viking, London.
Sen, A. (1988), 'Property and Hunger', *Economics and Philosophy*, Vol. 4.
Unger, P. (1996), *Living High and Letting Die*, Oxford University Press, Oxford.
Van Dyke, V. (1982), 'Collective Entities and Moral Rights: Problems in Liberal-Democratic Thought', *The Journal Of Politics*, Vol. 44.
Walzer, M. (1987), *Spheres of Justice*, Martin Robertson, Oxford.

Contributors

Alison Assiter is Dean of Economics and Social Science and Professor of Feminist Theory at the University of the West of England. She has published a number of books and articles in the field of feminist theory, of which the most recent is *Enlightened Women*, Routledge, 1996. She lives for part of the week in Bristol and the rest of the time in London, with her partner and their son.

Phillip Cole writes on issues in social philosophy, and is currently working on a project concerning political theory and immigration. He lectures on political philosophy and applied ethics at Middlesex University, London.

Gideon Calder (b. 1971) is associate lecturer in Philosophy and Continuing Education at Cardiff University, UK. Much of his recent work has explored ethical and epistemological tensions within pragmatist and post-modernist thinking. Sometime in 2000, he will publish a short book on Richard Rorty with Phoenix. He has been working on a PhD thesis (also on Rorty's work) since mediaeval times, but will finally submit it this summer. Next he plans to do some work on the philosophy of historiography.

Justin Cruickshank has just completed a four-year Graduate Teaching Assistantship in the Sociology Department at the University of Warwick, UK; during which time he wrote a Doctoral thesis on the relationship of social theory to sociological methodology. This thesis defended the position of 'social realism', as advocated by Archer and Bhaskar. He is now beginning research on the underclass issue, drawing upon social realism, and teaching with The Open University as an Associate Lecturer.

Stephen de Wijze is a lecturer in political thought in the Department of Government at the University of Manchester, UK. His current research is in the area of contemporary theories of justice. He is also working on the problem of 'dirty hands' and more generally exploring the tensions that exist between strong and effective political action (*realpolitik*) and the constraints of morality.

Ian Duncanson graduated in law from Southampton and Durham universities in the UK and qualified in England as a solicitor. He taught law at Newcastle-upon-Tyne Polytechnic and Keele University before moving in 1980 to the Legal Studies Department at La Trobe University in Melbourne, Australia, where he teaches courses on legal theory and on the historical, social and legal aspects of discrimination on the grounds of ethnicity, gender and class in postcolonial and social and legal theory. Recent publications include: 'Cultural Studies Meets Legal Pluralism', in volume 12 of the *Canadian Journal of Law and Society*; 'Sexual Harassment and the Politics of Culture: Ormond College Incident(ally)', in volume 10 of the *Australian Feminist Law Journal*, and 'Close Your Eyes and Think of England: Stories about Law and Constitutional Change in Australia', in volume 3 of the *Canberra Law Review*.

Edward Garrett (b. 1967) lectures in philosophy at Middlesex University, London; he also teaches philosophy at The Open University. A recently completed PhD explored the limits of liberal justice within the context of the land question in Britain today (particularly relating to the Criminal Justice and Public Order Act, 1994).

Judith Grbich researches in taxation jurisprudence and political economy, taxation law and critical jurisprudence. She teaches taxation law, property law and Literature and Law in the Law Program at La Trobe University in Melbourne, Australia, and legal interpretation in the women's studies and legal studies programs. She is General Editor of the *Australian Feminist Law Journal*, an Editorial Board member of the *International Journal for the Semiotics of Law*, and in 1999 President of the Law and Literature Association of Australia. Recent publications include an edited collection, *Native Title Rights and Colonisation: Law and Humanities Supplements to Property Law in Australia*, (1998, Australian Feminist Law Foundation, Melbourne).

Byron Kaldis studied at the Universities of Kent and Oxford where he received his D.Phil. He has been Assistant Professor of Philosophy at the State University of New York and Senior Lecturer at the University of Teesside, UK. He currently teaches philosophy at the Economics School of the University of Athens and the Philosophy Faculty of the

University of Patras. He is a Member of the Equipe Internationale de Philosophie Pénale at the CNRS – Université II Paris, in France. His thesis on *Holism, Language and Persons* was published by Avebury in 1993. His current project is a book on the relation between ethics and political philosophy. His research and publications are in metaphysics and political philosophy.

Daniel Kofman is currently Stipendiary Lecturer in Philosophy at Balliol College, Oxford University, UK. He has previously taught at Lincoln, St-Anne's, St.Catherine's, Blackfriars, Kellog, Keble, University, and Harris Manchester colleges, Oxford University. His research interests are Political Philosophy (including International Relations Theory), Ethics, Philosophy of Mind, and Social Theory. His previous publications have been in the area of nationalism, self-determination, and secession; he has also published both academic and newspaper articles on various national conflicts, in particular those in the former Yugoslavia.

Petri Koikkalainen (b. 1971) is a researcher and teacher in the Department of Political Science and International Relations at the University of Tampere, Finland. His publications include articles on communitarian and republican critiques of liberalism, entitled 'Liberalism – A Historical Payload?' (in Finnish, forthcoming) and 'Leo Strauss and America as a Philosophical Nation' (in Finnish, *Niin & Nain*, 2/1999). He is working on a doctorate on the influence of political philosophy on practical politics in the United States. His other research interests include the history of political thought and the relation between 'theory' and 'praxis' in politics.

Kalle Pihlainen is a research fellow at the Department of Cultural History at the University of Turku, Finland. He has worked as Assistant and Senior Assistant in Cultural History and has published on the use of semiotic methods in the examination of poetry as well as on narrative theory and the significance of literary knowledge in historical research. His doctoral dissertation, entitled 'Resisting History', deals with the ethics of narrative representation with a focus on the thinking of Jean-Paul Sartre, Hayden White and Michael Riffaterre.

Doris Schroeder is an Honorary Research Fellow in the Centre for Bioethics at the University of Birmingham, UK. She read economics and philosophy/ politics/ English literature at two German universities, and worked as a strategic planner for Warner Music Europe before completing a philosophy PhD in the UK (December 1998). Her main interests are the economics of unemployment, the politics of the welfare state and political philosophy. She is author of *Work Incentives and Welfare Provision: The 'Pathological' Theory of Unemployment* (in press; to be published by Ashgate).

Jess Shannon graduated in Humanities from the University of Brighton in 1997. She is currently teaching religion and philosophy at a secondary school in East Grinstead, England.

Gulia Taghiyeva (b. 1961 in Baku, Azerbaijan) is an independent researcher whose interests focus on the study of contemporary problems of democratization in post-Soviet Azerbaijan, including those of nation-building and state-building. She graduated from Moscow State University as a journalist and worked for the Azerbaijan State Information Agency between 1985 and 1994. While working for UNICEF from 1994-97, she was actively involved in research on children's and women's rights and turned to study of issues around democracy and human rights. She was awarded a fellowship from the Open Society Institute to read for an MA in the Theory and Practice of Human Rights at Essex University, UK, received in 1998. She is currently working for ISAR/Azerbaijan and is involved in conducting comprehensive research on developments in civil society in Azerbaijan. She is fluent in Azeri, Russian and English.

Lubica Učník was born in Czechoslovakia, and at one time worked as a TV producer for Czechoslovak Television in Bratislava. She studied journalism at Komensky University, but in 1980, before completing her studies, she emigrated to Australia with her daughter. In 1992 she completed a degree in Communication Studies at Murdoch University. She is now writing a PhD thesis in Philosophy at Murdoch University and teaching part-time. Her publications include 'Genológia, Ideológia a Text', in Vaclav Macek (ed.), *On the History of Slovak Cinematography* (Conference proceedings, Banská Bystrica, 1996), and 'The Discourse of Liberalism in Post-Socialist Europe', in B. Brecher, J. Halliday and K. Kolinská (eds), *Nationalism and Racism in the Liberal Order* (Ashgate, 1998).

Majid Yar is currently a tutor in the Department of Sociology, Lancaster University, UK. He has recently completed a PhD exploring the relation between ethical inter-subjectivity, Hegel's concept of 'recognition', and the theorization of community. His primary research interests relate to the ethical dimensions of both European social thought and contemporary processes of social change, and he has authored a number of articles exploring these themes.